Raoul de Navery

Idols

Or the secret of the Rue Chaussee d'Antin

Raoul de Navery

Idols

Or the secret of the Rue Chaussee d'Antin

ISBN/EAN: 9783741163784

Manufactured in Europe, USA, Canada, Australia, Japa

Cover: Foto ©Andreas Hilbeck / pixelio.de

Manufactured and distributed by brebook publishing software (www.brebook.com)

Raoul de Navery

Idols

IDOLS;

OR THE

SECRET OF THE RUE CHAUSSÉE D'ANTIN

TRANSLATED FROM THE FRENCH OF

RAOUL DE NAVERY

ANNA T. SADLIER

NEW YORK, CINCINNATI, CHICAGO
BENZIGER BROTHERS
PUBLISHERS OF BENZIGER'S MAGAZINE.

CONTENTS.

CHAPTER		PAGE
I.	The Pomereul Household	5
II.	A Prodigal Son	18
III.	The Knights of the Black Cap	34
IV.	The Crime	47
V.	The Secret of God	60
VI.	The Accusation	73
VII.	Heart Trials	90
VIII.	The Inviolable Secret	105
IX.	A New Misfortune	120
X.	The Trial	137
XI.	The Dream Ended	154
XII.	An Artist Supper	169
XIII.	The Golden Calf	187
XIV.	The War	206
XV.	The Two Brothers	229
XVI.	Jean Machû	248
XVII.	The Barricades of Death	265
XVIII.	Lipp-Lapp	280
XIX.	The Dwarf's Secret	299
XX.	The Broken Idol	315

IDOLS;

OR,

The Secret of the Rue Chausée d'Antin.

CHAPTER I.

THE POMEREUL HOUSEHOLD.

Two men, who in age and appearance were widely different, sat conversing in a spacious study. The room was luxurious, though somewhat severe in its arrangement. It contained many fine representations in bronze of masterpieces of antique art. Antoine Pomereul, the elder of the two men, seemed upwards of sixty years of age. His hair, which looked as if a gale of wind might have passed through it, fell over his massive temples. His florid complexion, the smile on his lips and the frank expression of the face betokened a straightforward and generous disposition, and much business ability. His grey eye was wonderfully penetrating; the very position of his hand upon the desk marked the energetic man of business.

His companion, on the contrary, was scarcely twenty-five. His broad forehead bore the impress of genius upon it, and genius of a solid and somewhat serious character; his expression was earnest, with a tinge of mingled asceticism and ideality. His figure was lithe and graceful, his hair black, his complexion pale, his whole appearance most attractive. A voice true in tone and musical in quality completed the charm, and added no little to the confidence which his countenance inspired. Nor did it belie a nature at once ardent and sensitive.

"So, Benedict," said Antoine Pomereul, "you refuse to draw aside the envious veil which covers your statue. Your apprentice, Cleomene, has just brought it here, and I am longing to see it. But I assure you I respected its folds, as if they were those of the ancient Isis."

"O my dear master," said Benedict, seizing the old man's hand impulsively, "if I have kept it veiled, it is because I would fain see for myself the impression it produced upon you, and hear with my own lips the decree which will make me happy or miserable. I want to consult your heart and mind alike in the two-fold decision you are about to give."

"On my honor," laughed Antoine Pomereul, "the affair is more serious than I supposed."

"It concerns my whole life," cried the young man eagerly.

"You mean your future as an artist, I suppose," said Pomereul, "and as to that, my boy, many find themselves deceived who follow art. Yes, those who seek her most often go farthest astray. Unwilling to follow the beaten path, they take new and unknown ones; sometimes they lose the guiding thread; their mind gropes in darkness; they fail to realize the grandeur of their first conception. However, Benedict, it is better even to miss a lofty ideal, than to remain forever satisfied with what is mediocre and trivial."

"Judge for yourself," cried the artist, suddenly raising the veil which covered the statue.

It was about three feet in height, of the purest Carrara marble. It represented a young girl modestly clad in a flowing robe, such as is seen on fauns of the twelfth and thirteenth centuries. The eyes were raised to Heaven, in her hand she held a chisel and hammer; she seemed the very personification of the sculpture of that period, a celestial daughter of prayer, offering her sublimest work to the God who inspired it. The old man regarded the statue for some moments in silence, after which he grasped the young sculptor's hand with an air of conviction, saying,

"Good, my boy, good."

"Ah," said Benedict, "how happy you make me."

"This figure represents—"

"The daughter of Steinbach," answered Benedict, "architect of the Cathedral of Strasburg. She assisted her father in that mighty work, and the pillar *des Anges*, of the Angels, bear her name, Sabine."

"Ah, Steinbach's daughter was named Sabine, like mine," said Pomereul, smiling. "Well, you are satisfied now, I suppose. Your statue is charming. The style and conception of it are good. You have kept your ideal, and the skill of your chisel has not interfered with the purity of your inspiration. Bravo! yes, I say honestly and in all sincerity, bravo! Keep up your heart. If the figure is small, the execution is great."

"Master," said Benedict, "your praise confuses me."

"It need not," said Pomereul. "I am stating facts. I trust you do not suspect me of flattering. You remember when, as a mere child, you worked with my sculptors, how exacting I was. Exacting enough to discourage any one but you. Perhaps you thought me severe or even hard. I feared so myself, yet I continued in the same way. It is by the patience of the pupil that the reality of his vocation is determined. Those cowards who are overcome by the difficulties of the task, and the severity of the master, are not worth a regret. It is doing them a service to keep them tradesmen, rather than raise them to the dignity of artists. You blushed, indeed, at my reproofs, but less with anger than with grief at your own mistakes; indefatigable you began again; every day you made new progress, and were not vain of it; you looked rather at what you had yet to learn than at the facility already acquired. At last I was forced to turn you out of the workshop, for you were too modest to see that sculpture was calling you to her service, and that with me you were making merely models for industry."

"Yes," said Benedict, "you are right; it was necessary indeed to drive me from your house, as I would never have left it. You were anxious for my welfare; I was more anxious to keep my happiness. You aspired for me to artistic heights; I would have sacrificed everything at that time to continue making your pendulums and candelabras. You were right, but my heart sought to persuade me that you were wrong. I begin to be known, I may become famous; but who will assure me that I have as of old—"

"The friendship of your old master? But you are still part of the family, Benedict. I love you almost as much as Sulpice more perhaps than Xavier."

"Really?"

"Really."

"Then, if I should ask you a favor?"

"I am almost sure I would grant it."

"Even if it were something of importance?"

"Even is not the word, say especially."

"Well," said Benedict, plucking up courage, "will you allow me to offer this statue to Mlle. Sabine? To-morrow is her birthday, and—"

"You dear, big boy," said Pomereul, "you were afraid to finish the sentence. Yet you have lived ten years in my house. My severity towards you was only a proof of my attachment. When the big tears rolled down your cheeks on the day of your departure, it was because you left behind you a happy past, and your youthful dreams and ambition. But I wished you to have such a trial. It was needed to temper your soul. Sheltered by my care and forethought, you knew nothing of the dangers of the world. You thought that each one lived there in the dignity of his own purity, and the strength of his own convictions, without either struggle or effort. I wanted you to pass through that fiery furnace, and come forth tempered for the battle of life. The boy bade me farewell with swelling heart and tearful eyes; I hoped that the man would return to me. He is come. You have made no false steps upon your way. Your gaze has remained fixed upon one star, your heart was true to one attachment. It was well done; it is rare and beautiful. Artists of your age often drag their inspiring muse in the mud. But you begged her to raise you upon her wings, and she has kept you there. You have often called me your benefactor, to-day you called me master, there is but one more title you can give me."

"One title," cried Benedict, "then you understand, you do not despise my—"

"Your father gives you his hand," said Pomereul. Benedict grasped it, with large tears standing in his eyes, and thus the two men stood face to face for some moments, emotion keeping them silent. It was with regret they both heard Baptiste's voice at the door, asking,

"Can you receive M. André Nicois, sir ?"

"Of course," said M. Pomereul advancing towards the door.

"Then, my statue—" said Benedict.

"Is Sabine's property now," said Pomereul, "and by the way, we must let her have this surprise as soon as possible."

As he spoke M. Pomereul turned to the darkest corner of the room, calling,

"Lipp-Lapp!"

Hearing its name, a strange creature came out of the shadow where it had been hidden. It stood upright and firmly on its feet, letting its arms hang down beside its lean body, and came towards its master.

It was a chimpanzee of the larger species, with intelligent face, mild dark eyes, and a broad wide-open mouth, which seemed about to speak. Lipp-Lapp's eyes gleamed with intelligence. He wore a robe of brocade, ornamented with pearls and gold, such as is seen in pictures of blacks by Italian masters. He had a bright colored turban on his head, and seemed very proud of his fine clothes. He had been brought from Java to M. Pomereul by a friend, and had soon learned, as many of his race have done, to perform various little domestic services. He could carry a tray of fruit, liqueur, or coffee with perfect safety, distribute the letters, and could besides understand almost any order given to him.

"Lipp-Lapp," said M. Pomereul, "take this statue and put it on Mlle. Sabine's mantelpiece."

The chimpanzee showed all his teeth in a broad grin; he seized the figure in his strong and dextrous arms, and went off in the direction of Mlle. Pomereul's apartments.

"My daughter is out," said Pomereul; "on her return she will find the statue, and can thank you this evening. You must dine with us, my boy."

Benedict only wrung M. Pomereul's hand, exchanged salutes with M. Nicois, who was coming in, and left the house radiant with joy.

M. Pomereul perceived at once that the countenance of his visitor was anxious and troubled. Unlike many people, who seeing their friends in distress, begin an account of their own difficulties, for fear of being called on for assistance, M. Pomereul took a chair opposite Nicois, and said to him bluntly,

"What has gone wrong with you?"

"Everything has gone wrong," said Nicois. "I came on purpose to tell you, and now—"

"You hesitate," said Pomereul; "but I say, what is the use of having friends if you cannot ask a favor of them? It was just the same with that fine, clever boy who has gone out. He came to open his heart to me, and I was obliged to offer him Sabine in marriage. *You need money.*"

"Who told you so?" cried Nicois excitedly.

"No one," answered his friend.

"Can you assure me of this," said Nicois, "there are no rumors at the Bourse?"*

"On the contrary," said Pomereul, "the talk there yesterday was how solid you were. If you are in difficulties, no hint of it has got about. But I simply judge from this. Nothing else but financial embarrassment could make you look so down in the mouth, and what else could have brought you here just before the end of the month, if it were not to say, Friend Pomereul, open your money-chest wide. I want to put in both hands."

"You are right," said Nicois, "you are as clear-sighted as generous. I need money, a large sum."

"How much?"

"A hundred thousand francs," said the banker with much embarrassment.

"I have not that much in the house," said Pomereul quietly, "but I can get it for you. Come here the day after to-morrow, and it will be ready."

---

* Exchange.

"You will save my life," said Nicois.

"Ah, it is too much to put life in the scale with money," said Pomereul. "I simply do you a service, which in like circumstances I should ask of you. If friendship does not go as far as the purse, and a little beyond, there is not much use in making a parade of it."

"Pomereul," said Nicois, "you know what true friendship is, though you do not make a parade of it. But who could be more noble, more unselfish than you are, to your very workmen, to all who surround you?"

"Stop there," said Pomereul; "I object. What you call unselfishness, generosity, liberality, and so on, is only a knowledge of business. If I have laid a foundation of benevolence to others, it is only making a profitable investment. I am rich, and it gives me the very great happiness of being loved by those around me, respected without being feared, and the possessor of four millions, without having any enemies or being envied. Looking back upon my life, it seems that in all its circumstances I was blessed by Providence. There is one cloud upon the blue horizon, but that I trust will in time disappear. My father was a blacksmith, pursuing his humble trade, and gaining a scanty sustenance. I resolved to aid him by my earnings. As a mere boy I got a situation in a bronze factory. I was employed only to run errands, and to sweep the store. But I never loitered upon the way, nor left a speck of dust where my broom had been. So I won my employer's confidence. He made me an apprentice. I astonished the workmen by my facility in learning. My master began to take a special interest in me. He had me taught the intricacies of the trade, instead of leaving me to spend my life toiling at its lower branches. I attempted first the casting, then the setting or the carving of large pieces. At twenty, few workmen could equal me. If my education was not classical, it was at least sound and practical. From that time my lot was cast. The proprietor had a daughter. He gave her to me in marriage. The firm name became 'Bernard et Pomereul.' It continued so for three years. Then Bernard died, and my name alone was on books or invoices. I succeeded him. I had three children, and our happiness was, indeed, enviable, when the greatest grief of my life came upon me. My wife died. I thought at first I should never be consoled for her loss, but though I have never forgotten her, time has softened my sorrow. My children remain to me—Sulpice, whose intellect is far in advance of his age, Xavier, whose good heart redeems his folly, and Sabine, the angel of our house."

"Ah, yes," said Nicois, "you are a happy father."

Pomereul sighed, and resumed.

"What was done for me, the poor child of Paris, without any other recommendation than his own desire to do right, I have always tried to do for others. I have striven to be rather the father than the master of my workmen. If I do all that is necessary in paying them their salary, I love to do more for my own satisfaction. You must see some time how I have organized their dwellings at Charenton, near the factory. Each family has its own house, which is simple and comfortable. There is water to purify and take away the bad properties of the gas, which gives it warmth and light; a little plot of ground to supply it with vegetables and to grow flowers; the children can likewise raise rabbits there, and the good wife, chickens. I have, besides, a hospital for the sick, a crib for nursing infants, a workroom for girls, an infant school for the little ones. My factory really includes a complete city, of which I am chief magistrate."

"And of which your son Sulpice is the apostle," said Nicois.

"Yes," replied Pomereul, in a voice of considerable emotion, "you may well say Sulpice is an apostle. What I do through philanthropy, he does from pure charity. I bring to one corner of the earth comforts, improvements, worldly goods, but he brings Heaven there. He teaches catechism to the children, guides the family, is the adviser of the father, and is beloved and respected by every one. He has made my workmen doubly honest and faithful in the discharge of their duties. There is perfect harmony between their principles and conduct. Seeing the son of their master, the millionaire, Sulpice Pomereul, working among them in his poor cassock and coarse shoes, they cannot doubt the divine character of a religion which inspires such sacrifices. Sulpice translates the Bible into action, and he might say, with the noble pride of an apostle, Be ye also my imitators, as I am the imitator of Christ Jesus. Truly I love Sulpice as a living part of my own heart. But at times the veneration I feel for his virtues is even greater than my affection. There could not be a finer spectacle than that of a young man endowed with every gift of mind and fortune, renouncing the privileges of the upper few to devote his life to the education of poor children, the consolation of the wretched, and the relief of human misery. Therefore Sulpice is beloved and venerated by all who know him. They knock much oftener at the door of the humble room which he keeps for himself in the attic, than at that of the rich merchant, member of the Municipal Council, and Judge in the Tribunal de Commerce. Every one in the house feels the influence of his gentleness and piety. I do not speak of Sabine, she is an angel, but customers, friends, servants, all, except Xavier."

"You exaggerate these youthful follies of Xavier," said Nicois; "why the deuce take it, Pomereul, a boy must sow his wild oats."

"What they sow they must reap," said Pomereul.

"Ah, well, he will come out right," said Nicois; "perhaps he needed a friend and adviser of his own age in whom he could confide. Sulpice is rather too austere for your youngest son, and Sabine's very innocence prevents her being of service to him."

"And what of me?" asked Pomereul.

"You, why confound it, man, you are his father. Besides you are of that disposition which difficulties to be overcome in early life naturally make a man, and whose character forbids Xavier to confide in him. Things will improve when Benedict Fougerais is your son-in-law, for you said, did you not, that you meant to give him Sabine?"

"Gladly, my friend," said Pomereul. "Benedict is one of those young men who left my workshop to become masters in their turn. For I have the deep satisfaction of knowing that my house has produced men who will be an honor to their country. One reason why I love my calling is that it enables me to aid deserving talent. Once a boy gains the special interest of his professor in drawing or modelling I keep my eye on him. I inquire as to the condition of his family. If they are poor I give the boy a pension, stipulating that he will pay me back, by yearly sums, till he has paid all I have advanced. This, in turn, is used to open a future to some other boy. It has another advantage, for it teaches them the proper value of money; that they must regard it, not as an idol, but as a power; that it must be used less for our pleasures than our necessities; that its worth may be increased a hundred-fold by the use made of it. Many artists owe their future to this plan of mine: Luc Aubry, the landscape painter, Jean Leroux, who painted the interior, which you bought last year, Benedict Fougerais, who is likely to take a front rank among our sculptors if he does not degenerate."

"Degenerate, when he is Sabine's husband?"

"I do not mean degeneracy of hand or of intellect."

"What then?"

"A moral degeneracy."

"That will be impossible when he is surrounded by such an atmosphere as this."

"I hope so, but who can tell? You know how fatally easy and insidious is the descent of an artist. Benedict only knows the great art, pure, religious, Christian, the art which is the softened shade of religious feeling. He is of the school of Fra Bartolomeo and Fra Angelico, who painted their Madonnas on their knees. But the current of fashion and of popular taste does not run upon that side. Art has become pagan. It has descended from the sacred heights. The Muse has become a Bacchante and dances with satyrs; a modest statue or a decent picture loses half its chance of success. The churches are no longer endowed with works of a religious inspiration, but rather the drawing-rooms are decorated with profane or indecent figures. Therefore, woe to the artist, however gifted, who sacrifices his power of inspiration to every passing whim, who says to himself, not, I am going to create something great, but, I am going to make a group which will sell. First, he tries to succeed, then to succeed again, then to be talked of in the papers. So far Benedict has escaped these perils. God grant he may continue so."

"Rest easy," said Nicois; "not only will he do that, but he will bring back your prodigal son."

"You believe so?" said Pomereul.

"Most sincerely; we were all foolish at his age, except you perhaps."

"And you too, I hope," said Pomereul, looking fixedly at his friend.

A dark shade passed over the banker's face.

"My friend," said he, in a troubled voice, "I paid to folly one tribute, which though brief cost me dear. My hair has been always white since you knew me, has it not?"

"It is true."

"It grew white in a single night."

"In consequence of some terrible misfortune?"

"Yes, you name it right, a terrible misfortune," said Nicois.

Seeing his friend's astonishment at this unexpected confidence he continued:

"It is since that, I have had such a passion for money. Till then I only thought of it as a means of obtaining an independent position; now, I want it to gratify my pride, my wife's follies, to excite the envy of others, and plunge myself into such a whirlpool of business and of pleasure that I forget, or at least for an hour lose that one recollection."

"Will you not confide to me the cause of your suffering?"

"Ah," said Nicois, "if you knew all. But some day the friend will come to your fireside and open his heart to you. To-day, the banker alone has told you his misfortune."

Pomereul took his friend's outstretched hand. Nicois rose to go.

"You say that the money will be ready for me the day after to-morrow?"

"The day after to-morrow," said Pomereul, "a hundred thousand francs will be in this portfolio for you."

As Nicois passed out, Lipp-Lapp brought him his overcoat and cane.

CHAPTER II.

A Prodigal Son

In the Pomereul household everything, even to the smallest details, was as orderly as possible. The merchant himself fully appreciating the value of time never permitted it to be wasted in idleness. Many people by delaying lose a few minutes now and a few minutes again, which at the end of the week amounts to several hours. The clocks always went to perfection, and the manufacturer of bronze daily found that rare phenomenon so eagerly sought by Charles V., all the clocks struck at the same moment. At six precisely the family sat down to dinner. Pomereul never waited for anybody. He considered want of punctuality a breach of good manners, towards which people are usually too indulgent. When Xavier dined out he generally let his father know. But on this particular occasion, when the butler announced dinner, Pomereul, Sulpice, Sabine and Benedict were in the drawing-room, but no Xavier.

Sabine's face was bright and joyful. She sat at a window talking to her betrothed, and a ray of the setting sun falling on her golden hair formed of it an aureola. Her only ornament was a white rose, which she had added to her simple toilet from the bouquet Benedict had brought her.

Pomereul and Sulpice were conversing in a low voice of Sabine's betrothal, and the young priest seemed very much pleased about it.

"It is one of those unions," said he to his father, "which are too seldom seen nowadays. On the one hand is Sabine with all the virtues which form the highest charm and special strength of a woman; on the other, Benedict, with his energy, love of work and lawful ambition. You know Benedict's talents, his moral character, his strong religious principles, and you do well to place my sister's hand in his. They both know full well, despite the illusions of their age, that the future will have many trials for them, but they know also that they can overcome these trials. The blessing of heaven must surely rest on such a marriage, and I shall gladly perform the ceremony which unites them."

"You remind me," said M. Pomereul smiling, "that Benedict and I have not yet spoken of Sabine's dowry."

"Your lawyer will attend to that," said Sulpice.

"No," said M. Pomereul, "when you want a thing well done do it yourself."

As he spoke he turned to the young people.

"Come here a moment, Benedict," said he.

The young man came.

"My good son-in-law," said Pomereul, "you acted somewhat thoughtlessly yesterday about a certain matter. I must say it did not give me a very high opinion of your business ability. How can you possibly sign contracts for your work, or make agreements if you know so little of the value of money, that you did not ask me what dowry I would give Sabine?"

"A dowry to Sabine?" cried Benedict. "I do not want any."

"You do not want any?" said Pomereul.

"Most assuredly not," said Benedict. "Is it not enough that I am to become the husband of such a girl as that without receiving a large sum of money? Do you think that while you live I would ever take a penny of your fortune from you? By doing so I would offend Sabine and degrade myself. I am only twenty-five. I am willing to work and I may add I have talents. I can easily supply our little wants. No, dear father. I refuse to accept her dowry, and I am sure Sabine thinks as I do."

"Yes," said Sabine, in a voice full of emotion, "you are right, perfectly right."

Pomereul shook his head incredulously.

"Believe me," said Benedict earnestly, "it is better that young people should not have too much money at first. Sometimes their future is marred rather than made by premature good fortune. Money is rather an incentive to idleness than to work. The rich are more apt to gather round them a crowd of parasites and flatterers. For an artist, wealth is a positive misfortune. It induces him to waste his time, and the very praise bestowed on him is often given less to the artist than to the rich man, so that it blinds him to the real value of his work."

"You are right," said Sulpice, pressing Benedict's hand.

"It seems to me, too," said Sabine, blushing, "that it robs the wife of half her merit; it condemns her to idleness, by making her rich all at once. A wealthy bride seems to owe everything to her family, and nothing to her husband. What will it matter, dear father, if the daughter of the millionaire Pomereul be without horses or diamonds? I can use your carriage at need, and Benedict shall see that I know how to dispense with these things cheerfully. My surroundings will be humble; so much the better. I shall go out of my world in marrying an artist, and yet I will remain myself. I do not need large means, which would render work useless, lead me to love the world, and to rival other women in dress and extravagance. We will live upon my husband's earnings as my mother was content to live upon yours."

Pomereul opened his arms to Sabine.

"Dear daughter," he said, "and dear son, more touched than I can express, I yield to your youthful wisdom. You are now voluntarily poor. But you will permit me once and a while to give you a little surprise."

"We will permit whatever will be a pleasure to you," said Benedict.

"Very well," said Pomereul gayly, recovering from his emotion, "we shall serve up surprises, like truffles, under a napkin."

At that moment Lipp-Lapp threw open the doors, and drew aside the curtains, while the voice of Baptiste announced,

"Dinner."

The great clock struck six.

The same thought occurred to Sabine and Sulpice. Xavier was not there.

Benedict, who read what was passing in Sabine's mind, said to M. Pomereul, in a half entreating way,

"Shall we not wait for Xavier?"

"No, my boy," said M. Pomereul firmly, "it is his duty to be punctual, he has not done his duty."

"He forgot that this night was not like every other."

"He knows that he owes me respect and deference," said Pomereul, "that should suffice. Give Sabine your arm, Benedict; we must not let the dinner cool."

They went into the dining-room. It was a large square room, made octagon in shape by great sideboards, laden with massive silver. The bright light of the lamps shone on choice pictures; the table linen was snowy white; vases of flowers ornamented the table; comfort and taste reigned supreme at this board, where the finest crystal rivalled the choicest of porcelain.

Taking up her napkin, Sabine uttered a cry of delight; a magnificent bracelet of diamonds lay beneath it.

"Ah, father," said the young girl reproachfully, "already!"

"It belonged to your mother," said M. Pomereul quietly.

Sulpice was at his father's right hand, Sabine to the left, while Benedict sat facing his future father-in-law.

An empty chair awaited Xavier.

The commencement of the meal was cheerful, spite of the young man's absence. M. Pomereul himself gave the tone to it, and besides an incident at once touching and comic added to its gayety.

Lipp-Lapp was a great pet of Xavier's, and the honest chimpanzee always took great delight in serving him at table. Not seeing him in his accustomed place, he showed the utmost vexation. His eyes were anxiously fixed upon the door. Seeing, however, that dinner was going on without Xavier, he was determined to perform his office, notwithstanding. He placed a share of all the viands before the empty chair, and changed the plates with as much care as if his young master had really partaken of all these good things. As time passed, however, Lipp-Lapp became sadder and sadder, and at the dessert his face was the picture of misery. All at once, when the coffee was being served, the chimpanzee gave a little cry of joy, and rushed towards the door, opening from the dining-room to the antechamber.

He heard his young master's step.

But Xavier did not appear.

Lipp-Lapp's instinct had not deceived him. Xavier had just passed up stairs. Instead of entering the dining-room, he had gone at once to his own apartment.

The little party, meanwhile, returned to the drawing-room. Sabine, who could read her father's thoughts, saw that he was deeply grieved. She went to the piano, hoping by music to chase away his gloomy thoughts.

Benedict turned the pages, not so much because she required this service, for Sabine played well without music, but simply to be near her, and leave Sulpice and his father to converse the more freely. They sat, in fact, at the other end of the apartment.

"Father," said Sulpice, "you seem to take Xavier's want of punctuality very much to heart."

"Yes," said M. Pomereul, "in the first place because it is a want of respect. In the second, because it is one step further in the course he has pursued for five years. I will not deny that your brother is a constant source of grief to me."

"He will do better, father," said Sulpice, "he is so young."

"So young," said Pomereul, "and can you too offer such an excuse for him? Why, his very youth condemns him. At twenty-three he neglects every duty; he has no other pleasures, but foolish extravagance and excess, he lives his whole life in idle or vicious society. He despises his home, and prefers his club or the green-room of theatres. Why do you defend him, Sulpice, when you should be the first to blame?"

"I do blame him," said Sulpice, "but I would not that his faults should bring down on him merited but perhaps excessive severity. Besides he is my brother, I might almost say my son. I first taught him the truths of faith. I too suffer and am unhappy on his account, but I know that the lost sheep are often found, and I trust that the prodigal son will return to the fireside of home."

"What have I left undone for that ungrateful boy?" said Pomereul, scarcely heeding Sulpice's consoling words. "I readily gratified his every wish. His apartments are more luxurious, his equipages more sumptuous than mine. He is fond of horses, and I gave him a stable fit for a prince. I thought each sacrifice I made for him would attach him more and more to me. And now, to my bitter sorrow, I perceive that if he is dutiful and affectionate for a few days, it is only that he may profit by my joy to get some thousands of francs from me. At first I gave him a fixed allowance, and he owed every one. At the end of the year, they all drew upon me. I scolded him, but I paid his debts. It has been the same every time. I am tired now of being banker to an idle boy, whose sole occupation is to discuss the pattern of a waistcoat or the tying of a cravat, who brings into my house the language of a horse-jockey and the manners of the Café Anglais."

"Father," said Sulpice, with great tenderness, "I do not deny that you have cause for grief; the facts suffice, and like you I see that Xavier is upon the downward path which leads to ruin. Now, do not suppose for a moment that I wish to cast any blame upon you. If your affection exceeded your prudence, far be it from me to criticise your actions. But, perhaps, you were too generous.

"Most assuredly I was," said M. Pomereul; "of course you are right. When he, a boy of eighteen, finished his studies, I should have said to him, 'Take your turn at the hammer and chisel, learn each branch of the trade, as I did. You are to succeed me. I do not want the firm of Pomereul to change its name.' I yielded partly through affection, partly through vanity, to Xavier's desires. I often smiled at sight of the handsome, witty boy, extravagant, perhaps, and inclined to swagger a little. Ah! what a mistake. Scarce had he set foot in the clubs, than the clubs took him from me. He became a spendthrift, an idler, a coxcomb, a trinity of names which form the same person, an idle and prodigal being, the offshoot of an *effete* society. I saw

the danger, and would have averted it. It was too late.
Xavier had lost among his boon companions that respect for me, that deference and affection, which are only cultivated at the home hearth. My remonstrances only estranged him; he answered me sharply, and left me irritated and resentful. I loved him, and too often called him back to comply with his request. This has continued for five years. I repeat that I am tired of humoring this elegant idler. I feel that I am not justified in paying the expenses of an ungrateful boy, who takes me to be his dupe. Henceforth, the bank is closed."

"Let it be so," said Sulpice, "but the father must open his arms."

"To the repentant son, most certainly," said M. Pomereul. "But you cannot know, Sulpice, what I suffer from his conduct to-day when I compare him with Benedict. My true son is that orphan boy, who calls me father, and who finds genius and industry sufficient capital, without seeking to add money thereunto. Xavier's absence to-night was the drop which made my cup of bitterness overflow. To-morrow Xavier must go to work, and take direction of the factory under my superintendence."

"Good," said Sulpice; "I approve of your resolution to cut the evil short. A time may come when it will be no longer possible. Only, I beg of you, be gentle with him. His heart is not bad. His friends are all attached to him. Sabine loves him with all the fervor of her innocent heart, and I too, father, love Xavier with the love that mothers give to afflicted children. If I deplore his faults, I hope to see him conquer them and efface their traces. Vice fills me with horror, but vicious men sadden me. Like Christ I have come into the ministry, not to bring the just but sinners to repentance. We must not deceive ourselves. Xavier is the Benjamin of the family, and if he has been hitherto unworthy of a partiality in which we all had our share, I am sure that sooner or later he will deserve it."

"God grant it," said Pomereul.

"Promise me, dear father, to speak mildly to him," said Sulpice.

"Mildly," said Pomereul, "but firmly."

"All will be well then, believe me," said the priest; "and now, to celebrate this betrothal day with something a little less dismal, listen to Sabine's music which is almost as fine as Benedict's sculpture."

The young girl had just left the piano, but she took her seat at the organ, and played one of those marvellous sacred melodies, the *O Jesu*, of Haydn. This sublime prayer of supplication, in which the man's cry of agony is followed by the child's caressing entreaty, was interpreted by Sabine with rare depth and tenderness. Few could perform this piece as she did, and Benedict closing his eyes, beheld above him the groined arches of a chapel, heard a mighty organ taking on its wingéd notes the prayers of the kneeling multitude. When he opened them, he caught such a look of inspiration upon Sabine's face that he cried out to her in a subdued voice,

"Stay like that for one minute more. Next year I will send a Saint Cecilia to the Salon."

When the last notes of the music had died away, Benedict rose to take his leave. He shook hands with M. Pomereul and Sulpice, took a flower which Sabine offered him, and left the house, and the family, whom he thenceforth considered as his own.

"Till to-morrow," Pomereul had said to him; "henceforth your place will be set at the table every day."

When the young artist had gone, Sabine said good night to her father.

"I hope you are not going to work late," she said.

"Only to write a letter, dear child," he answered.

"I understand," said Sulpice, "you are going to wait for Xavier."

"Yes, he must hear my decision to-night."

"Remember your promise."

"Have no fear, Sulpice. Rest in peace my good son!"

The young priest went up to the top floor, where his room was situated.

Sabine went to her little apartment, just between her father's and Xavier's.

The young girl, who had begged her father to retire early, seated herself at a table, and began to write with the rapidity of inspiration and of joy.

Meanwhile M. Pomereul rang for Baptiste.

"Let me know when M. Xavier comes in," he said briefly.

"M. Xavier has been in more than an hour," said the man.

"Then ask him to come to my study."

A moment more, and Xavier was face to face with his father.

His countenance bore traces of late hours and of premature excess; his eyes were dim, his lips colorless, his usually careful dress was disordered, his hands trembling with nervous excitement.

"Why did you not appear at dinner?" said his father.

The young man hung his head, but said nothing.

"Where were you?"

"At the club."

"So you preferred the society of your friends to ours?"

"I have not dined," said Xavier, in a low voice.

"What were you doing then?"

"I was playing."

"You were playing, and you lost, I suppose?"

"I lost."

"A large sum?"

"Yes, father."

"How much?"

"Forty thousand francs."

"Your gaming purse is large then?"

"No. I played on my word."

"Indeed. So there are people willing to risk forty thousand francs on your word. That shows considerable confidence in your honor."

"And my honesty."

"How is that?"

"It proves that if I make debts I pay them; if I contract a loan I make it good."

"With what?" said M. Pomereul.

"With—well with the money you are good enough to give me."

"Our interview is going to be longer then than I expected," said the father. "I intended to let you stand like a criminal before his judge, but I pity your evident prostration, so take a seat and listen to me."

It was the first time Xavier had ever heard his father speak to him with such icy coldness. He lost the little assurance he had on entering, and almost fell into an arm-chair.

"When I married your mother," began M. Pomereul, "she was poor; I was earning my living by my trade, and in those evil days we learned to know and appreciate each other. When fortune came, it found us prepared to encounter her perils. Your mother remained what she had ever been—a model of a woman and a wife. If she possessed jewels it was simply because it pleased me to bestow them. She never asked for them, and was never vain of them. She brought you children up without ever ceasing to be an accomplished woman, a charming and lovable companion to me. She watched over you as long as God spared her, and one day she left me alone. Yes, alone; for though she left me you three, and you fill a great part of my heart, there is still a large portion which must remain forever widowed. I was true to that dear memory. I devoted myself to your education and that of Sulpice. You both received the same lessons, and from the same professors. Sulpice, it is true, had been longer under your mother's care, and perhaps inherited more of her angelic character. Scarcely was he of an age to think when he became serious; scarcely was it time for him to choose a profession when he chose the perpetual sacrifice of self, the abnegation of his whole life. He became a priest, and is already an apostle. The seminary took him from me, you alone remained. You alone were to live the life of the world, and sustain the family name among respectable people. If that does not excuse my weakness, it at least explains it. For awhile I thought your folly was but the fleeting effervescence of youth; I did not put you under the yoke of labor soon enough, and every day I have felt that you are going farther and farther away from me."

"Father—"

"Do not interrupt me, you will answer later. Your superfluous wants grew in proportion as they were satisfied. You took me upon the weak side of affection and paternal vanity, and since then I have been nothing more to you than the purveyor of your wants, aye, the accomplice of your faults. But one can stop anywhere, even on the decline of a hill. I see the abyss, I would escape it, and I feel you are rushing into it. I have purchased your horses, paid your debts, and it is enough. The banker is no more. The father can be found at your pleasure; all that is necessary is a change of life. But I will not be content with promises. I want facts."

"Command me, father," said Xavier, dejectedly.

"You have incurred other debts?"

"Yes, father."

"Their total amount is—"

"About twenty thousand francs."

"Let us add five for the *about*," said Pomereul, marking the figures on a sheet of paper.

"I gave orders to an upholsterer to have my apartments refitted and my furniture renewed."

"Furniture only five years in use? Well, I can countermand the order, and if need be indemnify the upholsterer. As for the thirty thousand francs due to other creditors, the sale of your stable will suffice for that."

"What, sell my horses?" cried Xavier.

"Yes, at the Tattersall next week."

"But they will say I am ruined."

"I prefer that to being ruined myself."

"And to-day's debt?" cried Xavier, anxiously.

"You must make some arrangement about it."

"Make arrangements for a gambling debt, father? Can you dream of such a thing? Why, it is sacred. My honor is at stake."

"Sacred debt, honor!" cried M. Pomereul; "truly you have a singular way of altering the meaning of words. Why, I ask you, is a gambling debt more sacred than any other? Is it because gambling is in itself a vice? For my part, sir, I hold that debt truly sacred which I incur towards a tradesman struggling for his livelihood, or a workman living by his salary. By failing to pay such a debt you drive the one to insolvency, the other to the street. It is a more serious matter than to disappoint some hot-headed boy, who stakes at the card-table a portion of his inheritance. Honor! Why honor is to fulfil the duties imposed upon us by society and by our conscience. For the soldier, it consists in defending his flag at the cost of his life; for the magistrate, in unswerving integrity; for the artist or man of letters, in employing his talents to the best advantage; for the merchant, in preserving his credit; for the son, in showing his gratitude to his parents. Honor! I can speak of it, sir, for I have kept my own. But I forbid you to mention the word in connection with a gambling debt. And as for the law, it considers them so sacred that it takes no cognizance of them."

"Father, would you advise me to—"

"I advise nothing. I simply say that I will not pay this debt."

"Then, what am I to do?"

"Make an arrangement with this creditor, as you have made with many others. You must ask for an extension of time, which will doubtless be granted you. You do not know, for you take no interest in family affairs, that Sabine was betrothed to-day to Benedict Fougerais. I do not think it right to sacrifice her share and that of Sulpice to your extravagance. I will not throw their fortune into the pit you dig for it. To-morrow you will take control of the factory, and will receive a salary of twelve thousand francs a year. By means of that sum you will pay this gaming debt."

"Father," said Xavier, rising, his face livid, his limbs failing under him, "you will not compel me to do this, to admit my poverty, to ask for a delay! Give me this forty thousand francs, and after that refuse what you will. Do not reduce me to shame and despair. What are forty thousand francs to you?"

"Such a sum represents the careful savings of several families," said the father. "Forty thousand francs! How many small tradesmen would it save from ruin, how many people from despair. I tell you plainly you have spent more than your share of the inheritance. The rest belongs to Sabine and Sulpice."

"What use is such a fortune to my brother," cried Xavier, "who lives in a garret, goes barefoot from choice, and feeds on bread-and-water?"

"You forget the poor, sir."

"Oh, it is horrible, atrocious!" cried the young man. "I am willing to amend, to give up everything, even to go into the factory, and be content with twelve thousand francs a year. But pay my debt, father, pay my debt. It must be paid, it must, do you see. I want your word for it, your promise. There is gold in that safe. Give me some of it till I pay, till I pay."

"I have said no," said the merchant struggling to overcome the impression which Xavier's grief made upon him.

"Take care, father, take care!" said Xavier, wildly, and as he spoke approaching his father's desk.

"Wretch, do you threaten me?" said M. Pomereul rising.

Just as the father and son stood thus face to face, the one livid with rage, the other justly indignant, the study door was suddenly opened and Sabine, with a cry of horror, rushed between them. Xavier pushed her away, and the young girl weeping threw her arms around her father's neck. He gently disengaged himself, saying, "Leave us, dear child, leave us, I beg of you; my disagreement with your brother is painful, it is true, but it need not alarm you."

"O Xavier!" cried Sabine turning to her brother, "do not sadden by a violent scene this day of my betrothal. Beg father's pardon, for you must be wrong. He is goodness itself."

Xavier remained silent and morose.

"It is my turn to command, Sabine," said the father gravely, "go to rest and come to me early. I want to speak to you."

Sabine addressed a last entreaty to her brother, who looked at her with a sullen and lowering eye, then embracing her father she went away.

"You refuse me," said Xavier, "you finally refuse me?"

"I do," said his father.

"Then," cried the young man in a despairing tone, "it is your doing if misfortune comes upon this house."

CHAPTER III.

THE KNIGHTS OF THE BLACK CAP.

IN the very heart of Paris, near the quays and bordering upon the river, in the broad light of day and in a pleasant neighborhood is a street or rather a narrow lane, through the centre of which runs a muddy stream and where high dark walls shut out the rays of the sun. The Rue Git-le-Cœur, one of the oldest streets in that ancient Paris which has disappeared under the progress of modern improvements, remained what it was in the middle ages. But little more and it would require to have an iron chain stretched at either extremity of it, which together with the watch might enable honest citizens of Paris to sleep in peace.

About half way down this street, some four years before this story opens, stocd a squalid shop, full of rubbish, rusty iron, broken or mended china, old clothes, curtains ready to fall into dust, copper vessels covered with verdigris, instruments of all trades which men may lawfully and openly pursue.

We say lawfully and openly, for in dark corners of the shop were huge bunches of keys of every conceivable form, finely pointed chisels, files of exquisite perfection, pincers that were masterpieces in their kind, in fine, a whole collection of disavowed articles or articles which were seldom called for in any other language than that of slang.

Father Methusalem, who owed his surname to his indefinite age, was, within the memory of a whole generation of men, already old when he became proprietor of this shop and all its belongings. These belongings, be-

THE KNIGHTS OF THE BLACK CAP. 35

ginning by a court dark as Erebus, gloomy as a prison gate, ended in a building for the construction of which Father Methusalem had made use of the most heterogeneous elements. Wood and mortar had the principal share in it. The doors and windows had neither form, proportion, nor equilibrium. Several panes in the window were supplied by greasy paper; hinges creaked, window bolts had ceased to work, the ancient stove smoked, and yet there appeared in white letters on a black board, placed just above the entrance door, the sign, PENSION BOURGEOISE. These words set us thinking. What sort of kitchen could there be in the underground depths of this extraordinary structure? Who could be the customers of such a *table a'hote?*

In the middle of a large room stood a deal table, stained with wine and gravy, cut and hacked by the knives of the boarders, and set at the time when we entered with chipped plates, wooden spoons and iron forks. There were no knives, as the guests usually brought their own. Pewter mugs stood before each plate. Benches served for seats. There was but one chair in the room; it marked the place reserved for Father Methusalem.

A dark, winding staircase with rickety steps led down into the depths of the cellar transformed into a kitchen. Upon a long range or furnace, in stew-pans as large as boilers, over a hot fire boiled a strange mixture, the *olla podrida* daily served up to the boarders; it was in fact the invariable dish. In the steaming mess were rabbits, bones of mutton, chunks of beef, the tails of red herrings, sheeps' tails, remnants of calves' heads, beets, onions and lobster claws. A great lump of grease and several cloves of garlic gave all these components a certain similarity of taste. Some fine chickens, ready for broiling, veal cutlets and beefsteaks laid out upon the table proved that this establishment was capable of rising to the level of circumstances. Beside the heavy, sodden-looking potato-salad was delicate lettuce or fresh red cabbage; close to the livid cheese, the odor of which, *sui generis*, betrayed its quality, a superb basket of fruit awaited those who were equal to the expense of a dainty meal.

Among the tables, pots and kettles moved an extraordinary figure who seemed in perfect accordance with her sinister surroundings. It was a woman scarcely three feet high and apparently some fifty odd years of age. Her head was disproportionately large, her face sullen and dark in expression, enlivened ever and anon by a gleam of cold malice. Her grey hair, too abundant to be held in check by the red plaid handkerchief which covered it, hung loose upon her shoulders; in her great ears, which stood far out from her head, she wore a pair of ear-rings, such as might have belonged to some Norman peasant and so long that they touched her shoulders. The upper portion of this singular creature was of the usual proportions of a woman, but her lower limbs were unnaturally small. She had the appearance of a human trunk attached to a pair of broad flat feet. This horribly deformed being was dressed in a Brandenburg or hussar jacket, a faded blue skirt and shoes made from a pair of boots whence the uppers had been cut off.

How Methusalem and this dwarfish creature had become acquainted, and why this singular pair, similar in vice, continued to remain together no one could tell. If Methusalem were the head of the house, La Naine* was undoubtedly its right arm, and her influence upon the dealer in questionable commodities was very great.

The Naine was Methusalem's factotum. She went to

---

* Naine signifies a female dwarf.

market every day and made all necessary purchases; and also to the lowest restaurants, buying up at nominal prices the half spoiled remnants. A tin box received fish, meat and vegetables all in one, an earthenware jar, the coffee grains, tea-leaves, and crusts of bread, which were used for various culinary purposes.

Meanwhile Methusalem was taken up with commercial affairs; he kept the shop, and waited upon customers. He had customers of two sorts, those who needed tools, who wanted to hire a complete disguise for a day or a week, and those who wished to engage a room or take some meals at the Pension Bourgeoise. The ordinary meal cost ten sous. It comprised the daily dish, bread at discretion, a small bottle of wine and a cup of coffee. Dinners *à la carte* were such as might be provided at a second-class restaurant.

A worn-out clock, of which the cuckoo disdained to appear, struck out six. The Naine immediately seized a spoon of unusual dimensions, and plunging it into the pot dipped up the soup. After which, taking the earthenware tureen by both handles, she mounted the stairs with an agility surprising in a being so deformed. Just as she reached the dining-room the door leading from the courtyard opened, and a dozen or so of men, with Methusalem at their head entered. Each one took his own place, which was indicated by a square of copper, marked with a figure, and Methusalem began to serve.

"Well, well, boys," he said with a sort of grim jollity, "how goes business? Have you anything to sell or to exchange? Who wants any rabbit skins, rusty iron, or broken glass?"

"I do," said a man of ferocious aspect, who was known as Rat-de-Cave. "I have six silver forks and spoons which Providence has thrown in my way; they are first class, and should sell for twenty-three centimes the gram, but they might get one into trouble. People who forget these things on their dirt-heaps, dare to claim them before the magistrates, sometimes, but I'll not give them the chance. Once melted up, silver never reappears except in the pocket. Will you oblige me by making these into ingots, Father Methusalem?"

"With pleasure, comrade, with pleasure," said the old man, "but we must be quick about melting it, and you about selling it. Several silver mines have been discovered near Valparaiso, a pick is put into the earth, and presto, the metal gleams. So silver is going down in the Parisian market."

"Bah," said Rat-de-Cave, "there is a tariff for silver."

"There is a tariff, true; but just take your ingots to the mint, my lad, and see what price they will offer you. It is a fine establishment, we must not speak ill of our neighbors; but suspicious, inquisitive, meddling; one cannot go there with an ounce of gold but they must know precisely where he got it."

"How much will you pay for silver, then, Methusalem?" asked Rat-de-Cave.

"Sixty-five centimes the gram," said Methusalem, "and I lose on it, it is merely to oblige a customer."

Rat-de-Cave shook his head, incredulously.

"And you, Pomme d'Api," asked Methusalem addressing a boy about fourteen years of age, whose pallid, worn face betrayed an early acquaintance with vice, "did you open many carriage doors last night, or pick up any cigar ends?"

"I should think so," said the boy, proudly, "there was a beautiful actress; a piece, the 'Drame de la Misère,' the play began at three o'clock; there was a crush and a crowd, no one looked out for his pocket. But the coming out was best of all, the street was packed, every one wanted carriages at the same time. I had ten of

my men ready to my orders. When one of them told
me the carriage was ready, I ran to open the door. I
helped my lady in, I assisted a stout gentleman, and
nearly every time, a fan, a lace handkerchief, or a piece
of jewelry remained in my hands. Mère Fanfiche got
the best of me, but it's all one, I don't complain. I love
pretty actresses, as much at least as the great people do."

"So Mother Fanfiche had all the profits of the sale?"

"I kept whatever I could for you."

"And what do you want now?"

"A complete costume of velvet, with shoes and hat to match."

"You have some plan in your head?" said Methusalem.

"I am going to the ball at Vauxhall," said Pomme
d'Api, "and I must be smart; there is no smuggling in
in white blouses there; it is near the Custom House."

"I say, Pomme d'Api," said Rat-de-Cave, "be gallant,
and take the Naine there, so that you will have a dancer
ready to hand."

The Naine's eyes flashed, and she replied,

"I'd have you to know that I want none of his company, nor the likes of him either. If I had wished, I could
have been the wife of a man who could raise four weights
of three pounds each, with his arms extended, and who
could have knocked you all down with one blow of his fist."

At this outbreak, Methusalem's guests all laughed outright.

"And you refused a husband of that sort," said Pomme
d'Api. "By my faith, you're hard to please; are you
waiting for the King of Siam, or must your heart be
touched like the strings of a guitar?"

"My reasons do not concern you, miserable pigmy,"
cried the Naine.

"Then why do you confide in us?" said the boy; "and
if it comes to that, I know all about it."

"Stop," cried the Naine, "stop."

"If you get angry, I'll tell his name," said Pomme d'Api. "I know more than you think about the romance of your life, and it was queer enough how I got to hear it. It was one night at a gingerbread fair. The Mountebank saw his clown come in dead drunk, to the despair of the manager. I saw there were some pence to be earned, and I offered to take his place. The man thought me rather ambitious, but he questioned me about my gifts, and finding that I could receive a kick or a box in the ear gracefully, he engaged me secretly, saying never a word to his master. After the show, being charmed with my début and the receipts, they invited me to supper. I accepted, and at dessert Signor Guigolfo asked me to enter his troupe. I declined the honor, informing Guigolfo that I exercised the lucrative trade of opener of carriages, and dealer in theatre checks.

"I spoke of Father Methusalem's boarding-house, and of you, Naine, and Guigolfo exclaimed, 'By your description, I am sure I knew her once.'

"'Bah,' cried I, incredulously.

"'It is so.'

"'How and where?' I asked.

"'It is a long time, now, since such a woman became a member of our company. She brought with her a child some three years of age, pale and delicate, with eyes of clear amber, and dress that bespoke wealth. We could easily train the child, and as for the woman, she had only to show herself to make an audience laugh. I engaged her. During her engagement we went through Spain, Italy, and France; when I offered to renew our agreement, she said that she wanted to put the child under a regular course of study. Study indeed, a fine joke! I had taught her enough to gain a living in any city of Europe. But remonstrance was useless, she took the child, and I never saw her since. If she is in want, give me her address. There is always place for her in the company.' I promised Guigolfo to bring you to him, but I always forgot. Perhaps I should never have remembered this episode, if you had not spoken of your journeys, and the athlete who asked you in marriage."

An expression of pain and rage crossed the woman's face, and she would have thrown the bottle she held in her hand at the boy's head, had not Methusalem, seeing the danger, interposed, reminding Naine of her duties, and calling Pomme d'Api to order.

Supper went off gayly.

After it was over, the Naine lit a petroleum lamp which gave out a horrid odor, and each one of the guests lighting his pipe or his cigar, soon filled the room with a dense cloud of smoke.

Conversation had ceased, the Naine was about to bury herself in the black depths of the kitchen, when a young man of some twenty years of age opened the dining-room door. He quickly removed his hat, put it under his left arm with a graceful gesture, and drawing from his pocket a soft cap of black silk, placed it jauntily upon the side of his head, and advanced into the circle of smokers.

"Hurrah for the Knights of the Black Cap!" said he in a sonorous voice.

This was the signal; every one of the guests immediately put on a similar head gear, and once bearing this passport, became mutually confidential and communicative.

"Have you dined, Fleur d'Echafaud?" asked the Naine of the new-comer.

"No, bring me whatever you like, only see that it is

good, and in a private room. Rat-de-Cave will keep me company."

"Willingly," answered Rat-de-Cave.

"What," cried Methusalem, "concealment from the Father of the Knights of the Black Cap!"

"You will know all in a day or two, old man," said the new-comer.

"Agreed, I permit the consultation."

The Naine soon appeared, with a beefsteak deliciously cooked, salad and a bottle of wine. She laid the table in a neighboring room, and Rat-de-Cave was soon closeted there with his hopeful associate.

The latter, whom they called by the name of Fleur d'Echafaud (Gallows-Flower), was a good-looking, well-made youth, carefully dressed and intelligent. His face was a perfect oval, his eyes were blue, and not as yet dimmed by late hours, his brows finely pencilled, and delicately arched. If his lips were somewhat too thin, they had a trick of smiling pleasantly. His hands were white, his feet small. His hair, reddish in color, showed to advantage the delicacy of his complexion. Everything about him indicated a man who had led an easy life, and whose habits would seem to have led him far from the motley assemblage by which he had been so rapturously received.

"Well, young un," said the old thief, "I smell a rat."

"You are not mistaken, devil's limb," said the other.

"What's the game?"

"A hundred thousand francs to divide."

"And the danger?"

"The danger is little."

"All right then, youngster, the game's worth the risk."

Meanwhile the Naine from a convenient corner listened quite as attentively as did Rat-de-Cave, while his associate continued as follows:

"Here it is, then," said Fleur d'Echafaud: "my master, Antoine Pomereul, had a visit the other day from his great friend, Nicois, the banker. I met him by chance in the hall, and struck by the expression of his face, concluded that there was a secret on foot. So as soon as he had been ushered in, I listened to every word of his interview with my master. We can so easily make other people's affairs our own. I learned, then, to my great surprise that the banker Nicois, having been imprudent at the Bourse, ran the risk of being found out, and came to borrow a hundred thousand francs from the millionaire. To do M. Pomereul justice, he is goodness and honesty itself; he treats me, his secretary, as kindly as he does his son, M. Xavier. I was not therefore surprised to hear him promise the money to his friend, and I determined to profit by this circumstance. I have been three years in his house, and have had time to take the form of every key, and to have the most important ones duplicated. M. Pomereul got the money at two o'clock to-day. To-night it will rest quietly in his safe, and we must take it from there."

"But of course you have not the key of the safe?" asked Rat-de-Cave.

"If it had been in my possession for an hour," said his companion, "I would have duplicated it also, but my master always keeps it."

"During the day, yes, but at night?"

"At night he places it under his pillow."

"And we have to get it from there?"

"Yes."

"It is a dangerous game, an extremely dangerous game, my young friend," said Rat-de-Cave; "doors to open, chests to force, are in my line, but to get my fingers under a pillow I always find hard. If Pomereul should wake?"

"Then we will send him to sleep again," said Fleur d'Echafaud coolly, "that is all."

"I do not like that kind of work. It's a pretty steep business, when the share is doubtful."

"Do you refuse?"

"I don't say that, but—"

"Fifty thousand francs!"

"That's tempting, but still—"

"Bah, would you make me believe, that so old a monkey has never learned to make faces? That you were never surprised, embarrassed, and in a moment of mad fear or avarice used your knife?"

"Never," said Rat-de-Cave. "I am a thief, a robber, what you will, but it stops there. I know every kind of thieving, and if need be, could invent more. I could take away a horse and carriage as easily as a pair of shoes, no game is too small for me. When I can't find some old chap with a pocket full of gold, I am content with a box of spice from the grocer. I prefer petty larceny to grand, because it often brings in as much, and isn't dangerous. What makes a first-class pickpocket is his sharpness in running risks, without taking his chance of a free voyage to New Caledonia. I thought I taught you all this before."

"You did, and I generally follow your advice," said Fleur d'Echafaud; "but this time the temptation is so great that I cannot hesitate. Do you think, old chap, it's worth while having founded the most wonderful institution of the age, when it brings in so little profit? I live well enough, it's true, but I have no carriage."

"Such luxury as that will let up on you," said Rat-de-Cave.

"Oh, I'll manage that," said the other. "Once the capital is in my hand, I'll take a run at Monaco. I can risk a few thousand francs on the roulette-table, and whether I win or lose, it will matter little. I shall be known as a gambler, that suffices. I shall tell my friends I won, treat them at the Café Anglais, invite some newspaper men, and next day the morning journals will have it that I broke the bank at Monaco. Thenceforth I can have horses and elegant apartments, and no one will inquire where or how I got the means to keep them. You admit that I am good at inventions; give me your hand; have confidence in me, and lend me your help to-night."

"The merchant goes early to bed?" asked Rat-de-Cave.

"Very early."

"His servants?"

"Are on the fifth floor, and go up there as soon as M. Pomereul retires."

"His children?"

"Mlle. Sabine usually retires at nine. The eldest son scarcely ever dines at his father's table, and as for M. Xavier, he never comes in till daybreak, for he plays at the club all night."

"So we shall be alone."

"Entirely."

"The only danger is if M. Pomereul wakes."

"In that case, coward, I will take charge of him," said Fleur d'Echafaud, with a sinister smile, which rendered his face positively hideous.

Rat-de-Cave rose.

"Count on me," he said.

"Everything must be ready," said Fleur d'Echafaud; "we will wear tradesmen's clothes, take a carriage, which will set us down at the corner of the Rue de la Chaussée d'Antin, the overcoat which we carry on our arm will conceal a blouse, in case there is need of further disguise. At the door we shall ask for M. Sulpice Pomereul; his room is above his father's; the *concierge* will suppose we are engaged in conversation with the priest; we shall get into our carriage and go to finish the night at some theatre, and next day Jean Machû will return to his ordinary occupations, and Fleur d'Echafaud will go as usual to M. Pomereul's, to fulfil his duties as secretary."

"I shall be with you."

"Till to-night then, at the passage Choiseul, where we will take our carriage."

The two wretches arose; but closely connected as they were by their complicity in crime, it was with profound disgust that Fleur d'Echafaud gave his hand to Jean Machû, *alias* Rat-de-Cave.

As they went out of the room the man muttered, looking after the young man,

"He will stop at nothing, at nothing!"

The return of Rat-de-Cave and Fleur d'Echafaud was hailed with acclamation.

"Thanks, good friends," said Fleur d'Echafaud.

"There you have genius, coolness, daring," said Rat-de-Cave, pointing out his companion to Father Methusalem.

"And such a contour!" added Fleur d'Echafaud, with a gesture of indescribable insolence and conceit.

Then turning to the group of "Knights of the Black Cap," he said:

"Marc Mauduit, secretary of the millionaire Pomereul, must now show himself on the boulevard. *Sans adieu*, my friends."

Leaving the courtyard, Fleur d'Echafaud stuffed his cap into the breast pocket of his coat, put on his beaver, and soon reached the thoroughfare.

CHAPTER IV.

THE CRIME.

AFTER the terrible scene which had passed between Monsieur Pomereul and his son, Xavier shut himself up in his room. The idea of returning to the club without paying his debt was insupportable to him, and he knew his friends too well to hope to obtain from them the sum which he so urgently required. Once alone, he paced the floor in uncontrollable rage, giving vent alternately to threats, and exclamations of shame and despair.

The Abbé Sulpice asked to be admitted. Xavier obstinately refused. Yet he knew that, far from adding to his suffering, the young priest would, on the contrary, alleviate it; still, instead of being grateful for his kindness, he regarded it as an expression of contempt. It made him angry to think that Sulpice had money in the safe, without reflecting, as his father had told him, that Sulpice's possessions were the patrimony of the poor. Blinded by his passions, harassed by his urgent necessities, he could not believe that there was any one in the world so unhappy as he, or any situation so terrible as his.

Besides he was mistaken; all the abbé's savings had gone the previous week to save a worthy man and the father of a family from bankruptcy. Moreover if, in his strict integrity, the young priest, like his father, believed that all debts, even gambling debts, should be paid to the last cent, he thought it but just that Xavier should pay his by instalments. Had he not after that fashion paid debts as sacred as these? Sulpice would also have considered it wrong to abet Xavier in his evil ways by furnishing him with the means. There was no way to save him, except by letting the rotten planks of the vessel which was carrying him astray break beneath his feet. Although resolved to use his influence later with his father that Xavier might be relieved, he thought it best at the time to let him fathom the depths of the gulf which yawned before him.

But Xavier was in no mood to listen to sound reason, to take advice, to seek for truth and light. He thought of but one thing, and that was his debt. Already he saw his name placed at the club among the bankrupts, a punishment inflicted on all members who did not discharge their gambling debts after a short interval. He told himself he would rather be branded as a murderer than incur such disgrace. It would forbid him the *entrée* to all fashionable clubs; his most intimate friends would cut him on the street. So, as he believed it impossible to exist without going to the club and being on familiar terms with the men about town, he fell into a sort of despair and hated all whom he had hitherto loved. The life which he had led for five years had deprived him of all sense of justice and injustice. A quenchless thirst for new pleasures, each of which left a sting, consumed him. To struggle against the weariness of monotonous pleasures and mad folly he exercised his imagination to find amongst them all something new. Without taking any special interest in horses, he went to races; without being fond of dancing, he was forever at the ballet; without any real love for art, he bought pictures.

Having lost all idea of what was really good and beautiful he despised its true language. The slang of the clubs or the boulevards enlivened his conversation. He aimed at being witty, but cared nothing for real wit and intelligence. Most of his stories were those which he read in the daily papers. It must not be supposed, however, that the speech of his companions, the gentlemen of the Jockey Club, was very profound or that their opinions were expressed in studied phrases. Their judgment of books, theatres, equipages, everything in fact was expressed by "it has or it has not *chic.*" That meant all. Whoever was wanting in *chic* might possess all the cardinal and theological virtues combined with the rarest genius, but still be of no account.

Xavier sat absorbed in gloomy reflections when the door of his room opened and Sabine entered. At sight of her the young man could not restrain a gesture of impatience.

"Do not be angry, Xavier," she said, gently. "I know you refused to see Sulpice and yet I ventured to come. For, kind and indulgent as our brother is, his black robe frightens you, and you dread his advice. I do not come to offer any; I have no right, nor is it my place to do so. I do not even know what you have done wrong. I even forget that you threatened our father in my presence. All I want is for you to become yourself again and make peace with us all. I do not want my betrothal to be saddened by your suffering. For I was happy yesterday, until your sorrow cast a shadow upon my joy. You want money do you not? here is my purse; it is not very heavy, what with collections, charity, and one thing or another. It contains just two thousand francs."

Xavier smiled sadly.

"Thank you, Sabine, but two thousand francs would not pay what I owe the Count de Monjoux."

"But that is not all," said the young girl, putting her hand into her pocket; "here are my jewels."

Xavier took them with feverish hand, necklaces, ear-rings, rings, all that his sister offered him; he examined them, calculated their value, then threw them into Sabine's lap.

"I would get scarcely ten thousand francs for all," he said; "it would not be worth while depriving you of them for that."

"Then here," said Sabine, resolutely unfastening the bracelet which her father had given her the evening previous; "for great evils, great remedies; pawn this bracelet, Xavier, but do not sell it, it was our mother's. I will explain it to papa some way or another."

"You would make a bad liar, Sabine."

"Then I shall simply tell the truth," said the young girl, gently. "I may be scolded because of the principle. . . . But I love you so much, Xavier, that I really think I suffer more than you do. But, in acting as he does, our father wants to save you, to bring you back to us, and to the home circle where you come so rarely."

"Sabine, you promised not to reproach me."

"I am not doing so. I am pleading our cause, mine, my father's, Sulpice's. We all suffer on your account. Wherever you may go, believe me, you will find none to love you as we do. So, if you still feel any affection for your sister, accept what will restore you peace, sell the jewels, pawn the bracelet, discharge your debt and promise me never to act so again."

"You are a dear creature, Sabine, and I am far from being worthy of your goodness. But keep your jewels, child, I have forty thousand francs to pay to-night and what you possess represents but half."

"Ah! if I had my dowry!" cried Sabine.

"When you have, your husband will take care of that," said Xavier.

"He? how little you know him! Benedict says he wants me to be poor, very poor. Is he not a flatterer?"

"It is worse than flattery, my poor child; it is absurdity. A year or two of housekeeping will cure you both of this pretty folly and generosity."

"But how are you going to pay Count de Monjoux?" asked she.

"I do not know!" cried Xavier; "but there is no alternative. I must pay, or I will blow my brains out. I will never live dishonored."

"And you would die, O Xavier! die, and by suicide, for such a debt as this!"

"To judge of such a matter is not girls' work, my dear child. I have twelve hours before me to find an alternative which may save me."

"You must find it! Oh! tell me you will find it!" cried Sabine.

"I will find it," said Xavier, impatiently; "but you must let me seek it. If I should chance to need you, I will remember your offer. Leave me now, dear Sabine; I must be alone."

The young girl hesitated. Her brother's hardness alarmed her. She had hoped he might be touched by her tenderness; she expected one word, one look of the old affection; but Xavier's heart was hard, and the expected word did not pass his lips. The young girl took up her jewels and her purse in a kind of shamefaced way; she had reached the door, when Xavier suddenly followed and kissed her, saying:

"You are a good sister, Sabine. An angel upon earth."

The tears rushed into her eyes, and she hurried out.

Left alone, Xavier almost blushed at his momentary weakness. He covered his face with his hands as if seeking an inspiration. He remembered his sister's words: "If I had my dowry." "Yes, but even if Benedict does not repent of his chivalrous absurdity," he thought, "the marriage will not take place for a month at least, and I cannot wait. Her dowry? If I were to marry, my father would have to give me one. That money would be mine, to dispose of at my will. No doubt; but I must remain free. What would be the amount of Sabine's dowry? I think father spoke of five hundred thousand francs. Yes, since my majority, he puts it for Sulpice and me at twenty-five thousand pounds of interest, the principal to come later. So Sabine will have half a million; and in justice he owes me as much. One fifth of that sum would save me. I could pay that envious idiot, Monjoux, who is jealous of my horses and of my success. I could pay for the new furniture, and have a hundred thousand francs pocket-money."

Xavier began to pace furiously up and down the room. "To know it is here—in this very house—within a few yards of me!"

A dark flush passed over his face at the thought which occurred to him, and he threw himself heavily into a chair. Yet he did not drive the odious thought from his mind, but simply tried to put it in another way.

"Well, after all, would it not only be what lawyers call an advance of inheritance?" said he.

He went to the bookcase and took out a large book with sprinkled edges. He turned it over long and diligently, till at last he found what he sought.

"The law understands the matter," said he; "it is neither crime nor misdemeanor to borrow money from one's father, whether by making an appeal to his heart or opening his safe. Article 380 reads: 'Thefts committed by children, to the prejudice of their father and mother, can only be made good by civil reparation.'

"I run no risk; my father will be very angry, and may even curse me. But his curse may be withdrawn, his anger appeased, and I have no choice." Xavier took a sudden, irrevocable resolution. A moment before dejected, despairing, he was now full of hope and courage. But far as he was already advanced in his fatal path, what he was about to do, in spite of all his sophisms, seemed so desperate, so terrible a crime, that he felt the necessity of stupefying his faculties till the proper moment had come. The clock struck noon. He rang his bell; Baptiste appeared, and Xavier ordered breakfast in his room.

"Do not forget the Chartreuse and some good champagne," said he.

When his meal came, he drank more than he ate.

His repast ended, he lit a cigar and began to smoke. So passed the day. He wrote a note to the Count de Monjoux, begging him to excuse his slight but unavoidable delay in discharging his debt; and smoked on again till dinner-time. After that, he kept up his courage by brandy and green Chartreuse, observing from his room the various movements in the house. In that peaceful dwelling, where he was the only element of disorder, the greatest regularity prevailed, even to the minutest details. M. Pomereul retired early. Their duties ended, the servants went to their apartments in the highest story of the house. That he might be more free to exercise his ministry of charity and consolation at all hours of the night, the Abbé Sulpice occupied a room, furnished like the cell of a monk, on the same floor with the servants.

By half-past ten Sabine and her father were the only two upon the first floor, except Lipp-Lapp, who slept in a little alcove just off his master's bedroom. When the merchant was asked why he did not keep his faithful Baptiste near him, he always answered:

"I depend upon Lipp-Lapp; his courage and fidelity are sufficient for my safety."

The hours seemed to Xavier to drag painfully. Feverishly he watched the slow-moving hands of the clock. He dared not enter his father's room before midnight, lest he should have sat up late reading. But when he had counted twelve strokes of the clock he rose, and, barefooted, opened his door and crept cautiously towards his father's room. The old man slept, but some painful thought seemed to haunt his sleep. Shadows passed over that face, which was usually so serene, and the name of Xavier fell indistinctly from his lips. The criminal paused in affright. Had his father recognized him? But no! Pomereul was dreaming. Under the influence of his dreams he made a hasty movement, and disarranging the pillows, showed a little bunch of keys, amongst which was that of the safe.

Xavier's hesitation vanished; he seized the keys and turned away.

Pomereul slept on.

Xavier left the door half open behind him, and entered the study. Though his father had never confided the key of the safe to him, yet he knew the one which opened it. Taking a little bedroom lamp, he entered the dark room where M. Pomereul kept his books and valuables. That day Marc Mauduit, the secretary, had placed there the hundred thousand francs destined for André Nicois, and never had an occasion more favorable been offered to a son descending to the level of a thief to satisfy his expensive tastes and shameful passions. Xavier laid down the lamp upon the table, chose the key, fitted it to the secret lock, and the safe opened. Heaps of bank-notes lay before his eyes. He stood irresolute. Strange phenomenon! Why did he not eagerly seize the money which a moment before he had persuaded himself would give him rest? Why did he not remember the article of law which had sustained him all that day? He forgot that, but he

saw at last what he really was—a thief. In presence of
the gold, of the bank-notes for which he had so longed,
he judged and condemned himself. The hot blood
mounted to his face; as he drew back from the open
door with a gesture of horror his eyes fell upon the portrait of his mother, where it hung above the safe. Her
pure image seemed to reproach him with his crime, and
implore him to degrade himself no farther. Terror mingled with remorse, and Xavier drew back, farther and
farther, his eyes still fixed upon the features of the dead;
back till he had passed out of the study, leaving the
door of the safe still open, leaving the keys in the secret
lock.

"To-morrow I will confess all," he said, "and accept
whatever punishment my father may inflict."

When he had reached his own room, Xavier threw
himself still dressed upon the bed. Overcome with
shame, terror, and remorse, he relentlessly condemned
and cursed his own folly and wickedness, till at last he
melted into tears like a child.

While tardy remorse thus triumphed over Xavier's perversity, two men rang at the door of the hotel Pomereul.
They asked for the Abbé Sulpice. The *concierge*, half
asleep, uncertain whether he was in or not, allowed them
to go up. Instead of proceeding to the third story, the
two men, who were no other than Rat-de-Cave and
Fleur d'Echafaud, stopped at the first floor. Fleur
d'Echafaud opened the door with a dexterity which was,
to say the least, remarkable. The two men entered and
closed it after them.

"Was I not right?" said Fleur d'Echafaud; "there is
none to interfere with us; we are masters of the situation; let us try to make good use of it. Now for Pomereul's study."

Rat-de-Cave cautiously threw the light of his lantern

into every corner of the room; as it fell on the open safe he cried out,

"We are robbed; some one has been before us."

"Let us examine," said Fleur d'Echafaud.

The robbers knelt down and groped in the safe with their hands.

"Do not touch the bonds," said Fleur d'Echafaud; "they would only compromise us; let us stuff the bills into our pockets and be off."

Rat-de-Cave and his companion began to fill the pockets of their overcoats with bank-notes. They had almost finished when a slight noise made them turn. They scarcely suppressed a cry of terror. M. Pomereul, in his dressing gown, had come into the study. When Xavier, carried away by his intense desire to procure money at any cost, even that of crime, had entered his father's room, the latter was sleeping a feverish sleep, almost like nightmare. In his dreams he had a consciousness of danger. Threatened by unknown foes, he was defending himself fighting; a terrible shock caused him to awake with a start, his face haggard, the cold perspiration standing out on his forehead, his limbs trembling. For a moment he could not collect his thoughts, confusing the real scenes of the evening past with the more horrible ones of his dream. Xavier's name came involuntarily to his lips, and the pain at his heart convinced him that he suffered from nothing else than the misdeeds, the harsh words, the threats of his misguided son. Pomereul's eyes fell mechanically upon the door of his room; it was ajar, and he remembered perfectly having closed it when he came in. The thought that some one had been in his room while he slept crossed his mind. But who could it be? Sulpice? Why, Sulpice had told him he would be obliged to go to La Villette, and that he would not return till very late. Sabine?

Sabine never came into her father's room at night; she was asleep long ago. M. Pomereul had heard her light step going about her household duties, and then silence, the time for prayer and sleep. Xavier! oh, if it were Xavier!

This thought, and the deep anguish it caused him, instinctively led M. Pomereul to look under the pillows where he usually kept the keys. He could not find them. He turned over pillows and bed-clothes. "Ah! the wretch has robbed me," he cried.

He sprang out of bed, threw on his dressing-gown, and taking no light, lest it should betray him, stole softly to the study. The door was open, Pomereul looked in, and saw a man kneeling before the safe, busy emptying it. There could be no doubt it was Xavier. Full of just wrath Pomereul advanced hastily, and in his haste, and owing to the dim light of Rat-de-Cave's lantern, he overturned a stool. At that moment the robbers turned; and at that moment Pomereul saw their faces and knew he had to deal with burglars. Rat-de-Cave and Fleur d'Echafaud exchanged glances; they understood each other perfectly; above all things M. Pomereul must not be allowed to summon help. Rat-de-Cave sprang upon the merchant, and twined his bony fingers round his neck. A stifled cry escaped from the old man; he struggled desperately, his eyes rolling in their sockets. He collected all his energy, and by a desperate effort would have released himself from Rat-de-Cave's hold, but the latter tripped him, and he fell panting to the ground. A providential succor arrived. A guttural cry was heard from a corner of the room, and a creature, whose nature neither of the robbers could define, sprang upon Fleur d'Echafaud, as the latter was about to assist Rat-de-Cave in finishing their victim. It was the faithful Lipp-Lapp, who, hearing Pomereul leave his room at an unusual hour, became uneasy, and followed him, guessing with his wonderful instinct that the merchant would have need of him. With sudden and terrible force, which almost compelled Rat-de-Cave to loosen his hold, the chimpanzee threw himself upon the assassin, paralyzing all farther effort on his part.

"The devil is helping him," howled Rat-de-Cave.

"Why it is the ape," cried Fleur d'Echafaud; "finish the old man, I will look after him."

The brief moment in which Pomereul was released from his assailant gave him time to draw breath, and collect all his strength. While Fleur d'Echafaud was preparing to dispose of the chimpanzee by strategy rather than by force, Rat-de-Cave felt that his prey was escaping him. But Fleur d'Echafaud, drawing a dagger from his breast, struck the animal with it on the shoulder, and turned upon him the anger and vengeance of the ape. With one hand Lipp-Lapp seized Fleur d'Echafaud by his red hair, and in the spirit of imitation common to his race, took him by the throat with the other. Fleur d'Echafaud would have been strangled like Pomereul, whom Rat-de-Cave had again thrown down; but he struck the monkey once more in the breast with his fatal weapon; Lipp-Lapp relaxed his hold, and fell full length on the floor, howling piteously.

"That's one out of the way," said Fleur d'Echafaud.

"The old man is dead," said Rat-de-Cave.

"Let us be off quickly," said Fleur d'Echafaud; "we have provided a sensation for all to-morrow's papers."

Distrusting Rat-de-Cave, or fearing he was mistaken, he bent over the corpse, and questioned the pulseless heart. "All right," said he, "a first-class funeral. As private secretary, I shall follow the corpse."

The assassins pulled up the collar of their coats, drew their hats over their eyes, extinguished their dark lantern, went out of the room, and quietly descended the stairs. The noise of the street-door closing made them pause to listen. Some one had come in. A firm step sounded on the marble of the vestibule. The same thought occurred to Rat-de-Cave and his companion, "We are lost."

CHAPTER V.

THE SECRET OF GOD.

NOTWITHSTANDING their habitual effrontery, the two villains were now utterly terror-stricken. If it should chance to be a servant belonging to the house, he would undoubtedly ask their business, nor was it likely he would accept the excuse which had satisfied the sleepy *concierge*, that they wanted the Abbé Sulpice. He would in all probability call for assistance, and have them taken upon the very scene of their double crime. Whereas to murder him upon the stairs as he came up would be a most dangerous proceeding. In their suspense they went half way up to the second story, and leaning over the bannister, caught a good view of a dark figure on the stairs below. Recognizing him by his cassock, Rat-de-Cave whispered,

"The Abbé Sulpice."

As he spoke the wretch drew a silk handkerchief from his pocket, and muffling his neck and the lower part of his face with it, said to his companion,

"Watch whatever I do, and say whatever I say, and we are saved."

He went down as coolly as if he had come on some legitimate business. The Abbé Sulpice hearing the sound of footsteps, looked up, and saw the two men advancing towards him. Rat-de-Cave addressed him in a tone at once agitated and respectful:

"The Abbé Pomereul, I believe,' he said.

"That is my name," said Sulpice; "what do you want of me?"

"We were told by the *concierge* that you were at home, and came to ask for your ministry."

"Is it a serious case?" asked the priest.

"The salvation of a soul is at stake."

The poor priest was thoroughly exhausted, prostrate in body and mind. He had passed through one of those terrible struggles the secrets of which are known to the ministers of God alone.

He had remained for five hours at a death-bed. He had disputed a soul with the powers of darkness. He had wrestled with the ungovernable fear of death. He had prayed and implored and wept by turns; to soften a stony heart, he had chosen the most touching and most consoling promises of Christ, and when he saw that they had no power to soften nor to touch the hapless soul, which was then in its agony, he had called down, as it were, the avenging thunders of God, brought to those dying ears the sound of the angel's trumpet, pictured all the horrors of the dreadful valley, opened the depths of the abyss, and showed the awful vision of the eternity of the damned. Seized with affright, the dying man had clutched the priest, as the drowning clutch the object nearest them, and begged that he might be reconciled with his Judge. The priest having administered the sacraments, had gently and gradually calmed the wild terror of that soul, weighed down by the weight of its sins. And the faithful laborer had come home; the day was done, the sheaves gathered in, and he was about to rest from those toils, which are like unto no other toils, when the two men waiting for him said, "The salvation of a soul is at stake."

He did not hesitate a moment.

"Let us go at once," he said.

"It is a great distance from here," said Rat-de-Cave, "so we have brought a carriage."

"Very well," said the priest, as he knocked at the glass door of the *conciergerie;* it was opened, they passed out.

"Our carriage is just here," said Rat-de-Cave.

So short a time had elapsed since they went into the house that the driver merely supposed they had been waiting for the third person who now accompanied them. Rat-de-Cave gave an address which the priest did not hear, and the carriage drove off. No one spoke, and the abbé read his breviary in a low voice. After a while he lost all count of the various streets and places through which they passed. However the carriage stopped with a jerk, and aroused Sulpice from the drowsiness which had begun to steal over him. He felt somewhat rested, and in any case, the idea of a duty to be performed was new life to him. Rat-de-Cave paid and dismissed the driver. Fleur d'Echafaud drew back the bolt from a wretched looking door, and led the way into an alley, the priest following closely. The door closed behind them with a bang, and Rat-de-Cave lit a candle in a copper candlestick, which seemed to have been left in readiness. They went up stairs; the house was squalid and evidently inhabited by very poor people. On they went to the very highest story; Rat-de-Cave put his key into one of the doors and opened it. The room into which Sulpice was now ushered was so large that the feeble light of a candle at the far end by no means dispelled its gloom. The priest indistinctly perceived a bed in one corner surrounded by dark curtains.

"I suppose we will find the sick person here," he said addressing Fleur d'Echafaud.

That worthy made no reply; but having allowed Rat de-Cave to follow the priest into the room, he locked the door on the outside, and his steps were heard descending the wretched stairs. The face of Rat-de-Cave was still concealed by a muffler, but when he approached the priest his voice was tremulous with emotion as he said

"I told you the salvation of a soul was at stake, but I did not say anything about a sick person."

"A sinner is a sick person," said the priest gently. "In what is my ministry required?"

"Father," said Rat-de-Cave, drawing near to the priest and pointing towards the door, "if *he* were to hear me, he would kill us both. He has brought you here for a purpose of his own. He will return presently. You shall know all. But I, having seen your face, having heard your voice, which, O my God! I have such cause to remember, the desire seized upon me—"

He paused in agitation so extreme that he trembled like a leaf. "To make my confession!" he cried hoarsely, and as if in desperation.

"Here, and at this time of night, my friend, and you in apparently excellent health?" objected the priest; "I can see no necessity for administering sacraments in this room. To-morrow—"

"To-morrow may never come for me," cried Rat-de-Cave with strange energy. "A sudden quarrel, the least suspicion of my having revealed this much to you, and all might be over for me in this world. Something urges me now to do what I have not done for years—to bend my knee to a priest; to you who, as you shall presently know, were once my preserver. If you refuse, on your head the consequences."

So terribly in earnest was the manner of the man, that Sulpice dared no longer hesitate.

"I spoke as I did from reverence for holy things," he said gently. "I prefer, except in extreme cases, to administer the sacraments in a church."

"Mine is an extreme case," urged the wretch. "I, who am spied upon, followed, certain to be promptly denounced to those who think little of human life, I dare not approach a church for such a purpose."

while ne was the prey of one of those dark presentiments of evil which sometimes precede disaster. He overcame a sense of doubt and fear, in view of the duty which seemed to him so pressing.

"But if your companion should return?"

"He is safe for twenty minutes at least; so, priest, I beg of you do not delay."

"I am ready to hear your confession," said Sulpice quietly.

"We are face to face now, as man to man," said Rat-de-Cave solemnly. "One of us possesses a mysterious power to which the other appeals. What I say to the man, he is free to repeat. When does the office of priest begin?—from what moment is he obliged to hear without making use of the knowledge he may gain? Speak, Father, I am a desperate man!"

"Kneel down," said the priest, struck by the man's persistent inquiries, "make the sign of the cross."

Rat-de-Cave did so.

"Say the *Confiteor*," instructed the priest.

Rat-de-Cave dimly remembered such a prayer; by the aid of the priest he managed to go through it. The abbé Sulpice continued:

"Now say 'Father, bless me, for I have sinned.'"

Rat-de-Cave shuddered; he was trembling in every limb, but he repeated the words in a harsh, guttural voice.

"Now," said the priest in a tone of sweetness and tenderness, "now you may speak, for in this solemn moment it is no longer the man who hears you, it is Christ, your Judge and mine. Confess the sins which weigh upon your heart. When I part from you I shall have forgotten them, and you can count upon my silence as I count upon the eternity of my God."

Little the priest knew that for the first time he had really touc--- ---dened wretch whom he believed so truly penitent. But Rat-de-Cave overcame the momentary weakness, and proceeded hastily:

"Father, at your feet, before God, under the awful seal of confession, which it would be sacrilege to violate, I confess that I have this night stolen a hundred thousand francs."

"Ah!" said the priest, "you must make restitution."

"That is not all," said Rat-de-Cave; "the owner of the money, hearing a noise, came in, I struck him;—I killed him!" added Rat-de-Cave hoarsely.

"Have mercy on that soul, O God, my God!" cried the priest; "receive it, O Lord, into thy bosom! Be merciful to one so cruelly hurried into eternity. Have mercy on him, have mercy on him!"

After this hurried prayer, the priest, recovering himself, bade Rat-de-Cave proceed with his confession.

He led him back, through the years of crime, and when he had come to an end of the recital, which Rat-de-Cave, the more completely to deceive the priest, had made as full as possible, the priest made a brief but fervent exhortation to the wretch to prepare for absolution. He was interrupted by the sobs and tears of the supposed penitent. So completely was the priest misled as to the sincerity of Rat-de-Cave, that, fearing lest no other opportunity might occur, he had resolved to give him solemn absolution. He raised his hand, when Rat-de-Cave stopped him:

"There is more that I must tell."

"What more, O my God! what more?" said the priest.

"The name of the murdered man," said the other.

"His name, then, if you so desire," said the priest.

"Antoine Pomereul," answered the murderer.

Utterly stricken by the blow, the priest rose, a mist floated before his eyes, he stretched out his arms in the form of a cross, and fell face downwards on the earth. For some moments, as Rat-de-Cave stood by and watched, consciousness seemed to have deserted Sulpice. But with returning feeling came to the priest the full remembrance of his anguish. Remembering the agony of his Master, silently endured, Sulpice gave no sign. He thought upon another day, when prostrate thus he had renounced the world, its passions, its desires, its ambitions; a day when he had died that he might live; in short, the day upon which he had taken his vows. And now the whole extent of his duty was before him: the struggle between the son and the priest. He knew that the murderer of his father stood by him, laden with the spoils, reddened with the victim's blood, and he, the priest, had no right to remember even what had passed, when once he had set foot across the threshold of that house. He might not bring the criminal to justice, though the dearest interests of society demanded that it should be done. The priest must forget the very voice of that man, and if before others he should meet him, must feign forgetfulness. For a time he lay half stunned, repeating ever and anon: "Thy will, not mine, be done."

Rat-de-Cave sat upon the edge of the table, waiting till Sulpice should find strength to rise. All at once the thought of his murdered father came into the abbé's mind. By an effort he raised himself upon his knees, and holding by the chimney-piece, got upon his feet.

Rat-de-Cave, now no longer afraid of recognition from the priest, had thrown aside his handkerchief and greatcoat. He wore a blue blouse open at the neck, so that the cruel and even brutal expression of his face was revealed in all its repulsiveness. For the first time the abbé saw him distinctly. He fancied he was mistaken, made a step forward and stopped.

"It is I," said the wretch; "I, Jean Machû, who once asked you for a night's lodging somewhere in the neighborhood of Brest."

"Ah!" said the priest, "how have you kept the promise made to me that stormy night? I saved you by my silence, and I find you now the murderer of my father."

The abbé seemed to have somewhat recovered his strength; he continued:

"Well, whatever you have done, or whatever may have come to my knowledge, I am sworn to secrecy, so let me go."

"Not yet," murmured Rat-de-Cave.

"Why add such unnecessary cruelty to your crimes?" said the priest; "let me go home. The victim may be still alive; in the hurry of the moment you may have mistaken unconsciousness for death. Let me go, Jean Machû, my father's dying voice seems to call me."

"He is dead beyond all doubt," answered Rat-de-Cave with feigned emotion.

"Be it so, then," cried the priest, in a voice full of anguish. "If the soul has indeed left that beloved form, my place is at its side—if not to save my father, at least to watch beside his corpse. I am a priest, and I must be silent; but I am also a man. You have robbed me of what I held dearest upon earth, and I implore you, by the memory of your own father and mother, whom you loved, to let me go!"

"Ah, Father, you forget," cried Jean Machû, keeping up his pretence of sorrow, "it is not in my power. I dare not. An attempt on your part to leave here would be worse than useless. My comrade will not let you depart before morning."

By one of those miracles of zeal, known to the hearts of apostles, the priest dried his tears. Suddenly it flashed upon him that this wretched criminal was also a penitent, and that precious moments were being lost which might be turned to his salvation.

"Jean Machû," he said, "if I must pass the hours of this terrible night with you, I may at least spend them as I will." The latter bent his head in token of assent.

"I will speak to you, then, of the past," said Sulpice, ".not to reproach you, but as one may recall old memories to another. Seven years ago I made a pilgrimage to Brittany. I remained for some time after, recruiting my strength in a poor hut upon the sea-shore. One night such a storm was raging as is sometimes seen upon the coast of Armorica, with its lofty crags and its tremendous waves. It was very late; I was still writing, when a loud knock came to my door. I opened it; a man half clad and in miserably thin garments rushed into the cabin, dripping wet, slammed the door and stood against it, as if afraid of being driven out again into the storm."

Jean Machû clasped his hands and rested them upon his knees.

"The man," continued the priest, "who then came into the cabin was exhausted; I offered him wine, I gave him dry clothing, and my own bed in which to sleep. All at once I heard a sound rising, as it were, above the warring elements. I recognized the noise. 'It is cannon,' I said, 'it certainly is cannon!' Trembling in every limb, and shuddering violently, the stranger listened. He too knew the signal—a convict had escaped from the galleys. They were in pursuit of him. I looked at him; terror was in his face, his lips trembled; he sank upon his knees, and cried out to me in his distress, 'You can save me!' I was placed between society, which on the one hand demanded that he should be given up, and a poor creature who, on the other, cried to me for mercy. I listened to his voice. I kept the guest whom Providence had sent me under my roof, and cared for him. And while he slept I wrote a paraphrase upon the words of Scripture, 'There is more joy in heaven over one sinner who repents than for ninety-nine just.' I went to the village next morning, procured some clothing from a fisherman, and at nightfall Jean Machû, the escaped convict, left my house by stealth. Before departing, he had sworn to lead an honest life, nor was he without the means of so doing; for, besides my little savings, I gave him a letter of recommendation to a relative of mine who had large fisheries in Brittany, and who would have employed him at my request. Have I told the truth?"

"You have," answered Rat-de-Cave.

"Now I meet that man again," continued the priest, "not as then, protesting his innocence of the petty theft with which he was charged, but avowedly laden with the gold of an honest man and stained with his blood!"

"Ah!" cried Jean Machû, "the tiger will remain a tiger."

"In the name of that God who sees and hears us, I declare and maintain the contrary. A drop of water suffices to penetrate rock. So, too, a tear suffices to melt the heart of a criminal. You called me hither, and I came. You said, 'Here is a soul to be saved,' and by the grace of God it shall be saved. You have marred my earthly happiness; I am the more eager to secure your eternal welfare. You have deprived me of a father; oh, let me be the means of restoring you to God!"

Rat-de-Cave bent forward, as if scarce believing the evidence of his senses.

"A short time ago," said the priest, "you knelt before me to claim the privileges of a repentant sinner for one long hardened in the ways of iniquity. That pardon I freely promised you: I blessed you that you might have strength to open your heart to me. Kneel now, once more, I implore you, that the work may be consummated. Kneel, renewing your sincere and heartfelt sorrow, that I, the priest, may absolve you."

So noble and so lofty were the words and the gestures of the priest, and such was the authority with which he spoke, that Jean Machû felt his heart fail within him. He could not understand the source whence abbé Sulpice drew his magnanimity and his eloquence, but he was overcome by them.

At length he stammered: "Father, I was moved to contrition for my sins when I saw you and remembered the past; but how can I make restitution?"

"There can be no true repentance without restitution, as far as that lies in your power. Nevertheless, that that may prove no obstacle, I freely give you the hundred thousand francs you have stolen to-night. They can be deducted from my share of the inheritance."

"You will give them to me freely and without reproach, as if I had earned them honestly?" asked Rat-de-Cave in amazement.

"Henceforth they are your own," said the priest; "strive to make good use of them. I repeat that I freely give them to you. If poverty has led you into crime, you are now safe forever from want. So I beseech you to stir your heart to deeper, more heartfelt contrition. Let my grief and my tears supply for what may be imperfect in your sorrow. Reflect once more upon how awful a thing it is to take a human life, to send a fellow-creature, full of life and happiness, out of this world; to make orphans; to bring mourning and misery to a happy home; above all, how such an act has offended your Creator. Let your tears flow with mine, saving tears of holy penance. Have compassion on your own soul, and make your act of contrition from the depths of your heart. Oh, I entreat you, by the God who died on the cross, to make, above all, a firm resolution of amendment before I absolve you!"

"Oh, come, come!" cried a mocking voice, as Fleur d'Echafaud threw open the door, "I have been listening for the last five minutes, and I expected every moment to see Rat-de-Cave crying like a woman."

The priest stood confounded, while Fleur d'Echafaud continued: "Hold up, my dear Rat-de-Cave, you are on dangerous ground. As for you, my fine abbé, I do full justice to your eloquence. If ever the Sorbonne is threatened, I shall back you against all odds to set it right again. Just now, though, your oratory is unseasonable. It may be all very fine to preach sermons to that brute, Rat-de-Cave, but that he should be so much affected by your preaching as to go to confession with a view to changing his life, I say no, by Jupiter!"

The priest would have spoken, but Fleur d'Echafaud interrupted him.

"Had I known your game I should have come back sooner. It is almost sunrise. We must get out of here, but we will not take you home just yet. I will call a carriage; you will get in with Rat-de-Cave, and, as I know all the roads, I will drive. We will go about for four hours or so, and at eight o'clock I will bring you back to Paris. Meantime you need not try to soften me; it is useless. Like green wood, I do not kindle."

This man's intervention had completely prevented the priest from completing what he supposed to be the work of regeneration in the soul of the wretch beside him. When he attempted to urge upon Rat-de-Cave the necessity of kneeling but a moment to obtain the remission of his sins, the latter only implored the priest to consider the danger in which they both stood, promising to avail himself of the first favorable opportunity to receive absolution. In another moment the sound of carriage-wheels told Rat-de-Cave of his comrade's return. He touched the priest on the shoulder, saying briefly, "Come."

They went down the dark stairs together, and the priest, who could admit of no compromise with his conscience, was purposely as unobservant as possible, fearing to see anything which might make him remember the place; and once out in the street, he glanced neither at the house nor its number. Without a word of remonstrance, or an attempt at resistance, he got into the carriage which Fleur d'Echafaud was to drive.

The latter, unlike his companion, had never permitted the priest to see his face. He kept his hat drawn down over his eyes, and was so disguised that it would be impossible to recognize him again. They drove about for four hours, sometimes passing over hard pavements or macadamized roads, going in and out among the suburbs, or round and round in a circle, that the abbé might have a confused idea of the way by which they had come, and in all probability be unable to remember it.

When day broke, Rat-de-Cave pulled down the window-blinds. Meanwhile the priest prayed on in a low voice, waiting till the last act in the drama should be accomplished. At eight by his watch Fleur d'Echafaud was driving along by the Palais Royal. He pursued his way as far as the Chaussée d'Antin. Stopping at the most deserted side of the new opera-house, he opened the carriage-door, and said to the priest,

"Get out now; you are almost at home."

Sulpice got out.

"*Adieu*," said Rat-de-Cave in a husky voice.

"*Au revoir*," said the abbé in a low and feeble tone.

Tottering, so that he was obliged to lean against a wall for support, the priest went home.

"It is queer," said Rat-de-Cave, addressing his companion; "we are strong, of course, but there goes one who is stronger than either of us."

CHAPTER VI.

The Accusation.

The Abbé Sulpice caught a glimpse of his father's house. A great crowd had collected about it. The Chaussée d'Antin in that vicinity was thronged with people. The fatal news of a crime soon spreads.

At six o'clock that morning M. Pomereul's man had come down with duster and broom, to do his master's study as usual. On the threshold he was arrested by a terrible spectacle.

Stretched upon the ground, with distorted features and protruding eyes, lay M. Pomereul, in all the rigidity of death. Clots of blood stained his clothing and his face. Near him the man heard a feeble moaning. It was Lipp-Lapp pressing his gaping wound with his hand, dragging himself feebly towards his master, and weeping after his fashion. Baptiste's first thought was to see if there was any life in the body. Ascertaining the contrary, he called the butler, the concierge, and Sabine's maid.

"A dreadful deed has been done," he cried; "M. Pomereul was murdered last night. Let us keep Mlle. Sabine from seeing this horrible sight. The police must be notified, and the deposition taken before M. Xavier awakes."

The butler went for the magistrate and for a doctor. In about an hour the police commissioners were upon the scene. The examining magistrate installed himself in the study, and dictated to his secretary an official report of the position in which the body was found. The evidence of theft was manifest. The murderer had emptied the safe, and probably had not thought of murder, till M. Pomereul's interference had decided his fate. This first duty accomplished, the doctor made his statement.

"Sir," said he, addressing the magistrate, "from the traces of blood on the face and clothing of the deceased, I was led to believe that he had received a wound from some blunt instrument which had fractured a portion of the skull. But having washed away the blood, I can discover no wound, except a mere scratch; the tumefaction of the face, and the finger marks upon the neck, are indisputable proofs that he came to his death by strangulation."

"But the blood?"

"Is that of the ape, who has received two wounds, inflicted by a three-sided dagger; one in the shoulder and one in the breast."

"What is your conclusion, doctor?"

"I will suppose the occurrence to have been as follows: M. Pomereul discovers the burglar and rushes upon him. The burglar seized M. Pomereul by the throat, Lipp-Lapp interfered, anxious to save his master, and the poor brute was rewarded for his humanity and intelligence by these two wounds. The murderer fled, Lipp-Lapp, pressing his hand to his wound, dragged himself towards his master. He put his hand upon the body, and upon the head, and that is how we find the bloody marks upon clothing and face."

"Then will you write out your report, doctor?"

"Yes, and I have dressed Lipp-Lapp's wound," said the physician. "I am of those who believe that the instinct of brutes is often wonderfully illustrated. No clue must be lost in such a case as this. One thing strikes me forcibly."

"What?" asked the magistrate.

"This," answered the doctor, placing a tuft of red hair covered with blood before the magistrate.

"What is it?"

"It is hair. A tuft of fiery red hair, which Lipp-Lapp held in his clenched fingers. In his extreme suffering he held it fast, and pressing the hand which contained it to his breast, dyed it a deeper red in his own blood. Staunching the wound with it may have saved the brute's life."

The piece of hair was consequently sealed and put aside, with anything else that could be used in evidence. The magistrate, out of consideration for the children of the deceased, would not permit them to be called till the examination was over. Both Sabine and Xavier were still asleep, and the Abbé Sulpice had not yet returned as it was only seven o'clock. The examination of the servants was very brief. None of them knew anything of the crime, and could therefore throw no light on the subject. The concierge was the only one who could give any information.

But the fact was that when Rat-de-Cave and Fleur d'Echafaud had rung the bell, that functionary, sleeping profoundly at his post, dimly remembered to have heard the abbé's name pronounced.

His replies to the questions put him were as follows: The bell rang. I answered. A voice asked for the Abbé Pomereul. I supposed he was in and said, Go up. Almost immediately after the abbé came to the door. He must have met the men who had asked for him on the stairs, for they all went out together.

"Is the Abbé Pomereul in?" asked the magistrate.

"No, sir."

"You will let us know when he comes. You can retire."

"Does it not seem to you," said the other magistrate.

that the proper person to inform Mlle. Pomereul and her brother of the terrible affliction which has befallen them is the Abbé Sulpice? His sacred character of priest will enable him to break it to them as we could not do. He will console them; he will bid them raise their eyes to Heaven, instead of directing them to earth."

The other reflected a moment, then said:

"It will be more humane, and besides it will be easier for us."

Baptiste was summoned. Like the other servants, he slept on the fourth floor of the house, and was utterly ignorant of all details of the terrible drama which had been enacted that fatal night. His deposition was taken, and the magistrate said:

"You have been a long time in the service of the family? Your young master, the abbé, will soon be in. Tell him all, and let him prepare his brother and sister to obey our summons."

The magistrate sat down at the desk upon which they had placed:

1st. The bunch of keys belonging to the murdered man.

2d. The tuft of bloody hair found in Lipp-Lapp's hand.

3d. A piece of fine linen, evidently torn in the struggle, and which had been found near the door of the safe.

The examining magistrate, M. Gaubert, was somewhere about fifty years of age, tall and sparely built, with a high broad forehead, a bald head, a slender nose with dilating nostrils, thin, bloodless lips, and pale face. His eyes were bright and unusually penetrating, and their expression was so searching that it seemed to read one's very soul. M. Gaubert was indefatigable in the discharge of his professional duties, wherein he displayed remarkable judgment and energy. The strictest integrity characterized his decisions. Nothing could either influence or soften them. But it was scarcely his fault that this constant contact with criminals had left him but little confidence in his fellows.

The other magistrate or police commissioner, M. Obry, was a totally different person. Though still young he was already eminent in his profession, and endowed with a clear head and a certain aptitude for literature. He saw fewer criminals than his brother magistrate and more unfortunates. Under the brazen shield of a magistrate he still kept a loving heart and one susceptible of great tenderness.

Whilst these gentlemen were in the discharge of their duties Sulpice Pomereul came staggering home. We have said that he had observed from afar the crowd which had gathered round the house. When they recognized the young priest, the groups of curious men and women made way for him with mingled pity and reverence.

"Ah, how dreadful for him!" cried one; "he loved his father so much."

"The Abbé Sulpice is a saint," cried another; "why has God stricken him so cruelly?"

"To make him even more perfect," said still another.

"Look how pale he is. He has come no doubt from the bedside of the dying, and O my God! think of what is before him."

Whilst these questions and exclamations were passing amongst the eager crowd, Sulpice went up the steps; he grasped the balustrade; he tottered. He rang the bell with feverish agitation. Baptiste opened the door. Scarcely had he entered the hall, when the good old servant fell sobbing at his feet.

"My master, my dear young master," cried he, "have courage."

"My father?" stammered Sulpice.

"Come, come and see him, come and pray."

Baptiste led or almost dragged the young priest into his father's room.

The body of the victim lay on the bed; a reverent hand had covered the swollen face with a handkerchief. Sulpice raised the cloth and looked.

With clasped hands and breaking heart he prostrated himself beside the bed. At first only sobs, then prayer rose slowly from his heart to his lips, and gradually a sort of calm succeeded the storm of his terrible anguish. When Sulpice felt himself strong enough to meet the others, he said to Baptiste,

"Sabine?"

"Mlle. Sabine has not appeared yet.

A moment after Sulpice was in his sister's room. The young girl's apartments, separated from her father's by a parlor, dining-room, and boudoir, were still so far distant that she had not heard any noise, either during the night, nor in the early morning hours. Besides there was often so much noise in the house, that a few comers or goers more or less never disturbed her. She always remained in her own rooms till the breakfast hour, which was ten o'clock. At that time she went down and found her father in the dining-room. Xavier sometimes joined them, but rarely; and as for Sulpice, the monastic frugality of his life forbade him to partake of this first meal. When no duties interfered, he usually came down after breakfast for a half hour's chat with his father and Sabine. Until breakfast time, Sabine usually occupied herself with some sewing or fancy work. She had just finished dressing when Sulpice came in. Sabine uttered a cry, for she saw the traces of tears on his face.

"Ah! What has happened?" she cried.

Then remembering what her brother had said the night before, she fixed terror-stricken eyes upon Sulpice, saying simply,

"Xavier?"

"He knows nothing of it as yet," answered Sulpice.

"You are weeping. Xavier knows nothing—then something has happened, and in this house. Something' but what? Ah," said she, with a terrible cry of anguish, "my father!"

"My sister! Sabine, my dearest Sabine," cried Sulpice, supporting her half-fainting form. "God is the master. He has given, and has taken away."

"Taken away," cried she, "taken away, and suddenly like this, without any warning sickness, without any alternatives of hope and fear to prepare us for the worst ! I am not so near to God as you, Sulpice. I cannot be resigned like you. It cannot be. It is a trance, but not death, no, not death. The doctors are mad, they do not know what they are saying. Oh, think what mistakes they make every day; they say a man is dead, and he comes to life in a few hours. Their remedies are sometimes powerless. I will take him in my arms, and with my tears and caresses bring him back to life. And if a miracle be necessary, you are a saint, Sulpice, my brother; you will ask God, and He will work a miracle."

"No," said the priest, in a voice which betrayed the terrible anguish of his soul. "We cannot ask for a miracle; it would be tempting God. No; our father will never wake again, except with our Father who is in Heaven. When I have given up hope, Sabine, be assured there is none."

"No hope?" cried she; "and you say this? But of what did he die? Was he stricken by a thunderbolt?"

"The thunderbolt which often falls upon unsuspecting victims; a crime—"

"My father murdered!" cried Sabine—and oh, how terrible was the horror of her voice.

"Murdered," said Sulpice, in a low voice.

"But why, why? He was so good! He had no enemies. Who could have done it?"

"That, my poor, heart-broken Sabine, justice is seeking to discover," said Sulpice, "and you will presently be called upon to aid it in its work."

"To aid it!" said she, bewildered. "But what do I know? I was asleep. I was sleeping while my father was being murdered. I was sleeping, and perhaps he was calling me! Why did not a secret presentiment warn me? I was sleeping—I who pretended to love him!"

"Do not reproach yourself, Sabine. Whilst this monstrous deed was being done I was far away, and Xavier did not hear."

"Does Xavier know?" asked Sabine.

"Not yet," answered Sulpice. "I still have the second part of my task to accomplish. Help me, Sabine. My burden is heavy; I almost sink under its weight. The daughter, indeed, is on the verge of despair; but the Christian should arise. Keep the dignity of your sorrow. Suffer and pray, but no tears or outburst of grief, if you can help it. Promise me that, for the present at least, you will not ask to see our father's body; later, when the magistrates have left the house, we will keep watch beside him—keep our vigil together. Will you give me your word?"

"I give it, Sulpice," she said. "Go to Xavier, go!"

Sabine sank down upon her *prie-dieu*, and kissed the feet of the crucifix, her tears streaming upon it.

"Lord," said Sulpice, "comfort her soul and strengthen mine."

When the priest was on his way to his brother's room, he was told that the magistrates desired his presence. The priest collected all his strength: the strength of his heart that he might not fail; of his mind that he might not betray, by word or sign, the secret which was the secret of God.

Just as he was entering his father's room, where the magistrates were in waiting, Xavier, coming suddenly to his door, questioned Baptiste as to what was going on.

"Sir," said the presiding magistrate, addressing Sulpice in a tone of deep respect, "will you take a seat? I beg your pardon for having to discharge so unpleasant a duty at such a time; but justice cannot wait."

"I am ready to answer your questions, sir," said the priest.

M. Gaubert made a sign to his secretary, who prepared to take down the deposition.

"You went out early yesterday evening?"

"About eight o'clock, sir. I was sent for on a sick call."

"You came in after that?"

"A little before half past twelve. As I went up stairs I met two men coming down, and one of them said to me, 'We need your ministry; the salvation of a soul is at stake.' I went whither I was summoned; I fulfilled my task, and returning—"

"You have nothing more to make known to the law?"

"Nothing more."

"You can retire. Mlle. Pomereul's testimony is also necessary. We are now awaiting her."

"I will go for her," said Sulpice.

After a moment's pause, Sabine, supported by her brother, entered the room. The expression of her face was pitiable. It was plainly to be seen that, trying to follow the example of her brother, she was making heroic efforts to control her grief.

"Mademoiselle," said the judge, "you were alone last night with your father on this first floor of the house?"

"Alone? I am not sure," she said. "My brother Xavier may have been in the house."

"I thought your brother spent his evenings, and, usually, his nights, at the club?" said the magistrate.

"Usually, yes," she said; "but as for that, he will tell you himself."

"You heard no unusual noise?"

"No, sir. I left my poor father at half past nine. I left him there sitting where you are. I went to my room. For about an hour I was writing in my journal little incidents of our domestic life, as I do every day. I went to bed. This morning Sulpice came and told me all."

"To your knowledge, had M. Pomereul any enemies?"

"Some people may have been ungrateful to him, but he had no enemies," she answered.

"Then there is nothing that occurs to your memory? No light flashes upon your mind? There was no one about him who entertained any ill feeling towards him on account of having been refused a favor, or the like?"

"My father never refused a favor which it was in his power to grant. I know that the day before yesterday his friend, M. André Nicois, asked him for a hundred thousand francs before the end of the month. My father sent for that amount. People always found him ready to oblige, or to give in charity."

"You can retire, Mademoiselle," said the magistrate. "Should it be necessary to question you further, you will hold yourself in readiness."

Sabine slowly left the room. As she passed through the hall, a storm of passionate grief reached her ears. Xavier, to whom Baptiste had told the whole truth, had, in spite of all the efforts of the faithful servant, rushed into the chamber of death. Throwing himself upon his father's corpse, he strained it to his breast, and spoke to it with the eloquence of despair. He implored it to answer him, he addressed vain prayers and supplications to it, the word pardon came again and again to his lips, and the excess of his grief bordered on frenzy. Vainly did Baptiste repeat that the magistrates awaited him. He could not be torn from the place. What could the law do? Could it with all its idle forms restore his father? Justice could do its work later, but only a few hours remained in which he could clasp the dear dead form in his arms, that form which another and more inexorable law must soon take from him.

Baptiste went to the magistrates and told them how useless were all his efforts. M. Gaubert rose.

"Let us go there," he said, "and question him where he is."

They went thither and stopped on the threshold. Terrible was the spectacle that met their eyes: The disfigured corpse and the young man half mad with grief; it was a sight to touch the hardest heart.

"How terrible his grief is," said M. Obry.

"Somewhat too demonstrative," said M. Gaubert.

"Let us for humanity's sake leave him time to recover himself," said M. Obry.

Xavier held one of his father's stiffened hands, and thus addressed the rigid clay:

"Father," said he, "is all over? You will never look at me again, your lips will never more call your son, you are lost to me, lost irrevocably and beyond appeal, lost, mute, dead. It is horrible, horrible, and when your eyes last met mine it was in anger, and your lips, instead of affectionate words, spoke but to drive me from you, almost cursed me."

M. Obry would have approached Xavier, but his companion stopped him.

"Listen," said he, authoritatively, "listen."

"Ah! I have been wicked and ungrateful; I repaid your goodness by causing you grief. I responded to your tenderness by indifference. My faults embittered your life, and my crime—'

Xavier stopped, for convulsive sobs choked his utterance. M. Gaubert waited till this storm of grief had passed, pressing his companion's hand significantly. Xavier continued·

"For money, that cursed money which I spent in folly or debauch I embittered your life. I needed money for my suppers and my horses. I needed it for gambling, gambling. Pardon, pardon, father, I implore you, pardon, pardon. Can you never let me know from that other world that you have forgotten everything, even—? I am indeed lost, forever accursed--"

M. Gaubert whispered to his friend,

"Let us retire quietly."

When they had returned to the study, M. Gaubert rang the bell. Baptiste appeared.

"I wish to put some further questions to Mlle. Pometeul. Ask her to come here."

When Baptiste had gone M. Gaubert said:

"You see, M. Obry, our task is being simplified. It seems to me—"

"You suspect—"

"What do you think yourself?"

"I? Nothing, nothing, I swear to you."

"You deceive yourself. The same thought which occurred to me a moment ago also flashed upon your mind."

"It is impossible," cried Obry.

"Everything is possible," said the other; "you are still young, but you will become in time as skeptical as I am."

Sabine came in, and the conversation ceased.

"Mademoiselle," said M. Gaubert, "in such a matter as this everything tends to enlighten a court of justice. We must have a perfect knowledge of this household and its habits to guide us in our researches. Do not have any fear, conceal nothing from us. Your duty is to tell the whole truth, you should be the first to desire the punishment of the guilty."

"My sorrow is too great to think of vengeance," she said.

"In what frame of mind was your father when you last saw him? Had he not been annoyed in some way?"

"Yes, he had some slight annoyances, but it did not amount to much. My father was so good."

"Was it not on account of some money which your brother had asked from him?"

"It was."

"M. Pomereul refused to furnish him with means for his superfluous expenses?"

"Yes, but he would have yielded. I offered Xavier my jewels and my savings, but he refused, such confidence had he in my father's generosity and affection."

"Perhaps, too, the amount he required exceeded the resources at your disposal?"

"That might be, sir."

"Did you witness any scene of violence between M. Pomereul and your brother?"

Sabine hesitated.

"Your duty is to speak, mademoiselle," said the magistrate almost sternly.

The young girl raised her tear-dimmed eyes to M. Gaubert's face; he did not heed her distress. M. Obry on the contrary cast a look of compassion upon her.

"The night before last," said Sabine, with an effort, "my father had a long conversation with Xavier. I do not know what they said, only the sound of their voices reached me. I was alarmed. Anxious to reconcile them I came here. My father seemed angry, Xavier had lost all control of himself. Ah! only for that he would never have said it. Xavier was wild, extravagant, but never wicked."

"What did he say, mademoiselle?"

"He said: 'You refuse me; then something terrible will happen in this house.'"

Sabine could scarce pronounce these last words. The effort overcame her, and she fainted.

M. Obry sprang to her assistance.

"It is like putting her to the torture," cried he.

"Yes, but the torture has brought out the truth," said M. Gaubert. He summoned Sabine's maid.

"Take your mistress to her room," said he, "Dr. Arnal is still in the house. He will take care of her."

Then he turned to his associate.

"We must proceed with this affair," said he.

The secretary was sent to bring Xavier from the chamber of death to the presence of the magistrates, despite his resistance. At first Xavier paid no attention to the magistrate's polite request; a more imperative summons was necessary.

When he came into the room his face was livid, his clothing disordered, his limbs trembling, his manner full of fierce excitement; he refused to sit down; advancing to the desk he placed his two hands upon it, and leaning forward, said in a strange unnatural voice, addressing M. Gaubert,

"Could you not leave me to weep for my father? Cannot justice come after the first outburst of filial grief?"

"Sir," said the magistrate in a cold, impassive voice, "the Abbé Pomereul and your sister complied with our demands as representatives of justice; have the goodness to imitate them."

"What can I tell you of this crime?" said he. "I knew nothing, I suspected nothing. This cowardly murder must be avenged, and I will help you with all my heart. But not now, not now! Oh, leave me in peace to weep beside the corpse of him who was my father!"

"You loved him very much?" said M. Gaubert.

"Ah, yes, I loved him very much."

"And yet you gave him a great deal of trouble?"

"I committed faults, serious faults it is true, but their memory weighs heavy enough on me now; you need not reproach me with them."

"You have debts?"

"Yes, sir."

"Arising from your extravagant habits, or from losses at the gaming table?"

"From both sources."

"You have lately, in particular, lost a large sum?"

"A day or two ago I lost forty thousand francs."

"Lost upon your promise?"

"On my promise."

"And your father refused to pay this debt?"

"He refused."

"Did not his refusal occasion a violent scene between you?"

"With which I bitterly reproach myself."

"You went so far as to threaten him?"

"No, sir, my grief led me only as far as despair. I saw myself dishonored, and I thought—"

"Of commiting a crime?"

"Yes," answered Xavier in a husky voice.

M. Obry looked at Xavier in amazement.

M. Gaubert proceeded with the examination.

"Your father was a man of regular habits. You knew

he retired early, and you waited till he was asleep to enter his apartments. Is it not so?"

"It is so," cried Xavier, overcome by the recollection.

"Taking off your shoes, you stole into the room where he was asleep; you took his keys and approached the safe to take the sum you required."

The young man hid his face in his hands.

"It was not surprising that a son should know the secret of his father's safe," continued M. Gaubert, laying an emphasis on each word, and giving them further significance by impressive pauses; "you opened the safe. It was full of valuables, and contained amongst other things the hundred thousand francs intended for M. André Nicois. The sight of the gold, the bank-notes, agitated, fascinated, bewildered you?"

"It is true, O my God true," cried Xavier, overcome.

"You bent down, you filled your hands with the gold and bank-notes, and laden with your spoils—"

Xavier brought his clenched fist down upon the table.

"That is not true," he cried, exultantly; "I was tempted, I took the keys, I opened the safe, but I did not steal; on my soul, I did not steal!"

He pronounced these words with such sincerity that M. Obry was deeply moved.

M. Gaubert continued in an unmoved tone:

"You came for that purpose, however?"

"It is true, I freely confess it. I said to myself substantially, My father's fortune, or at least a portion of it, will revert to me some day. I am only taking what will be my own. The thought of his anger was less terrible to me than the thought of being disgraced at the club. All that evening I encouraged myself with dangerous sophistry. I silenced my conscience and listened to my passions. Even the sight of my father sleeping did not touch me. But as I was about to take the money which I so much needed, when I was about to discharge my debt by committing a crime, my terrified eyes fell upon the portrait of my good mother, and my courage, if it could be called courage, left me abruptly. I saw the act which I was about to commit in its true colors, and I fled. I fled from myself."

"And yet the money is gone and your father is dead?"

"Then, sir," cried Xavier, fixing horror-stricken eyes upon the magistrate, "if you accuse me of having stolen the money, you also accuse me of having murdered my father!"

"An hour ago I came to that conclusion," answered M. Gaubert.

"I, the murderer of the best of fathers?" cried Xavier.

"The best of fathers to an unnatural son," replied the magistrate. And rising with more than his usual severity, he said with all the authority of his office,

"You will answer at the bar of justice for the crime of parricide."

"Parricide!" cried Xavier.

"Henceforth you are in the hands of the law."

Xavier's eyes dilated with horror, wild thoughts passed through his mind, and he fell unconscious into a chair.

CHAPTER VII.

Heart Trials.

Whilst the doctor was in attendance upon Xavier, who was slowly recovering from the terrible paroxysm which had ensued, M. Gaubert and M. Obry were left alone in the study.

The former seemed calm, like a man who had come to a foregone conclusion. He sorted his papers, numbered and labelled them. M. Obry, on the contrary, seemed anxious and nervous. His face changed from white to red. At last he got up abruptly and began to pace the room. M. Gaubert, raising his eyes, and observing the alteration in his companion's face, asked him kindly,

"Are you unwell, M. Obry?"

"Yes," cried M. Obry, in a voice which plainly showed his inward emotion. "I am suffering from a malady, which I see has passed you by while it tortures me; this malady is called doubt."

"Then you doubt this young man's guilt?"

"Yes, I do."

"But can you deny the evidence?"

"I feel a certain conviction to the contrary, an impression; I yield to the imperious dictates of my conscience, and I have a presentiment, which I am sure does not deceive me. This young man's sorrow is sincere. His horror and repugnance when he heard himself accused of so terrible a crime were not feigned."

"It was a well-acted farce, I admit," said the other; "but it should not mislead a man of your experience."

"That may be, sir," said M. Obry; "but there is something else."

"What?"

"This," said the other, holding up a tuft of red hair covered with Lipp-Lapp's blood.

"You understand, however, that very little importance can be attached to such a circumstance. Lipp-Lapp comes and goes about the house; he even goes out sometimes; who can explain the whim of this singular animal? Of course we cannot account for the presence of a tuft of hair in the hands of a chimpanzee, but it does not in the least influence my conviction. Let us look at the matter, M. Obry; let us discuss it, or rather let us lay the facts before ourselves. I would not wish the shadow of a doubt to be left upon your mind, because I know you, and know that it would be torture to you. The luxurious habits, the extravagance, the folly, the dissipation of Xavier Pomereul are well known. He admits that he is heavily in debt, and owes a gambling debt, or debt of honor as it is called, of which the amount is forty thousand francs, an enormous sum, so enormous that, wealthy as the father was, he refused to pay it."

"I know all that," said M. Obry.

"Xavier is bent upon having the money; he begs, implores, threatens. He threatens, do you understand? His sister heard him; he himself confesses it."

"True."

"His father having refused, the young man shuts himself up in his room, not daring to go to the club till he could pay his debt. He seeks some means by which to obtain the money, and loses sight of all honor and honesty. In the examination made by us a moment ago we found upon this young man's table a penal code, marked at the page containing Article 380. That proves a premeditated robbery. Then, a letter addressed to M. de Monjoux, informing him that the money owed him will be at his disposal the following day. That note was written during the evening. In the son's mind the hour of his crime was fixed; he could commit it fearlessly, in the certainty of impunity, the code having taught him that in such a case the law is powerless, the authority of the head of the family being supreme."

"The unfortunate boy has admitted all this himself," said M. Obry.

"He waited," continued the other, "till his father was asleep, took the keys from under his pillow, opened the safe, was in the act of taking the money, when his father stood before him, calling him thief. He grew frenzied; he was afraid of his father; he did not want to give up the money; a terrible struggle ensued; the son was the stronger; the parricide fled. All prudence deserted him. He forgot to close the safe, left the piece of his shirt upon the ground, and throwing himself upon his bed without undressing—horrible to relate! goes to sleep."

"You may be reasoning logically from the premises," said M. Obry. "You have drawn these conclusions from proved and admitted facts. Most men would think as you do, and yet is it not possible that, as he himself says, seized with terror and remorse he fled? His intention cannot be here established from the fact. He stole the keys and opened the safe, then, horrified at the thought of the crime, fled."

"If he fled, who took the hundred thousand francs, and who killed M. Pomereul?"

"That is what I do not know, what I cannot guess, and that is what remains for us to discover."

"The most we can admit is the presence of an accomplice," said M. Gaubert, "and that may require another trial. I believe, sir, that I am as deeply impressed as you with the sacredness of my office; my whole life is a proof of this; my conviction is unalterable, yet I will use every means to throw further light on this terrible affair, which will stir public opinion to its depths. And if, by your efforts, you should discover some proofs in support of your *presentiment*, I shall be deeply indebted if you will communicate them to me."

"You authorize me then to pursue my inquiries?"

"It is your duty so to do, and mine to urge you thereunto." Just then the doctor appeared with Xavier.

The latter fell into an arm-chair, weak, exhausted, utterly overcome.

"Sir," said he, addressing M. Gaubert, "I swear to you that I am innocent. I perfectly understand, with natural fear and horror, that circumstances are against me. And yet, however foolish and dissipated I may have been—sufficiently so to give ground for such an accusation—I loved my father; ah! indeed I loved him."

"Had you any accomplices?" asked M. Gaubert, coldly.

"Accomplices!" cried Xavier. "Do you not hear me say that I am innocent?"

"You must prove your innocence, sir, before the law," said M. Gaubert. "And now would you like to say good-by to your brother and sister?"

"Then you are going to take me—"

"To prison," said the other, briefly.

"Oh, I am lost, lost!" cried Xavier.

In this cry of despair, M. Gaubert saw only an evidence of a criminal's hardened conscience overcome at last by the evidence against him. It certainly seemed that a young man of irreproachable conduct and regular habits, accused of a parricide committed under such circumstances, would have protested against so horrible an accusation with more vigor and eloquence. But the circumstance of his intended theft weighed upon Xavier. His own admission, Sabine's testimony, in which that of Sulpice seemed to concur, all were against him. Yes, he felt that he was lost; his punishment was indeed heavy.

His nature was weakened morally and physically by his nightly vigils; his mind, too, prematurely enfeebled, lacked the energy which it would have required to sustain him in so terrible an ordeal. Xavier had no strong, living, overmastering plea to offer; he felt weak as a woman, helpless as a child.

"Sir," said he, "I would prefer to spare Sulpice and Sabine the pain of such a parting. They will be allowed to come and see me?"

"Yes, when the affair is made known to the public."

"Let us go, then—quick! For humanity's sake, send for a carriage, and, if possible, disperse the crowd outside; I can hear the murmur of it even here."

M. Gaubert gave an order to his secretary, who went out. Xavier wrote a few lines to his brother, and left the letter open on the table.

While the doctor and Sulpice were still busied with Sabine, Baptiste, weeping, kissed his young master's hand, and the latter, accompanied by the two magistrates, went down stairs.

M. Obry whispered hastily to Xavier,

"Keep up your courage. I will not desert you."

The unfortunate boy gave him a grateful look.

The two carriages had arrived. In one went M. Gaubert and his secretary; in the other, M. Obry and the policemen who had charge of Xavier. During the drive M. Obry was obliged to keep silence, owing to the presence of the policemen; but Xavier knew that he could regard him as a friend.

Whilst Xavier was passing through the first stages of the long and sorrowful way which lay before him, Sabine was slowly recovering consciousness. The first word she uttered was Xavier's name. Sulpice promised that she would see him soon, and went out to ask the magistrates if the three sorrowful orphans could be left together beside their father's corpse. It was then the priest first learned that Xavier had been arrested by order of the examining magistrate. At first he could not, would not understand. The note left by Xavier told him of the horrible accusation which had been made against his brother.

"But he is innocent!" cried he; "he is innocent! I will speak to the magistrates, and beg them to give me back my brother, my poor brother."

Returning to Sabine, he threw his arms round her with mournful tenderness, saying,

"Pray, oh, pray, Sabine; our trial is harder than I thought."

Sulpice went to the jail. He spoke with convincing eloquence; he pleaded for Xavier, answering for him—soul for soul, honor for honor. Every one showed the greatest respect and sympathy for the young priest; but, as regarded Xavier, could only give him an evasive answer.

"Alas! sir," said the magistrate to whom the priest addressed himself; "to save your brother, we must find another criminal."

"But then—" cried Sulpice.

He did not finish; he knew the real criminal; he had seen his face—knew his name. With one word he could prove Xavier's innocence and bring the murderer to justice. If his magnanimity had been so great as to pardon his father's murderer, must he then leave his brother under so monstrous an accusation? Did his duty oblige him to sacrifice Xavier and leave unpunished the escaped felon, Jean Machû? Was the secret of the confessional then so absolute that, placed between the honor and the life of his own brother, he, the priest, was obliged to see the family dishonored and his brother dying upon the scaffold, rather than betray a wretch's secret? A sudden and awful doubt flashed into the abbé's mind.

Had that man of blood, when kneeling before him, the priest, *really* repented? Suppose that Jean Machû had played a sacrilegious farce, had used Sulpice's power to ensnare him? Would he then be indeed bound to a man who had made a mockery of the sacrament, who had used the secrecy imposed upon the priest for a shield to save himself, as he would be to an ordinarily repentant sinner? In one rapid moment Sulpice thus questioned himself. His heart beat high, his head seemed burning. Alas! he had been only too certain of the criminal's sincere repentance. He had accepted his confession in good faith. These doubts came all too late. A terrible struggle was going on in his breast. By one word he could save his brother; but by one word he would become unfaithful to his oath, perjured alike before God and men. He wiped the cold sweat from his brow, and muttered in a feeble voice,

"I am sure of Xavier's innocence, but I cannot furnish any proof of it. Let me at least go and console him."

"In a day or two the secret will be made known, and the doors of the prison thrown open to you," they replied.

Sulpice getting into a carriage drove back to his home. He found Sabine in the chamber of death. The room had been arranged by her direction; tapers were burning at the four corners of the bed; a silver vase of holy water stood at the foot; a crucifix was laid upon the dead man's breast, and the curtains were drawn to conceal the face, changed, alas! beyond recognition. The perfume of flowers standing in vases about the room mingled with the air which had already become close and almost stifling.

Sabine burst out crying when she saw Sulpice, and said but one word·

"Xavier?"

"I told you, my poor child," said Sulpice, "to pray, and to be courageous. Let the sister rely upon her brother's words: let the Christian be resigned. There are afflictions which surpass human strength, and to sustain such we must ask our Lord to let us carry the Cross with Him. Do not question me, for I cannot answer. Do not tell me to act; I am powerless; but God is above us, and God knows all!"

Sabine sobbed aloud. An hour passed thus. The young girl was still weeping, and Sulpice begging mercy of Heaven, when the door of the room opened noiselessly, and Benedict Fougerais, pale and trembling, came in and knelt beside the orphans. Adopted on the very evening before the murder by M. Pomereul, he came to share in the grief of the family. Sabine raised her heavy eyes to his for an instant; Sulpice made place for him, but not a word was spoken.

All three remained absorbed in a grief which was deep and beyond expression. Ever and anon Sulpice recited some psalm, thus pouring the words of faith and trust in God into their desolate hearts. A strong cry went up from his soul to God with the lamentations of the royal Prophet. Once a sob which burst from his overcharged heart broke upon the stillness of the room.

Meanwhile, a scene scarcely less painful was being enacted in the drawing-room, in the dining-room, and, in fact, in all the apartments of the house, each one in turn being examined by the officers of justice.

Somewhere about eleven o'clock, a short time after the inquest, Marc Mauduit appeared upon the scene to fulfil as usual his daily duties.

These were the correspondences, the management of money, and the keeping of private accounts. M. Pomereul had thought very highly of Marc Mauduit, and was wont to praise his discretion, promptitude and good habits. In fact this well-dressed young man with the soft voice and intelligent face always inspired sympathy. Yet certain signs, by which physiognomists are rarely deceived, might have led one to believe that his employer rated him rather too highly. The lips were thin, and the expression of the face not wholly devoid of cunning. But, as we have said, these details were lost in the pleasing whole.

Marc Mauduit, lithe and graceful of figure, was always well and carefully dressed, but without affectation or display. He was fond of fine linen and the choicest perfumes. People often jested about the great care which he bestowed upon his hair, but he always answered in the same strain, that such care was more necessary for him than any one else, because he had to make up for its color by great attention to its arrangement. The servants, though not over-fond of him, always showed him the greatest deference. Xavier alone regarded him with positive hatred, which was easily accounted for by the fact, that the elder Pomereul so often drew a comparison between his son's extravagant and irregular habits, and the irreproachable conduct of his secretary.

When Marc Mauduit appeared at the door, the *concierge* said to him in an agitated voice,

"So you have not heard, M. Mauduit?"

"What is the matter? what is going on?" cried he.

"M. Pomereul was murdered last night."

"Murdered? By whom?"

"By whom no one knows. But you know how it is with the law; it must always have a victim and make some arrest, and so M. Xavier has been arrested."

"Ah!" cried Marc Mauduit.

He said no more; he seemed overcome by emotion.

"You are amazed, and no wonder," continued the *concierge*; "a boy can be fond of gaming and of horses, without being capable of such a crime. What do you think?"

"I? Why I can answer for M. Xavier's innocence."

"Right you are, M. Marc," said the other, "and it does you honor."

"But," said the secretary, "when such a dreadful affliction comes upon a family, notwithstanding their grief, many things have to be attended to. Have the funeral arrangements been thought of?"

"Nothing has been thought of, sir; every one is overcome with grief and horror."

"Their grief must not be disturbed," said Marc Mauduit. "I will consult with Baptiste, and see how I can be useful."

Marc Mauduit went up stairs and found Baptiste in the dining-room.

"My poor Baptiste," said he, "all I can do is to try and spare M. Sulpice the mournful duty of attending to the funeral. A certificate of burial is required, a coffin, a hearse, and printed announcements. I will attend to the legal formalities at the Mayor's office, and bring the news to the workmen in the factory at Charenton. I have lost a protector, a second father, in the person of M. Pomereul; looking down on us from above, he will see that I deem it my sacred duty to honor his memory."

Baptiste highly approved of the young secretary's devotion, and the latter proceeded to the Mayor's office, to the undertaker's, and lastly to Charenton. The news of M. Pomereul's terrible death spread general consternation among the workmen at the factory. They asked themselves what would become of them, now that they had lost the master who had sweetened their laborious existence, and made their domestic life so honorable and so happy. The old men who had known him when he and they were still young, and who had seen his hair grow grey with their own, wiped away bitter tears. Each one recalled some act of benevolence or of generosity on the part of that excellent man.

Moreover if he had only died a natural death, if they had been prepared for it by a long illness—but murdered! That good man! A cry of detestation against the murderer followed the first natural outburst of astonishment and sorrow, and when Xavier's name was mentioned the excitement was intense.

"It is impossible," cried a young workman, whose dress was somewhat above his station; "he may have kept late hours, and been fond of good dinners and the theatre, but that does not lead to such a thing as this."

"It does lead to such things," replied an old workman, slowly, "and before one thinks, too, laziness leads to drunkenness. First is spent the money earned, next the money borrowed, and lastly the money stolen. I do not mean this for M. Xavier, for I saw him first when he was a little fair-haired boy, and the sight of his rosy face did my heart good, but I say it for you and such as you, who want fashionable coats and despise the blouse, who read papers which are much more Rouge than Blue in their principles, and who play billiards in low coffee-houses; you make light of all this, my lad, but if anything bad happens in your neighborhood you're like to get the credit of it. M. Xavier, I can answer for it, never murdered his poor father, but his conduct was bad. Circumstances which are almost proofs rise up against him, and God knows where it will all end."

"Yes," echoed Marc Mauduit, "God knows where it will all end."

"Meanwhile," said Blanc-Cadet, the old workman, "we have a double duty to do, to pay the last tribute of respect to our good master, and if we can to help his son. We are only laborers, but the Son of God vouchsafed to be a carpenter, to show us the value of work. We have hearts, souls, arms, and intelligence, let us place all these at the service of the orphans. What say you, comrades?"

"We say yes, a thousand times, Father Blanc-Cadet," they answered, vociferously.

The old man now approached Marc.

"We thank you, M. Mauduit," said he, "for having come to tell us the sorrowful news; this afternoon a deputation of us will go to pay our tribute to the remains of our poor master, and to-morrow all the workmen will attend the funeral." The secretary then got into the carriage and drove rapidly homeward. The workmen were full of honest grief, never had they so fully understood M. Pomereul's constant kindness as now. When they thought of the infant-school, the work-room, and the hospital, all founded by this noble-hearted man, this model master, this generous capitalist, so delicate in his generosity, they could only repeat that no one could take his place towards them, and that they, too, like the Pomereul family, were orphans.

Each among them wanted to go to the Chaussée d'Antin to pray beside the mortal remains of the victim; it was at last decided that only the heads of each department should go in the name of their comrades. In about two hours afterwards they reached the Pomereul homestead. Sulpice, informed of their arrival, himself threw open the doors of the room, transformed into a *chapelle ardente*, and when he saw them kneeling, praying, stifling back their tears, the refreshing dew of heavenly consolation fell upon his heart.

"O God most good!" he said aloud, "God of mercy and of clemency, receive into thy eternal peace him whom thou hast so suddenly withdrawn from life. Shall not the memory of his many virtues, of his benevolence suffice for Thy justice? We venture to hope so, Lord! but if aught remains against this man who lived to do good, if the alms so lavishly given were not offered fully and entirely to Thee, if he forgot to send upwards to

Thy throne the feeling which prompted him to relieve the poor and to assist his brethren, then, O my God! hear the voice of those who weep, accept our prayers and tears in suffrage for the imperfections of his life, and let the pain and horror of his last hour obtain for him mercy in Thy sight."

All hearts were wrung, all eyes were streaming with tears, and all hands were outstretched towards the corpse as if for a parting benediction. Sulpice vainly tried to persuade these worthy men to retire; they insisted upon remaining to watch beside their master and benefactor, to share the vigils of the family. Both Sulpice and his sister consented, too much touched by this mark of grief and respect to insist further.

The night passed solemnly in the chamber of death. Sulpice prayed aloud by turns, and the others answered. Notwithstanding her weakness, Sabine had insisted on remaining beside her father. Kneeling by the bed, her hands resting upon the coverlet, she seemed utterly unconscious. Orders had been given that the funeral should take place very early in the morning. But, despite the unusual hour, a dense crowd had assembled in the Place de la Trinité. According to promise, the workmen of the factory at Charenton had come thither with their wives and children. An effort was made to spare Sulpice the pain of saying the Mass and giving the final absolution. But, heroic to the last, the young priest would not permit any one else to pronounce, in the name of the Church, the last farewell to the beloved dead. As soon as the coffin had been placed in the hearse, the children of the employees advanced, each one laying a wreath upon it. The procession passed on to Père-la-Chaise, where the Pomereuls had a vault. No panegyric was pronounced over the remains: not because the merchants, and the Municipal Council, of which M. Pomereul had been a member had excused themselves from accompanying the funeral, but because of the charge against Xavier. To speak of the death would have been the same as mentioning the name of him whom some already called the murderer, and would thus have inflicted another pang upon Sulpice. Every one present came forward to shake hands with him; he kissed the younger of the children, and took his place with Benedict in M. Nicois' carriage. The banker was in despair.

"Ah!" said he, in a tone of deep grief, "it seems as if I were, indeed, the cause of my poor friend's death. For had I not asked for the hundred thousand francs, no one would have thought of robbing him."

"You had every right to apply to a friend for the loan you required, M. Nicois," said Sulpice, "and I shall consider it my duty to render you the service my father had promised. The sum which you require shall be placed to your credit at the bank, and you can use it at your discretion; accept it from me, as you would have done from Antoine Pomereul."

"But under such circumstances—"

"Our affliction will not lessen your anxiety, sir; my father's friendship for you must survive him, for we are heirs to it. If ever you find yourself in trouble, believe me always ready to sympathize with you."

M. Nicois did not ask to see Sabine, but Benedict returned home with Sulpice.

"Do you think your unfortunate brother has chosen a lawyer?" asked he.

"He will not hear of it, my dear Benedict," said Sulpice, "he disdains it."

"Let me go and see M. Renaut for you;" said Benedict; "he is a young man of great talent in whom I have every confidence."

"Do as you like, my brother," said Sulpice, extending his hand, which the other warmly pressed.

"Will you not give me yours also?" asked he, addressing Sabine.

The young girl hesitated; but seeing the look of pain and reproach upon the artist's face, she could not refuse.

"A brother may indeed take his sister's hand," she said, gravely.

Benedict started, and looked at her with sad surprise; but Sulpice whispered,

"She has suffered so much that you must pardon her dejection."

Benedict soon went away, and Sabine threw herself into her brother's arms, with an outburst of grief.

"I can bear no more!" she cried. "My God! it is too much for a feeble creature. You are a saint, Sulpice, but I am but a woman, and my strength has given way."

CHAPTER VIII.

The Inviolable Secret.

However exhausted in mind and body, the Abbé Pomereul was none the less resolved to settle everything which his father's sudden death had left unsettled. His first important step was to proceed to Charenton, to secure the interests of the laboring population there, and also those of Xavier and Sabine. He sent for the foreman of the foundry, the heads of each department of carvers, mounters, or other workmen, and said to them frankly and kindly:

"My friends, your prosperity as well as ours rests with yourselves. I can guide you in the right way, teach your children the lessons of the gospel, and to love the things of God; but I am powerless to direct you in the affairs of the foundry, or bear so heavy a burden. If we give up—do not look well to the control of affairs at present—it is more than probable that more disastrous times will follow. There are rumors of war on all sides; hostilities with Prussia may begin any day; trade will inevitably suffer. The wisest course is, therefore, to continue what my good father so well commenced, thanks to your honesty and devotion. Henceforth you will no longer be the workmen or employees of the house of Pomereul, but its proprietors. Our commercial prosperity will be yours. You will have full charge of the laborers under your orders. If their conduct has been hitherto good, help me to make it still better. I will now have many cares; therefore I beg of you to supply what I cannot do; give me this consolation in my heavy sorrow: say to me, 'The men, their wives and children, still continue in the way of virtue, from which nothing will turn them aside.'"

"So it shall be, I swear to you, in the name of my companions," answered Blanc-Cadet. "As for our interest in the profits, we will accept it willingly, as upon it depends the future of our families. God grant that the loss of your poor father may be the last of your troubles."

"But will you not come any more to officiate in our chapel, sir?" asked one of the men.

"I will devote Sunday to you, as usual, my friends," said Sulpice. "My greatest consolation hereafter will be to live among you. Farewell, or rather *au revoir*. My mind is now at peace."

Touching was this scene between the Abbé Pomereul and the workmen of the factory. All of them had tears in their eyes, and Sulpice could scarce restrain his own emotion.

However, he felt better after leaving Charenton. The interests of his brother and sister would be protected, and these good people, whom he considered as a part of the family, would not suffer. When he got home, he went to Xavier's rooms. He found them in the greatest disorder. The servants, with a sort of superstitious feeling, had not ventured to go in since the legal formalities had been gone through with there. Sulpice opened the secretary. He examined all the papers. They were principally bills. He classified them by dates, catalogued them, and added the total. It was, indeed, a large sum, but Sulpice sent word to the creditors that he would meet their demands on Monday. He sent to the Count de Monjoux the forty thousand francs which his brother had lost, praying him to excuse the slight delay in the payment of the debt. That done, Sulpice breathed more freely. At first he thought of selling Xavier's horses and carriages.

"But, no," he said; "that would seem like casting a reflection upon him, and might add to the gravity of his situation."

He had just finished making up the accounts, and concluded his arrangements, when, coming out of Xavier's apartments, he met the doctor.

"You have come to ask for Sabine, M. Morvan?" said he. "I thank you for your kindness. The poor thing is very weak and broken down."

"She is in no danger, however," said the doctor. "She is a heroic child, and, being a true Christian, seeks strength from on high. I am less uneasy about her than about her unfortunate brother. M. Xavier has lost that wonderful vitality, which is one of the privileges of youth. He is in such a state of despair that I fear for his mind."

"Doctor! what are you saying?" cried Sulpice.

"It is a terrible truth, sir," said the doctor. "Late hours and dissipation have told upon his constitution. Another shock would finish him. Happily, however, there is only an accusation as yet. He may be speedily released. Of course, I am perfectly convinced of his innocence; but will he be able to prove it?"

"Ah! you believe in him; you—think him innocent."

"Why, I am certain of it," said the doctor; "and M. Obry is of the same opinion. Unfortunately, M. Gaubert has accumulated evidence, and the sole witness of the murder is a creature who, though gifted with the greatest sagacity or intelligence, is unfortunately deprived of speech."

"Lipp-Lapp?" asked the priest.

"Yes; the poor creature seems to know that he is needed. Sometimes his eyes question us, and his lips, too, tremble. He gives a cry, and great tears roll down his cheeks. Have no fear; I will cure Lipp-Lapp, and set him on the trail of the murderers, and I warrant you he will find them out quicker than a whole squad of police."

"You are right," said Sulpice, after a moment's silence. "That poor creature may be the means which God will employ to make known the truth—the truth which has escaped the magistrates, and which it is not in my power to make known."

Just then a mournful sound was heard in the adjoining room, and the doctor said:

"He has recognized your voice, and is calling you."

They went in. As soon as he saw his young master, the chimpanzee rose and held out one arm towards him. His eyes, dimmed by suffering, sparkled with joy, but, overcome by weakness, he sank back exhausted.

"You see," said the doctor, "your young master loves you; he has not forgotten you."

Lipp-Lapp moved upon the pillow, and with an effort put his hand to his head, making a movement as if pulling out hair, and then to his breast.

"See," said the doctor, "Lipp-Lapp is telling you how it was he plucked the hair from the murderer's head. The murderer wounded the poor chimpanzee, and it is for us to find the wretch."

"Yes," thought Sulpice; "for that is not Jean Machû, but the accomplice, to whom I have promised nothing, nothing!"

When Lipp-Lapp saw that his master was going away, he held out his long hairy hand, which Sulpice pressed, remembering that it had defended his father.

Sulpice had not seen his sister since the evening before; he found her in her little room, gazing, through her tears, at a photograph which Benedict Fougerais took care to have taken some hours after M. Pomereul's death. This representation of violent death was frightful, and yet the young girl could not take her eyes from it.

"Sabine, I implore you," cried Sulpice, "give me that horrible picture. Forget that you saw your father after his terrible death agony. Remember him only as he was when last we embraced him."

"I remember him so, Sulpice," she answered, "and yet my eyes seem to fix themselves upon this photograph, as if it would reveal the secret of our father's death, and tell us the murderer's name."

"God will make it known, if He so wills, Sabine," said her brother; "but, meanwhile, for us courage, for Xavier, resignation."

"And can he be resigned?" said Sabine; "must he not hate both the law and society at large? Who knows but that he curses me, for did not my replies to the magistrate help to draw on him their odious suspicions?"

"We must submit to whatever the will of God permits," said Sulpice; "Sabine, my sister, do not reproach yourself; you have done your duty."

"When can you see Xavier?" asked she.

"The day after to-morrow, I hope," replied Sulpice.

"May I go with you, Sulpice?"

"I do not feel strong enough to have you with me during that first interview, Sabine," said he; "let me go alone and receive the first outburst of his grief and despair. You will come afterwards like a consoling angel, to soften the bitterness of that poor heart. Alas! If your sorrow for Xavier's situation be not greater than mine, at least you have a better right to console him."

"But promise me that you will let me go every other time," said she.

"I promise," answered the priest.

"Then," said she, "I must dry my tears; if Xavier were to see us so overcome, he would believe his case hopeless. I will take your advice and put away this picture which renews my grief."

Sulpice left his sister to go to M. Renaut's; the lawyer, engaged by Benedict, to place his talents and eloquence at Xavier's service. He had not been able to see him until the matter was made public. When they reached the prison, Xavier, as was usual in exceptional cases, was received by the director of the jail. He was ushered into a room, of which the architecture resembled a chapel; and the first legal formalities were attended with so much courtesy and kindness, that Xavier warmly thanked the director. The latter, upon a word from M. Obry, had promised to pay every attention to Xavier, and to spare him as much as possible the horrors of prison life. A well-lighted cell, with newly whitewashed walls, was given him; a narrow bed, a table, and a chair constituted its furniture. At his request they brought him writing materials. As soon as he was left alone he began a long letter to Sulpice. When it was finished he re-read it, and remained absorbed in thought, his elbows resting on the table, and his head buried in his hands. A jailer coming into the cell aroused him from his meditations.

"What do you want?" asked Xavier. "I did not call."

"People never call here," replied the jailer; "I brought your supper."

"I am not hungry," said Xavier.

"As you please, sir," said the jailer; "but M. Gaubert has ordered a new examination, and it is better in such cases to keep up one's strength."

"What! is he going to question me again?" said Xavier.

"Most likely," answered the jailer.

"How many times does he mean to put me to the torture?" said Xavier.

"Until his opinion changes, or his conscience is satisfied."

The keeper went out. Xavier did not touch the coarse

food set before him; he threw himself on the bed, though he could not sleep, his wearied brain seeking for some infallible means, some indisputable proof by which to convince the judge of his innocence. But he could not find any. His past career condemned him in anticipation. He could find no means by which to escape from the burden of this fearful accusation. Not one act of virtue or of self-sacrifice arose to plead for him from out the long years of his unprofitable youth. His time had been always spent in pursuits which were useless if not dangerous. He could number many companions of the gaming-table, of his suppers and his revelry, but he could not count upon one friend. Benedict Fougerais alone had stood by him, and that not so much through liking or esteem for Xavier, as for Sabine's sake.

Sabine! What did she think of him? And Sulpice! With what anguish, he asked himself, would they too consider his past offences as sufficient reason to accuse him of such a crime! What mattered the opinion of the multitude if Sabine and Sulpice believed him innocent? The director of the prison came to see him. Xavier begged him to forward the letter which he had just written to his brother.

"You are still under secrecy," said the director, "but I shall send it as soon as possible."

The doctor also came to see him. He advised him to eat and keep up his strength; the director sent him in some lighter food, and Xavier managed to eat a little. During the evening he was summoned into the presence of M. Gaubert to undergo a second examination. When the summons came the prisoner trembled in every limb; since the evening previous he had been frequently seized with such nervous attacks, and they left him too weak and helpless to pass through this terrible ordeal. The jailer was obliged to repeat the magistrate's orders then Xavier rose with some difficulty, and followed him in silence. When he found himself in presence of the magistrate Xavier did not even hear the words addressed to him, but said in a broken voice:

"Sir, I am innocent; of course you do not believe it; you accumulate, to my ruin, a monstrous collection of facts and suppositions, in which you place the proof of my guilt. I repeat to you, as I shall repeat at the bar of justice, and as I shall proclaim to the world, that I did not murder my father. Your questions are horrible tortures to me; I am free to remain silent, and I declare that whatsoever you may ask me, I shall refuse to answer."

"Take care," said the magistrate, severely.

"What more have I to fear?" said Xavier. "I spoke to you at first with perfect frankness. I confessed my folly and my debts; my criminal attempt to rob my father of the sum he had refused me. I concealed nothing; I did not dissimulate. You had my effects searched. Did you find the money which you accuse me of having taken?"

"Your accomplice of course has the money," said the magistrate, sententiously.

"But I have no accomplice, nor am I a criminal myself," said Xavier.

"Let us look at things in their true light," said the magistrate. "You took the keys and opened the safe. While you were busy abstracting the money, your father, awakened by the noise, appeared. You, the son, were bewildered, stupefied, overpowered, by fear and remorse. Your accomplice, on the contrary, hoping to escape punishment by a new crime, threw himself upon M. Pomereul. A terrible struggle took place, in which, I admit, you may not have taken any part. A third actor appeared upon the scene; it was Lipp-Lapp, who attempted to defend his master, and fell wounded in his turn. Your accomplice fled and you crept terrified to your room. I admit that you may have been merely the passive spectator of a murder. But a murder was committed. If you did not strike the blow, who did? Name the murderer if you do not wish the consequences to fall upon your own head."

"Sir," said Xavier, "my mind seems to wander and grow hazy. I scarcely know myself when I hear you picturing, with such terrible distinctness, events which you seem to see, to render visible, tangible, and which weigh upon me and oppress me like some horrible nightmare. I will not answer you farther, because I scarcely understand. I cannot answer farther, for I am becoming crazed."

"Of course I cannot force you to do so," said the magistrate; "but for your own sake I regret the attitude you have taken, and I will not conceal from you that your refusal to answer will have an unfavorable effect upon the minds of your judges."

"M. Gaubert," said Xavier, "I have always heard you spoken of as an honest, incorruptible judge, and a man whose great skill and experience were coupled with wonderful perception. Therefore, if you accuse me, they will accuse me. I must be resigned; and, however great the effort, I must be brave. There are misfortunes which cannot be foreseen, and under which we fall and are crushed."

The magistrate turned to the jailer. "M. Pomereul is remanded," he said. Then to Xavier:

"From this time forth you are no longer under secrecy."

"I shall then be allowed to communicate with my family?" said Xavier.

"As far as the rules will permit," said the magistrate.

"I have written a letter. Can it be sent?" asked Xavier.

"After the director has examined it," replied the magistrate.

"You tell me that I am no longer under secrecy," said Xavier; "but what is more sacred than a letter wherein I show to my dearest friends, without any shame or disguise, a heart crushed as mine is?"

"It is the rule," said the magistrate.

Xavier followed the jailer. When he reached his cell he tore up the long letter which he had written to Sulpice, and contented himself with writing simply,

"Come! I am waiting for you!"

The unfortunate prisoner passed a sleepless night. He counted the time told by the great clock, which he could hear striking the hour. The night seemed interminable to him. He paced his narrow cell, listened to the step of the jailer in the corridor without, half hoping, with a sort of vague hope, that it might be Sulpice coming to visit him. At last a jailer appeared.

"You are wanted in the parlor," said he.

Xavier barely suppressed a cry of joy, passed through various halls till he found himself in a large room. He looked for Sulpice, but saw no one. At last the jailer pointed to where his brother stood motionless at a little iron grating, separated by a strip of wall from a similar one. Xavier could not throw himself into his brother's arms, nor even press his hand. Bitter was the disappointment, but he approached the grating and said, in a tremulous voice:

"Sulpice, my dear Sulpice, it is really you. You do not accuse me of this crime. In your heart you believe me innocent. And does Sabine know that I am not guilty?"

"We both pity you, and in your trial hold you far dearer than ever before. You were foolish, extravagant but, oh! you were not wicked."

"You do me so much good, Sulpice," said Xavier; "but, oh! if others could hear you."

"God will make known the truth," said Sulpice.

"Weak and foolish as I have been, Sulpice," said Xavier, "I did not deserve that Heaven should send so terrible a punishment for my sins. I am innocent, but how convince the world of it—how prove it to the judge, who questioned me again yesterday evening and found so many strong arguments against me? Everything worked with such infernal smoothness, and there is so fatal an array of circumstances that, were I a judge and did such a one as myself appear before me, I believe that I would condemn him, as M. Gaubert has accused and condemned me."

"Ah, misguided man!" said Sulpice.

"He is right, as a man and a judge," said Xavier. "The crime was committed and I was alone—alone. He told me I must find the other."

"The other, yes, the other," repeated the Abbé Sulpice, turning pale.

"The wretch whom he calls my accomplice," cried Xavier, excitedly, "I call the true, sole, and only murderer. But I am in prison; I cannot go in search of him nor assist justice. It seems to me that, were I free, I should know him without ever having seen him, such horror and remorse must his crime have left upon his face. Ah, that accursed wretch; who will bring him before the judge and the tribunal of justice to confess his crime and restore me my honor?"

"I will find him in this Paris, large as it is," cried Sulpice, half frenzied. "I will recognize the house. I will throw myself at that man's feet. I will say, to him, Release me from my oath. I will not be like Cain—the murderer of my brother."

Xavier gave a cry.

"You know him," he cried; "you know him!"

But the Abbé Sulpice had already recovered from the brief hallucination during which he had disclosed the fact that he possessed the clue to the terrible drama that had convulsed the Pomereul household. Pale and tottering, he clung with both hands to the grating which separated him from his unhappy brother.

"So then I am saved," cried Xavier. "You will go at once to M. Gaubert and give up the murderer, and I will be cleared from the horrible stain which rests upon me, and the wretch will undergo the full penalty of his crime."

"I cannot do it," murmured Sulpice.

"Well," said the prisoner, "of course, that is right; you are a priest, and must pardon even the murderer of the best of fathers; you would pardon your own murderer. You will, of course, do what your conscience dictates, and grant to the wretch that mercy which he did not show his victim."

"I cannot even do that, brother," said Sulpice. "I cannot go to the magistrate and say, 'I know the man, and will tell you his name.'"

"Do you forget that the honor of our name is at stake?" said Xavier.

"I do not forget," replied Sulpice.

"And that my life is in danger?"

"I know it."

"Yet you hesitate between your brother and this wretch!"

"It breaks my heart to see my brother here, but I do not hesitate."

"I do not understand—I am going mad!" cried Xavier. "You have discovered the murderer, and will not denounce him."

"I did not discover him," said Sulpice; "he confessed it all to me"

"And what matters your oath of silence, if you did give such an oath to a murderer, when it will lead to my destruction? Who can release you from it? The archbishop? the Holy Father himself? Why, he would tell you to speak."

"But," said Sulpice, "it is not merely a promise made to the criminal himself, Xavier; it is an oath made to God—a solemn oath from which no one can release me, not even the Pope. Yes, I know the name of him who murdered our father, and I cannot speak it. One word from my lips would set you free, and I must still be silent. I beg your mercy and forgiveness, brother; for, even were you to die, I dare not disclose the name nor unveil the face of our father's murderer. Know that that which binds, and at the same time is killing me, is the sublime and terrible thing which they call the secret of confession."

"Ah!" cried Xavier, "but it does not oblige you to let me die. I respect that secret; it guarantees the inviolability of a penitent's avowal; but when my head is concerned, it is different. You will not let me die, that you may remain faithful to your vow. When you swore inviolable secrecy as to the confessions received by you in the tribunal of penance, of course you could not foresee being placed between your own brother and a murderer. If you are silent, Sulpice; it will not be the law that condemns me to die, but you. I will no longer blame the judges, but I will curse you."

"Ah," said the priest; "what you ask is impossible."

"You will let me be tried and condemned?"

"Yes."

"You will see me brought before the Court of Assizes, sooner than reveal the truth?"

"I would give my life to save you, Xavier," said Sulpice, "but I cannot be false to my duty."

"But your duty will make you a fratricide," said Xavier.

"My God, my God!" said Sulpice, falling on his knees, "the trial is too great."

Xavier thinking that he had shaken his brother's resolution, continued:

"I know how sacred you hold the word duty. I respect no other man or priest as I do you, Sulpice; yet, if you persist in this cruel silence, I shall no longer regard you with veneration, but with horror."

"Xavier," said the priest, in a broken voice, "you remember when we were all children, we read books which described the agony of the martyrs. To urge them to apostacy, a mother, sister, or friend was sent into the cell. They cast themselves before the new-made Christian, begging him to burn incense before the idols, and renounce the Crucified. They said to him, what you now say to me, 'Sell your soul for love of us!'"

"Yes," cried Xavier, frantically; "sell your soul, renounce your God, be false to your priestly vow, risk eternal damnation if it is necessary, but oh, save me!"

"Wretched boy!" cried Sulpice, "you have lost your faith."

"I would trample the image of your God under my feet, if He obliged you to doom me to death. He is a cruel master who strikes me through your unrelenting honor as a priest. If you persist, Sulpice, I will appeal to the court, to the jury, to the whole world: He knows the guilty one, and will not reveal his name. And the law will oblige you to tell."

"You mistake, Xavier," said Sulpice; "it respects the rigorous law which seals my lips."

"And I who do not respect it," cried Xavier, "will curse you when the evidence accumulates against me. I will curse you when I hear my sentence from the judge, and when the foreman of the jury gives the verdict of his colleagues. I will curse you when the presiding judge reads the death penalty, and my last words upon the scaffold will be to curse you."

"Miserere mei, Deus," murmured the priest.

His face was deathly pale; a mist gathered before his eyes; his brother's words seemed to pierce his very soul. Meanwhile, Xavier clutched at the iron bars, his features were distorted, his lips covered with foam, he seemed the very image of despair. His brother's heroic virtue roused him to fury. Unable to conceive the martyrdom which the hapless priest was undergoing, he overwhelmed him with cutting reproaches and bitter taunts. At last, maddened at sight of him, who was even then offering his life in exchange for his brother's, Xavier cried, shaking the iron bars in his fury,

"Go, I say, go!"

"May I come again?" asked Sulpice.

"No," cried Xavier; "the very sight of you fills me with horror. May you be accursed! Cain! Cain!"

The priest crept away from the bars pursued by the horrible cry,

Cain! Cain!

CHAPTER IX.

A New Misfortune.

The Abbé Sulpice was in his father's study, looking over some papers, when Sabine entered. The young girl dressed in black bore even more in her heart than in her costume the deepest mourning for her father and her own happiness; she paused a moment mute and motionless before her brother. She regarded him with compassion mingled with profound admiration; and yet it seemed that the deep, tender affection she had once felt for him was lessened somehow in her heart; he was henceforth too great, too far above her. Something of that fear was upon her which kept from their side the wives, daughters or sisters of the prophets, of those whom the Lord seemed to draw near to His own glory, and cover at all times with His shadow. Sabine had just come from the prison.

She had gone thither attended by Baptiste, who waited without in the anteroom, and had learned from Xavier's lips the scene which had taken place between the brothers on the previous evening. Her first feeling was one of profound astonishment; her second, a species of awe inspired by Sulpice's exalted virtue, which seemed to human eyes so near cruelty. From that moment her whole heart went out towards Xavier. He alone seemed suffering; she pitied only him. Xavier's affliction was so entire, so horrible, that she forgot the agony which Sulpice was enduring. She did not renounce him, but her heart no longer sought him.

Alas! in those hours of terrible suffering, during that ordeal, to which few men were ever subjected, Sulpice had even more need of a friendly and consoling voice. Never had Sabine's affection and tenderness seemed more desirable than in this hour when both failed him. Yet he did not reproach her even in thought. Could he expect from this child the superhuman strength which he owed to his priestly character? Had he a right to raise Sabine to the same height as himself?

He knew that he would be censured by men, cursed by Xavier, that his brethren in the ministry would alone approve of the course he had taken, and that God only could console him. These thoughts flashed across his mind, whilst Sabine, in perfect silence, stood regarding him with painful intentness.

"You saw him?" asked Sulpice.

"I saw him. He was expecting M. Renaut."

"Did he speak of me?"

Sabine hesitated.

"Oh, do not fear to tell me all," said the young priest; "one pang more or less matters little."

"I do not understand," said Sabine, shaking her head. And she added in a low voice, as if half ashamed of her own words,

"I do not understand myself. I thought I had been early formed by you in the school of sacrifice, and it once seemed to me that however hard a duty might be it would find me ready. But it is not so. No, it is not so, Sulpice. All my compassion remains with Xavier. I will not tempt you, I do not reproach you, but I feel with a sort of horror, that I have forsaken you and preferred him."

Sulpice took his sister's hand.

"Do not reproach yourself," said he; "go to him. Console him, for consolation springs from your heart and flows from your lips. Meanwhile, if the priest's lips are sealed, the man will labor none the less unceasingly

There is a person whom I must seek, find, soften, that he may release me from my oath, and whose confession I will purchase with my entire fortune. Heaven can bring this man in my path, and I will hope. To each his part, Sabine. If I must journey through the desert with no angel hand to point out the spring of pure water, if I must bend beneath the burden of a sorrow misunderstood by men, do not pity me. God will keep account of it. But comfort Xavier, devote yourself to him. Bring resignation into his soul. Though innocent of this crime he has been guilty of many faults; teach him to accept the punishment patiently, that the hand of the Lord may not weigh heavier upon him. We may not see much of each other during the next few days; the work of justice is done in the shadow and I must struggle against it."

"Forgive me that I cannot rise to your height," said Sabine.

"Alas! my sister," said the Abbé Pomereul, "were I abandoned to myself, I know too well how far my weakness might lead me."

They held each other's hands for some moments, their lips trembled, their eyes filled with tears; at last they bade each other a reluctant good by, and Sabine went to her room.

Whilst the priest continued his task, and Sabine wrote in her diary the painful impressions of the day, Léon Renaut proceeded to the prison for a first interview with Xavier. The young lawyer was only twenty-eight years of age. A native of the South, he had brought from that land, where a burning sun looked down upon the sea, his taste for all that was great, his youthful ambition, his poetry and his eloquence. His examinations at the law school had been perfect triumphs, and his *début* had astonished even the veterans of the profession.

Renaut possessed in a rare degree the quality of perception. Inferior to many as a consulting lawyer, little versed in the arts of lying and deceit, he had a perfect passion for difficult, intricate or dramatic cases, upon which he often threw a sudden light, and seizing the more human side of the case, dwelt upon it with the skill at once of a novelist and a lawyer.

His whole appearance had contributed to the success to which he had already attained. He had a finely formed head, regular features, pale complexion, and large, brilliant eyes. His finely modulated voice had chords in it which went to the heart. He had a knack of using unexpected expressions and producing spontaneous effects. If he did not carry the judge with him, at least he made a deep impression upon the jury, and the opposing lawyer dreaded so formidable an opponent. He feared him all the more that the young lawyer always adhered strictly to oratorical or parliamentary forms. None knew better than he how to pay a tribute to the talent or experience of his adversary, and to wind up by showing in the most conclusive manner that he was wrong both in fact and in point of law. When Benedict Fougerais went to ask Renaut to undertake Xavier's defence the young lawyer held out both hands to him.

"Have no fear," said he; "skill will be of little avail in such a case as this; heart must win the victory, and, thank God! I have one in my breast. Certainly the case seems almost hopeless, and the unfortunate boy has got himself into the meshes of a net, which encloses him on every side, but we will find means to break the net and let the poor fellow out. How often I have seen him, gay, careless, light-hearted! How he did throw his life to the four winds of pleasure! What a prodigal youth has his been! What mad infatuation! The handsome gamester, the agreeable boon companion has come to this! An accusation which incurs capital punishment! I will see him this very day, and I swear, Benedict, that as surely as God has given me some talent I will use it to defend him."

"Thanks," cried Benedict, "thanks! I not only regard Xavier as the friend and companion of my youthful days, the son of my benefactor, but almost as my brother."

"You are to marry Sabine Pomereul?" said the lawyer.

"Her father gave his consent to our engagement the night before his death. Since then, though, I do not know what Sabine has in her head, but she avoids me. Yesterday she refused to receive me, sending word that her mourning did not permit her to see any one. Her mourning! as if I had no part in it. She has no right to deprive me of being with her, and trying to console her, once she has placed her hand in mine and said, 'I will be your wife.' You must save Xavier Pomereul. Then I shall have my hopes for the future."

"Yes," said the lawyer, "I understand what Mlle. Pomereul has not yet told you. Young, wealthy, of high social position, she was willing to become your wife; but if Xavier Pomereul be condemned, the poor girl will wear all her life two-fold mourning for the honor of her family and her love for you."

"Yes, yes, you are right, Léon," said Benedict; "procure the brother's acquittal and the sister will be restored to me. Sabine must be the guardian angel of my life. Ever since I remember, whilst the father gradually developed my intellect and my artistic sentiment, whilst Sulpice placed my inspiration under the guidance of faith, Sabine has seemed to me the very personification of domestic virtues.

"Well," said Léon Renaut, "this is another powerful incentive for me to espouse her brother's cause with all possible zeal."

The young men parted at the prison gate. Benedict went home, and the lawyer was admitted to the cell of his client. He found him utterly prostrate. The occurrences of the past two days had broken him down both in body and mind. His paroxysm of rage once passed, he began to remember Sulpice's words, and to repeat to himself that the murderer of his father was in Paris, and that one word would be sufficient to bring him to justice and restore himself to liberty, but he remained as if stricken by a sudden blow. Hitherto he had struggled against the accusation and protested his innocence; but now his courage seemed utterly to fail him. Where was the use, was not his cause already lost? The sight of his lawyer seemed to arouse him from his stupor. This handsome, brave young man, so full of life and vigor, who declared himself his champion, won his heart, and finding the lawyer convinced of his innocence he blushed at his own weakness.

For the first time he opened his heart, displayed its wounds, and related even the smallest details of the drama which seemed so incomprehensible, look at it as he would. Whilst Léon Renaut took notes and classified the facts, he became more and more convinced that his client had never even handled those bank-notes, which in a moment of frenzy he had dreamed of appropriating. But still the difficulties were many and serious. Would his own conviction influence the jury? In presence of facts would presumption in favor of Xavier have any weight? Certainly he had never undertaken so difficult a case, and the battle would be greater than any as yet lost or won by the young lawyer. Public opinion ran strongly against Xavier. At the time instances of wild and dissipated sons were becoming every day more frequent. Some robbed their father, others ended their career of folly by a cowardly suicide. Xavier capped the climax in the long list of those who ended a precocious youth spent in extravagant folly by a terrible crime. Of him an example must be made for other young men. Society had long been crying out that the new generation was rotten; therefore a gangrened member must be cut off. Arrayed against Xavier were the envious whom he had outshone in extravagance and luxury, the rivals of his successes on the turf, or at the theatre, fathers of families, and magistrates. They rang the changes in every key on the fact that an example was needed. Renaut knew all this and knew that it was harder to struggle against public opinion than to carry the jury. He did not conceal the truth from Xavier, but he used the very difficulties which lay before them to stimulate his courage.

"Alone I can do nothing," he said, "but with you I am strong. Your attitude in the court, your replies, will assist me greatly. Between this and the great day of our struggle collect your thoughts and take note of everything that may be useful to me. Meanwhile, I will see the Abbé Sulpice."

"You will get nothing from him," said Xavier.

"You are mistaken," said Renaut; "I will obtain from the man and the brother what is due to justice. He can give a certain amount of evidence without betraying his sacred office. He can tell that two men were upon the stairs when he went in, that they declared they had come for him, and I believe from my soul," added the lawyer with sudden vehemence, "that he may justly declare what followed to be a sacrilegious farce, a base subterfuge to deceive him."

"Even would he do so," said Xavier, "who will believe in the reality of so dark and mysterious an act in this

"It will be believed, because your brother will declare it," said the lawyer; "his reputation for sanctity will leave no room for doubt. However brief his testimony it will suffice. The presiding judge, jury, etc., will divine the truth, which it is forbidden the ministry of God to reveal. They will understand that the real culprit exists, and that nothing remains for them but to release you."

"You are right," cried Xavier, "and I will cling to this hope. If you believe in me, I must not lose faith in myself. I owe it to Sabine, Benedict, and the few friends who refuse to believe me a ruffian."

"Well, keep up your courage," said Renaut, "the battle has commenced. I will come every day."

Whilst Sabine went daily to console and encourage the prisoner, whilst Léon Renaut endeavored to keep up his strength, and whilst Xavier alternated between hope and despair, Sulpice was scouring Paris for the escaped convict, who held in his hands the destiny of his family. It seemed to him that God must put the murderer in his way, and that he must conquer him by gentle persuasion. It seemed that his sufferings were great enough to merit such a reward. Every day he set out and wandered hap-hazard through the streets, having but one object in view. He visited the prisons, the lowest parts of the city, scanned every group, peered at dark figures by night, and followed men whose gait or appearance reminded him of Jean Machû. He was forever consumed by this burning thirst. His nerves seemed strained to the utmost, like the cords of an instrument where the tension is so great that but little more will suffice to snap them. He returned home late at night, utterly exhausted, his head burning, his feet swollen and painful. Prayer seemed to refresh him unspeakably. He found in it, not, indeed, forgetfulness, but strength;

and the next day, sustained by his brotherly affection, he set out again on his wearisome quest, ever hoping and expecting to find himself, some midnight, perchance, face to face with his father's murderer.

Once he went to the quay. It was full of gaudily dressed, showy looking people. The day was one of bright sunlight. Every one seemed happy in the very fact of existence, though the political news was anything but hopeful. A declaration of war, however, seemed to every one the sure precursor of victory. No one feared for the future of that great army. The past was the best guarantee for the approaching struggle. When the sound of trumpets or the measured tread of a battalion struck upon the ears of the crowd, dispersing them to right and left, a murmur of delight greeted the soldiers. Their imposing appearance and martial mien was freely admired; already the people saw them returning as conquerors, and bouquets were often showered upon them as they passed.

Sulpice loitered about that portion which lies near the prison. All along the quay dealers in second-hand books displayed their wares to the passers-by. At some little distance from the last book-stall a crowd were surrounding a man who stood behind a wooden table, so formed that he could close it up and move it at will. This table served as a balustrade, keeping the juggler apart from the crowd. Dressed in a sort of dark velvet blouse, holding in his hand a black felt hat, the actor, who seemed to be remarkably dextrous, changed the expression of his face with wonderful art, and with astonishing rapidity. The hat was twisted into every variety of form, and, each one being accompanied by appropriate movements of the muscles of the face, the man was rendered almost unrecognizable. If you have read Poussin's *Études sur les Passions de l'Âme*, you can form some idea of this man, reproducing by turns the most opposite expressions with a skill which was really artistic. Children laughed till they cried; nurses forgot their errand; urchins shouted for very glee, and every minute the crowd grew greater, till it became impossible to pass. The policemen, attracted by the spectacle, forgot to cry "Move on," and Sulpice, about to cross the street, found it impossible. Seeing that he could not get on, he remained unwillingly enough, waiting till some movement of the crowd might permit him to pass. By the merest chance he glanced at the performer. Like a flash came a memory to him. Yet at first sight there was nothing about this man to disturb Sulpice; he was a mountebank exercising his profession with the ease of long habit. He laughed, he made jokes and grimaces, his countenance seemed open and simple as a child's, and yet Sulpice was involuntarily convinced that this face with its multifarious expressions belonged to Jean Machû, the convict. The very intensity with which the Abbé Pomereul regarded him seemed to have a certain fascination for the performer, and the priest noticed a slight twitching of the eyes, and saw that he seemed to lose something of his animation. In fact there was a sinister gleam of feared defiance in the mountebank's eyes which would have dispelled all doubt as to his identity, if doubt had remained in the abbé's mind. A sort of struggle began at once between Jean Machû and the priest. The former sought to escape the latter. Sulpice, thanking God for having at last brought him face to face with the murderer, was resolved to follow him wheresoever he went, and to wait as long as he might be inclined to exhibit himself to the public.

Jean Machû felt his vivacity diminish as his irritation increased. Whatever the Abbé Pomereul might have to say, he dreaded an interview with him. Finding no farther inspiration for the performance with which he had hitherto regaled the crowd gratis, Jean Machû brought his hand down upon the shoulder of a boy of fourteen or thereabouts, in whom it was easy to recognize Pomme d'Api.

"Play an air," he said, roughly. "I want to bring out my soap."

While the boy struck up an air upon the organ as a sort of overture, Jean Machû, still keeping his eyes fixed upon the Abbé Sulpice, drew from the table some green phials full of red liquid, and some cakes of soap wrapped in gilt paper. He seemed to find less difficulty in pronouncing his customary panegyric on the articles in question than in improvising the jokes which preceded each of his facial changes. The overture ended, the farce had to be played, the receipts taken in, and then to get away from the place, or discover, if he could, what M. Pomereul's son might want with him.

The Abbé Sulpice, approaching one of the book-stalls, seemed to be intent on an old Latin volume, but his eyes never strayed from Jean Machû, and the wretch became convinced that there was no hope of escaping that watchfulness. He tapped Pomme d'Api playfully on the head.

"Enough music," he said. "You must not disgust the Conservatory people."

Then, tearing the gilt paper from one of the cakes of soap, he began:

"Ladies and gentlemen, this soap for removing stains, which I have the honor of offering to your enlightened appreciation, has been patronized by all the crowned heads of Europe. Her Britannic Majesty uses it for the hands; the king of Prussia for shaving. It is infinitely superior to the ordinary soap which housekeepers employ in washing, to carbonate of soda, Panama chips, and all such. Come here, my bashful lad," continued the charlatan, seizing upon a raw lad who was listening with gaping mouth. "You have received, through your mother's goodness, a new vest fresh from the shop. The price is still on it—thirty francs sixty-five. Why, you got it for nothing! Now, ladies and gentlemen, you see the freshness of this stuff. I will just spill this little phial of oil upon it, like that—"

And the rogue actually did spill the oil upon the poor boy's vest, while the latter made desperate efforts to escape from the charlatan's grasp, and only succeeded in splitting his coat.

"Have patience, good youth," said Jean Machû, with a sardonic laugh. "I would surely not destroy such a costly vest, had I not the means of restoring it to its pristine splendor. You see the stain, ladies and gentlemen; it has visibly increased; it has now spread over the entire back of the garment. Well, I will now rub it with my soap, my incomparable cleansing soap, and immediately it grows paler, becomes effaced, disappears entirely, without leaving a trace. I thank you, worthy youth, for having lent yourself with such good grace to scientific experiments. If your mother should not be pleased, go fearlessly to the shop at the Pont Neuf. Your money will be returned. And now for some music!"

Pomme d'Api played a waltz, and meanwhile twenty hands were outstretched for cakes of soap.

"Order, order! have some order!" cried Jean Machû. "Two cakes of soap for you, madame? One for that pretty little cook? And you, brunette? Come, come! only twenty-four cakes remain, at sixteen cents a cake."

Machû displayed his merchandise under the very eyes of the police, to whom he showed a license from the prefect of police which seemed perfectly regular. Meanwhile, the Abbé Sulpice continued looking over the books. At last Jean Machû thought he could escape those watchful eyes. Hastily he refolded his table, gave it to Pomme d'Api, whispering,

"Go to the right; I will go to the left. Get back as quick as you can to Methusalem's."

But this movement had not been lost upon the abbé. He had made up his mind to speak to Jean Machû, but he had also to consider his promise. His conscience would not permit him to compromise the ruffian in any way, nor say or do anything which might betray the secret. He feigned, therefore, to have lost sight of him; but scarce had Machû gone round the nearest corner than the abbé followed him. Jean Machû turned once, but the crowd of vehicles prevented him from seeing the priest, and supposing that he had eluded him, he rushed down the Rue Git-le-Cœur. When he reached Methusalem's house he turned again, but saw no one. The Abbé Pomereul had hidden himself in an alley way. He determined to wait till nightfall, and then have a decisive interview with the murderer. He leaned against the wall, perfectly motionless. He could easily see from his post of observation what manner of customers entered Methusalem's shop. They were not purchasers of its wares, for none came out of that sinister abode. He divined at once that he was in the vicinity of a most dangerous den, where a visit from the police would result in the arrest of many others as well as his father's murderer.

The day slowly waned, and night came—a dark night, moonless and starless. One by one Methusalem's customers quitted the "boarding-house." Pomme d'Api sauntered out, cigar in mouth, and went on his way to Chatelet to exercise his calling of opening carriage-doors in front of the theatre. Fleur d'Echafaud next appeared arm in arm with a showily-dressed young man. Soon afterwards a heterogeneous party issued, in every variety of costume.

Jean Machû came out last. The searching glances which he cast round did not penetrate the abbé's hiding-place, and just as he passed the dark alley way he made a gesture which seemed to say,

"All's well; why should I be uneasy?"

Jean Machû went through St. Michel's Square, and proceeding along the quay, passed the Hôtel Dieu and Notre Dame.

He seemed lost in the deep shadows of the night, when a footstep close behind him caused him to turn his head. He waited a moment to see whether it was simply a passer-by, or whether some one was following him of a set purpose. As he did so, a hand was suddenly laid upon his shoulder, and he barely suppressed a cry.

"You are not mistaken, Jean Machû," said a voice, which trembled with excessive emotion; "it is I."

"You promised to forget," cried he.

"I swore that I would not betray you."

"But don't you understand that your being seen with me is dangerous?"

"Yes; otherwise I would have addressed you to-day, in front of the prison, upon which your gaze was fixed, as if you feared lest its walls should claim their prey. You know, then, Jean Machû, the result of your crime, and of your diabolical ingenuity."

"Yes," answered the felon.

"You know that my unfortunate brother is accused in your place, and that in your place he will, perhaps, be condemned to death?"

"What can I do?" cried the ruffian, in a hoarse, unnatural voice. "All I want is impunity. The law has made a mistake; that is not my business. Your brother has his innocence to plead for him, and besides a famous lawyer."

"Do you not tremble lest I, seeing my brother in such peril, should save him at any price?"

"No," said Jean Machû, composedly.

"Beware, Jean Machû! I am but a man, a weak, frail man, whose reason seems at times to totter under the weight of a duty so cruel. Sometimes I can scarcely distinguish right from wrong. My brother cursed me. He will die in despair if sentenced by the law. Machû, remember that I saved you once. Remember that I promised to keep your secret, unconscious of the fatal consequences to my nearest of kin. I gave you the stolen gold; I freely pardoned you the blood which you had spilled; but can I bear to think that, in screening you, I am sending my own brother to the scaffold?"

"All this has nothing to do with me, Jean Machû, the thief and convict; what matters it who I am? remember who you are. My identity was lost in confession; you have promised, you must keep your promise."

"Are you altogether pitiless?" cried the priest.

"Listen, if your brother's head doesn't fall, mine will. I must defend my own life. I always stick to that through thick and thin, and I stick to it so closely that there's no use disputing about the matter. You will not speak. I will be outside the prison every day, and you will not follow me any more. I will be present in the court on the day of the trial, and you will be silent."

"But if I were to give you the means of flight, of going to America? If I were to double the amount of money which you stole, would you confess your crime? A letter from you to the magistrates would procure an acquittal, and you could save my brother, without endangering yourself."

"I could not," said Machû, "on account of the extradition."

"Then my brother is irrevocably lost."

"Why, I thought," said Rat-de-Cave mockingly, "that you depended on the justice of God."

"To it I submit," said the priest; "nor do I question it."

Jean Machû stopped.

"See here," said he, "there is no use prolonging this interview. You are sworn to silence. Keep your promise."

"I swore to be silent before the people, before the magistrates, the judge and jury, and that oath I have kept in spite of all my sufferings. But I did not promise that I would not make a last appeal to him who alone had power to release me from this oath. Listen, Jean Machû, the religion which I teach and profess must indeed be great and sublime to bind me to such obedience. Then, in the name of that faith, in the name of the God whom I serve, I promise you complete forgetfulness, the pardon of my divine Master, and even the indulgence of men. My brother is only twenty-three; he bears a name hitherto honorable. My sister is an angel upon earth, and we are all disgraced for you."

"Oh, yes, I understand perfectly," said Jean Machû; "it matters little for me, the escaped convict, the hardened criminal, who will fall into the clutches of the law sooner or later, for some other crime; who has passed through the galleys, and belongs in advance to the gallows. Ah, well, perhaps that is just why I cling so fiercely to the few years or months or days of life which yet remain to me. I have more money than I ever had in my life. I want to enjoy it, to wallow in luxury like a hog, to revel in pleasure. After that, Charlot* can do

---

* The executioner.

what he likes with me, and then it will be time for your sermons. Till then, to be plain with you, Mr. priest, you must not know me."

Sulpice clung to the wretch's clothes.

"Ah," said he, "it must be my fault. I have not explained things clearly. You do not understand my terrible anguish, the struggle which is consuming my very soul. Have pity, have pity on me! I do not think I ever injured any one in my life. I have lived for the poor and for God. Ah, see I am at your feet, praying, weeping; give me my brother's life, my brother's life!"

Jean Machû tried to extricate himself from the priest's grasp, but the latter, knowing well that no second opportunity would ever occur, held on with the energy of despair.

The wretch's anger, hitherto counterbalanced by a feeling of mingled pity and admiration, at last got the better of the other sentiments so foreign to his nature. He no longer beheld in Sulpice the man who was saving him by his silence, but one who was troubling and annoying him.

"Let me go," cried he, savagely, "some one is coming."

Jean Machû drew himself to his full height, put his feet firmly together, and with a sudden jerk backwards, shook off the priest with his whole strength, and the latter fell heavily on the pavement. His head struck against the parapet of the quay, and the blood gushed out. Jean Machû took to his heels, and ran from the spot with all possible speed.

CHAPTER X.

THE TRIAL.

A DENSE crowd had gathered around the court-house. The streets in its vicinity were packed with a curious throng; all the efforts of the police only succeeded in keeping a narrow passage for carriages and other vehicles. The court, the grand staircase, the halls and lobbies presented an unusually lively appearance on this day, when the court was expected to sit, and to surpass in interest a drama of the Boulevard.

The presiding judge had been fairly persecuted with applications for tickets of admission. Within the hall were to be seen numerous representatives of the very best Parisian society. One foreign ambassador had begged them to keep him an arm-chair. The Minister of Justice had announced his intention of being present; the ushers had to double the row of chairs usually reserved for distinguished guests. Never had so many professors and students of law assembled to hear so thrilling a case. Many were the strategies employed, and several young men borrowed a friend's cap and gown to secure themselves a place on the benches of the court-room. The holders of red tickets ostentatiously displayed them, while others held on to their buttonhole or even their hat, with an alacrity rarely seen anywhere outside of a steeple-chase.

Chase had in truth been made after tickets for the past eight days. Besides the privileged ones who had tickets, an eager multitude filled the staircases, halls, lobbies, even the court-yard outside; workingmen and women, tradespeople, pale, sickly children, all crowded about the place, discussing the Pomereul family, the nature of the crime, and the improbability of the prisoner's acquittal.

Many of the workmen from the factory at Charenton had come thither to give another proof of their interest and attachment to the family of their old master. None of them felt any great sympathy for Xavier. They remembered him as cold and haughty towards themselves; an idler and a spendthrift; in fact they hardly knew him. But Antoine Pomereul, whose name was on every lip, together with Sulpice and Sabine, still claimed their warmest affection and gratitude. As soon as it became known in the crowd that this little group of men had known the murdered man and his children they were immediately surrounded, and plied with questions as to the crime and its melancholy probabilities.

"Do you think," asked a woman, "Mlle. Pomereul will be at the trial?"

"Ah, she is an angel," said Blanc-Cadet; "and she will be there if she dies of shame."

"And the priest?"

"Ah, that is another thing. He will not appear."

"Why, does he disown his brother?"

"Then you don't know all that has happened," said Blanc-Cadet.

"Has anything else happened in that house?"

"A terrible thing," said Blanc-Cadet, impressively; "and is connected with the other affair, too. Some one tried to kill the Abbé Sulpice."

"To kill *him!*" cried several voices.

"Oh, yes, it was hushed up in the papers, out of pity for the wretch who did it; the Abbé Sulpice refused to denounce him. But one night, about twelve o'clock, the poor priest was brought home in a carriage, unconscious, and with his head split open. A passer-by found him lying on the pavement. Of course the parapet had blood on it, and the abbé may have struck his head in falling. But every one knows very well that it was not an accident. As soon as he came to, they questioned him, but he only said, 'I fell.' Since then his brain has been wandering, and he raves and raves, or keeps such a silence that it is sadder than any raving."

"There seems to be some misfortune in that family," said an old man.

"Just think what a burden Mlle. Sabine has to bear. She watched beside her brother every night except two, when M. Pomereul's former secretary took her place. I used to think that young chap selfish, but since his master's death he is all devotion. It is true, besides thanking him, they presented him with six months' salary; but even so, it is not every young man in Marc Mauduit's place that would take such trouble about the abbé's health."

"But won't his testimony be needed, and wouldn't it help his brother?" said a woman.

"Well, well, God wants to keep the secret to Himself, I suppose," said Blanc-Cadet. "But, if I was the judge, I'd do as I have read in books they used to do in old times. I'd bring the man of the woods into court."

"Lipp-Lapp?" said a child, eagerly.

"Yes, just Lipp-Lapp," said the old man. "You've got his name sure enough. A worthy beast, who was almost killed defending his master. The doctor who cured him is an excellent man, and if I belonged to the 'Society for the Protection of Animals,' I'd give him a medal, so I would. But, as I say, I'd bring Lipp-Lapp into court. I'd show him the knife which the murderer used, and I'd say to him as they say to the hounds, 'Catch him.' And if, when he came face to face with the prisoner, the man of the woods didn't strangle him, I'd swear that M. Xavier was innocent."

"Ha, ha!" laughed a bystander, "that would be too funny. It reminds one of Jocko, or the monkey of Brazil."

"It would be contrary somewhat to the dignity of the court," said another.

"Oh, well," said Blanc-Cadet, "the dog of Montargis disturbed the dignity of the 'judgment of God.' And that was as good a court as this any day. I maintain that if Lipp-Lapp alone knows the truth, Lipp-Lapp alone should be asked for it."

"And why not the Abbé Pomereul?" said a voice.

"But he wasn't there," replied Blanc-Cadet.

"He knows everything," said an old man.

"How could he?" asked the other.

"Well," said the old man, "I have followed all the trials at the court, and I am hardly ever mistaken, and mark my words, he knows all about it."

"Why doesn't he tell it then?" asked Blanc-Cadet.

"Perhaps he can't," said the other.

"What would prevent him from declaring it to the court, and saving his brother?"

"Oh, well, he's a priest, and some way or another they might have bound him to keep silent," said the old man.

"But his brother?"

"As for that," cried the other, "if it was himself, he'd have to keep silent just the same."

"That would be horrible!" cried a woman.

"Of course it would," said the man, "but heroic and grand for all that. It would show what the secrecy promised by the priest is worth. Things like this happening from time to time keep the people's faith alive. If it be so, though, I think the Abbé Sulpice as great a martyr as any that we read of in the *Lives of the Saints*."

This idea, started by the old man, spread like wild-fire

through the eager, breathless multitude. It produced a feeling of profound commiseration for all concerned, and deepened the interest which already centred around this mysterious case; and the regret became greater and greater that the Abbé Sulpice was unable to give his testimony.

When the great clock struck eleven, the soldiers who kept guard below, and regulated the admission to the court-room, stood back a moment as the ushers threw open the doors, and the crowd rushed in like a torrent which has burst all barriers. The reserved places, and the space without the barrier, kept for those who had no tickets, were simultaneously filled. The law-students mounted to their places on the benches, and the reporters seated themselves at their desks, some describing the appearance of the audience, and others preparing to stenograph the trial *in extenso*.

Women took out their opera-glasses to see whom they knew in the stalls. They exchanged smiles, while the men saluted each other by a wave of the hand. The costumes were for the most part dark, but rich and elegant. It was a play to be sure, but of such a character that costumes of neutral tints were in the best taste. The lawyers discussed the case among themselves in an audible voice, some condemning Xavier in advance, others defending him energetically. Every one looked forward to hearing Léon Renaut's defence, his fervid eloquence, and the replies of the much dreaded Solicitor-General. Near the benches for the lawyers sat some members of Xavier's club, smiling and careless, looking round them glass in eye. Foremost was the Count de Monjoux, indulging in reminiscences of the fine suppers he had had with young Pomereul. Taken in general, this assemblage of curious people in the court-room seemed rather as if awaiting the rising of the curtain, than sitting in expectation of a death sentence against a fellow creature.

All at once a sound as of the murmur of voices was heard in the adjoining room. The door was thrown open by two attendants, and the sonorous voice of the usher proclaimed,

"Hats off, gentlemen! the Court."

A sudden death-like silence followed the solemn entrance of the magistrates. The judges took each his place behind the great table covered with green cloth, upon which were piled huge bundles of papers. On a separate table were the deeds of indictment, numbered and sealed. The jury next appeared, each answering to his name, and then the judge gave orders for the introduction of the prisoner. Men and women rose tumultuously, and every eye was fixed upon Xavier Pomereul. He appeared between two *gendarmes*. He had summoned up all his fortitude for that moment of entering the court-room. He was deathly pale. His hands worked nervously, and as he took his seat in the dock he scarcely heard Léon Renaut's whispered words of encouragement The cruel, staring, eager crowd bewildered him, as the noisy pack bewilders the stag. He felt too well that to every tear which he might shed a cruel taunt would respond. He made a violent effort, and steeled his face to immobility, whilst the lawyer looked over his notes and deeds. Xavier, questioned by the judge as to his name, surname, and condition, replied in a voice scarcely audible. The clerk then began to read the accusation. Its logic was overwhelming. It was written in a sober, sedate fashion, by a man of tried integrity, with rare talent as a dialectician. Every point of the accusation was laid down with mathematical precision. Hearing it, there seemed no argument left for the defence, and not even a single objection to offer to that clear, concise statement, dictated neither by hatred nor prejudice.

Aware of his own innocence, Xavier was nevertheless completely overwhelmed by the force of the accusation. Thenceforth his mind entered upon a new phase. He seemed no longer the party concerned in all this; it was not his life, his future, which was being decided, but the existence of another. From being an actor in that terrible scene, the *dénouement* of the bloody drama of the Chaussée d'Antin, he became merely a spectator. His forced composure gave place to a sort of morbid curiosity. He asked himself what must be the fate of a man accused in such fashion, and forgot that his own life hung in the balance.

For a moment he thought of giving up the defence. Where was the use? His brother, who alone possessed the knowledge which could save him, was hindered from disclosing it. God did not will that his innocence should be made known. At least he could show the vulgar courage of dying well.

Meantime a lady in deep mourning appeared. M. Renaut recognized her and offering his arm led her to a seat near the prisoner. She raised her veil and showed the face of Sabine. It was deadly pale, and sorrow had written dark lines about the eyes. But it still retained, in spite of anguish, the imprint of her own pure and gentle nature. She could not speak to Xavier, but she gave him a look which seemed to say,

"For our sake, if not for your own, defend yourself, plead your innocence. Remember our honor is at stake."

The sight of Sabine revived Xavier's courage. He drew himself together, looked firmly and bravely, but without bravado, at the audience. The women seemed touched by his youth and his comely appearance, and Sabine attracted general compassion.

The witnesses were summoned. Each one related what little they knew of the matter. The doctor made his purely scientific deposition, and Sabine was called. The young girl advanced trembling to the bar, and spoke in a clear, musical voice of Xavier, at some length, before the presiding judge had the heart to interrupt her. She spoke of their happy youth, their friendship, of her father's great love for Xavier, which had made him weak. She touched briefly upon the dark morning when she had seen her father's corpse, and learned that Xavier had been taken away from home, and wound up by saying,

"Would Xavier have dared to look me in the face if he had murdered our father? The affection he shows me, and his caresses, are the surest proof of his innocence."

The Abbé Sulpice was then called for form's sake; the doctor came forward declaring him quite incapable of appearing. The presiding judge then bade the other judges and jury remark that his written deposition contained all that he would have said, and it was read. The testimony being thus ended, it behooved the attorney-general to speak. Contrary to the usual custom of solicitors-general, he did not commence by showing society shaken to its very base, and tottering, if the head of the accused were not sacrificed to law and justice. Disdaining these commonplaces, he took Xavier limb from limb, and totally ignoring his denial of the charge, overpowered him with proofs, showed him his punishment in all its horrors, and ended by saying:

"You despised honest work which made your father rich and respected; you despised the virtue which made your home a sanctuary. You allowed evil passions to take hold of you in the very flower of your youth, so that, from an idler and spendthrift, you became vicious, and ended by descending to the level of burglars and midnight assassins. There is no pity for you who have despised the example of such a brother as yours. Ask mercy and pardon of that God, who would have pardoned even Judas had Judas repented, but from men expect only justice, implacable justice, which throws over you in anticipation the dark pall of a parricide."

Sabine hid her face in her hands. Leon Renaut pressed the hand of the accused, murmuring,

"Keep up your courage, it is my turn now."

The young lawyer's powerful eloquence was of that kind which, without resorting to oratorical tricks, produced splendid and unforeseen results. His talents were well known, and people loved to hear his impassioned imagery, which took such a hold upon them. His past victories on the judicial battle-ground were cited, for he had saved criminals and gained when all seemed lost. But on this occasion, though no doubt existed in the minds of the audience as to Renaut's reputation as an orator, no one had any hope that it would suffice to procure Xavier's acquittal. Before the summing up, the audience were already convinced of Xavier's guilt, but after the discourse of the attorney-general, scarcely a single partisan for the accused remained. M. Renaut fully understood this, and rising impetuously he began:

"Gentlemen of the bench and of the jury, I see before me judges where I looked for witnesses. I hear a passionate, virulent accusation, and I demand proofs. You bring before me a deplorable scene—the blood of an old man, shed at midnight. I crave only day and open air; you intensify the darkness, and I want light."

It seemed to the audience as if a portion of the darkness were already being dispelled. The lawyer's very tones were so convincing, his gestures so full of authority, his face bearing a look of such sincere conviction, that many of those present forgot how, a moment before, their opinion of Xavier had seemed irrevocable.

"This whole case, gentlemen," he continued, "is enshrouded in mystery. You see but one criminal, I see two. You repeat that the deposition of the Abbé Sulpice should suffice, and I cry out that it does not satisfy me. You show me in this witness a priest, and I demand a man who holds the key to this terrible drama. A saint who is unquestionably bound to silence by the obligations of his dread ministry, and a senseless being who in the order of creation is mute; an angel and a beast; the one bound by his oath to a silence like that of the grave, the other a poor brute, condemned to everlasting silence. Yet Lipp-Lapp who was severely wounded by the murderer; Lipp-Lapp who defended himself, and in whose clenched fist was found a handful of the murderer's hair; Lipp-Lapp saw it all. You point to the accused and you say, 'He opened his father's safe, therefore he must have killed him.' And I say that he did not even rob him. Since when has temptation become an actual crime? He tells you that, when in the very act of committing a crime, he raised his eyes to the portrait of his dead mother, and drew back in shame and horror, flying from the room. No, this prodigal did not kill his father; during that night of murder and of mourning he was shedding tears of bitter repentance, and at the very turning-point of his career, at his very entrance upon a new way, you cast him into a felon's cell and call him—parricide. Ah, gentlemen, take care; it is not the first time I have had the honor of addressing you; it is not the first struggle I have made for the innocent, against the law, whose mission it is to protect outraged society, but which, without ever diverging from its end, sometimes goes astray in the means; never, never, did the cause of a prisoner seem more just to me than this one; never have I so much desired to convince you that my client is not a murderer, but a deeply wronged and suffering man. My God, my God! do You no longer work miracles, or will You not send thither, armed with full power to reveal the truth, the man who alone can do so? From suffering, aberration of mind, from the very jaws of death itself, it would seem to me that the Abbé Sulpice must appear before us."

"I am here," said a feeble voice beside him.

To the amazement of every one the Abbé Sulpice indeed appeared suddenly in the doorway leading to the witness-stand. A murmur of compassion was heard in the court.

The Abbé Sulpice, feeble and tottering, wearing his loose black cassock unconfined by any belt, his face as pale as a corpse, seemed like one summoned from the grave. A red mark divided his white forehead in two, and this scar, still fresh and bleeding, gave him a strange resemblance to one of the early martyrs. Sabine arose and made a step towards him. But his eyes were fixed upon Xavier.

Seeing his brother thus coming, as it were, from the verge of the grave to defend him, a sudden ray of hope entered the prisoner's heart. His eyes, dilated, feverish, red and burning, were fixed upon Sulpice in ardent supplication, seeming to ask of him at once his honor, his life, here and in eternity. This dramatic entrance concluded Léon Renaut's appeal. The greatest emotion was displayed by the jury, and the reporters wrote some rapid lines descriptive of the effect produced by this incident. The presiding judge declared that by an exercise of his discretionary power, he would hear the Abbé Sulpice's testimony. The hapless prisoner, clutching at the bar, grew paler and paler, seeming to fairly totter.

And how all this had come about was as follows: For

more than a month the young priest had been a prey to acute physical suffering. His mind had wandered in delirium, and lost sight of reality. On the very evening previous to the trial, the doctor had declared his almost certain conviction that he would never recover his reason. But that morning Sulpice had felt the darkness which enshrouded his mind gradually being dispelled, he strove to remember all that had happened. Sitting up, and pressing his hands to his forehead, he tried to collect his thoughts. An incident occurred to assist him. Lipp-Lapp, who, since the illness of his young master, had never left the room; poor Lipp-Lapp, who still dragged himself about, not having yet recovered his strength, had found upon the chimney-piece an old almanac. Sitting upon a low stool, he was going over the figures with his long hairy fingers, and seemed as if deploring that he could not, like others, comprehend the sense of them. Wearied with his efforts, he arose, and noiselessly approached the bed, just when Sulpice, sitting up, was trying to recollect events and to recall the past. Lipp-Lapp, holding out the almanac to him, attracted his attention. He seized the card covered with dates, and his eye fell upon one to which the animal was accidentally pointing. Providence, how wonderful are Thy ways! That date brought back the abbé's wandering thoughts.

"The eighteenth of August," said he; "the eighteenth of August."

He looked round in a sort of vague, helpless way, then suddenly light broke in upon him.

"Xavier," exclaimed he; "Xavier!"

He rang the bell, and Baptiste immediately appeared.

"Baptiste," said he, "where is Sabine?"

The old man bowed his head, but made no reply.

"She's gone there?" said Sulpice.

Baptiste made a gesture of assent.

"Listen," said Sulpice in a feeble voice, "I am going there too. Do not say no, for I will go even if it is my death."

"Go, then, dear young master," said the servant, bursting into tears, "and bring us back M. Xavier."

Sulpice took a few drops of cordial, and feeling stronger, sent for a carriage. Baptiste and he got in and were driven to the court-house. The young priest proceeded at once to the witness box and appeared as we have seen.

The deepest emotion was visible on every face.

The plot seemed thickening.

Xavier was for the moment forgotten. All eyes were turned upon that frail face with its bloody aureola. Profound silence reigned throughout the court. Every one felt that Xavier's life hung upon his brother's words.

"You being a near relative of the accused," said the judge, "I will not oblige you to take oath, being convinced that you will not speak one word contrary to the truth."

"Sir," said Sulpice, "I will speak the truth."

And turning to his brother he said,

"Forgive me, that it cannot be the *whole* truth."

"What have you to say to the court?" asked the judge.

"My brother is innocent," said the young priest, raising his hands to an image of the Crucified which was directly in front of him.

"Can you prove it?" asked the judge.

"On the night of the crime two men came to our house and asked to see me. They did not come up to my room, nor had they any need of me. It did not take them long to accomplish their purpose; the money stolen, the victim stricken, they were stealing out. The door of my father's room had just closed after them when I came in from a long drive. I suspected something at first. But it was necessary for them to secure my silence. It was easy to deceive me, as they knew my mission was entirely among the poor and suffering. One of them told me that my ministry was required for a man whose soul was at stake, and I went with them."

"Could you tell us where you were brought?" asked the judge.

"I could not," said the priest, "and even if I did remember I would have no right to make it known. When we arrived at a wretched house we went in, and immediately one of these villains knelt down and under the seal of confession told me of the crime he had committed."

"Did you see that man's face?"

"I did."

"Would you know him again?"

"I knew him before."

"Under what circumstances did you know him?"

"I once saved his life," replied the priest, quietly.

"His name?" asked the judge, "or do you know it?"

"I know it."

"In that case one word will be sufficient to save your brother."

Sulpice clutched at the railing.

"That name I cannot reveal to the court. He, whose image you have placed upon yonder wall, forbids me. You must believe me upon the honor of a priest and the word of a Christian, but you must not ask for proofs; I cannot furnish them."

Judge and jury alike looked at him.

Xavier who, in the agitation of new hope, had risen from his seat, fell backwards overwhelmed. Sabine sobbed aloud.

Public sympathy had reached a climax. Some admired the Abbé Sulpice, others were amazed at his silence, not comprehending the inviolable secret which bound him.

To Sulpice the judge said gravely, "The gentlemen of the jury will no doubt take what you have said into account. It does not come within our province to urge you to betray alike your conscience and your God. Your duty is rigorous, but ours remains inexorable."

The attorney-general, fully understanding that the appearance of Sulpice, and the simple words by him spoken, had done more for the defence than the eloquence of Léon Renaut, and unwilling that he should lose at any cost the cruel victory he had been on the point of gaining, arose to reply to the young lawyer, annihilating his fervent defence and endeavoring to efface the impression produced by the priest's testimony. He no longer cared to display his talents and fine language, but his cutting voice, his brief, incisive words, his unanswerable arguments, followed each other in quick succession like poisoned darts. He spoke of the Abbé Sulpice in terms of the highest praise, but briefly touched upon the illness from which he was scarce recovering. He declared that the confession of two mysterious men in an unknown house was undoubtedly one of the feverish visions of his delirium, and concluded by a scathing condemnation of the parricide. Sulpice was near Sabine, but unlike her, he heard, upon his knees, the terrible words of the attorney-general, realizing that he was henceforth powerless to save his brother. Léon Renaut again rose, but every one felt that his confidence in himself was weakened. He knew, in fact, that if Sulpice's deposition did not save Xavier it would injure him, seeming like the stratagem of a brother to deceive the jury and gain the sympathy of the house, by a plan preconcerted, perhaps, with the lawyer himself.

The jury retired, and Xavier was removed by the *gendarmes*. Meanwhile the spectators were divided into two parties: the one believed what the Abbé Pomereul had said and demanded Xavier's acquittal; the other shook their heads saying,

"You see it is merely a lawyer's strategy. Would confession be of any importance in such a case? Of course he would save his brother and let religion go."

Every one was busy discussing the attorney-general's speech and the eloquence of the young lawyer. Friends sought each other out, for must they not in some way pass the time while the jury was deliberating? It seemed to augur well for the accused that they were so undecided. After an absence of an hour and a half they returned. Then in a tremulous voice, amid a death-like silence, the foreman read the decision of his colleagues:

"Xavier Pomereul was guilty, but beyond all doubt the priest's testimony must be taken into account, and a plea for extenuating circumstances be admitted."

It was the only means of saving Xavier from the penalty of death, the only means of giving Providence time to work out its end. A murmur of astonishment greeted the foreman's fatal decision, and when Xavier was brought in he might have guessed his fate at once from the appearance of every one. But he saw nothing, his eyes were fixed upon the judges while he awaited the reading of his sentence. When he heard the words, "has been found guilty," he burst into tears, and when sentence was pronounced, "hard labor for life," he murmured,

"Far better death."

"No, Xavier, no, my brother," cried Sulpice, trying to take his brother's hand, "for God will permit light to come upon the darkness, and you will yet be free"

But with a gesture of abhorrence Xavier threw him off, crying,

"You, who might have saved me and would not, I disown you."

The judge then asked, "Have you anything to say why sentence should not be passed upon you?"

Xavier answered, "I am innocent! I am innocent!"

Sabine fell into Sulpice's arms, as Xavier was being led away.

"Ah, poor martyr!" she said, "who will console you in such an ordeal?"

Sulpice pointed to the picture of the crucified God.

"He will," said he.

And, assisted by Léon Renaut, he returned home with his sister in the carriage which had brought him.

CHAPTER XI.

THE DREAM ENDED.

THE studio occupied by Benedict Fougerais was on the ground floor of the house, No. 11 Boulevard de Clichy, which had been honored by numbering among its tenants at one time Jacque, the painter of fishes, and Diaz, the brilliant colorist. His studio was spacious, and furnished in severely classical style, to harmonize with the character of him who passed his life there. The draperies were dark red, showing to the best advantage the whiteness of the marble, the sombre tint of the bronzes, and the softened lustre of the burnished silver.

On a carved oaken buffet stood vases in bold relief, a lava plaque, painted by Joseph Devers, in imitation of one of those marvels of Lucca della Robbia, whose traditions it faithfully followed. Two highly-colored pictures, the tints of which were mellowed by time, hung upon the panels at either side. On pedestals covered with velvet draperies were the works of the artist, well placed, each in its peculiar light, and displayed to the utmost advantage. Vainly did one seek in this sanctuary of art the much-lauded conceptions of Pradier, Clodion's nymphs, or any of the works of that school, which, for want of an ideal, becomes realistic, and the decay of which is disguised by a word unknown to the ancients.

To be realistic is to make no use of what we find in the works of God, and which His Providence has given us, that we may add thereunto the inspiration of genius; it is to choose the low in preference to the beautiful—to give interpretation to what is base and expression to what is vile; for vile is the only word to express such degeneracy.

To belong to the realistic school means to produce no more such faces and figures as were sculptured by Michael Angelo upon mausoleums, or admitted by the popes into the great basilica, St. Peter's. The "Night and Day" of that master would not represent, according to the idea of the realists, the human form in its whole strength, draped merely in its own chastity. The artists of our day have brought into art a certain profligacy of conception—the licentiousness of the times. They work no longer for temples, but for drawing-rooms. Their work is trivial, commonplace, and unwholesome. But such art pays. It gives the artist at once money and a certain ready fame. None of these groups, heads, or basso-relievi will live; but the artist of to-day does not look beyond the present. He is indifferent to immortality, as he is skeptical of a future life. His faith in art is as dead as his religious belief. For him there is no God in heaven, and on his path of life no sublime poetry. There are some noble exceptions among the modern artists, who stand out from the groups of realists, either through pure love of the antique, or through a higher and worthier motive.

When Benedict Fougerais left off making designs for clocks and ornaments for M. Pomereul, he entered the studio of a member of the Institute, whose reputation was perhaps not yet equal to his solid merit. Jules Autran was a master at once kind and severe, and it was thanks to him that Benedict succeeded in finishing his artistic education.

He studied history, of which so many artists remain in ignorance; he devoted himself to archæology and numismatics, and all the branches of sculpture and architecture as practised by the ancients, whose works inspire in us at once admiration for their genius and a feeling of our own impotence. He studied the lives of those great artists of the middle ages and the period of the Renaissance, and drew thence this conclusion, that before becoming artists whose fame was to astonish the world, they had been men.

Without aspiring to equal such a master as Leonardo da Vinci, who reached a high degree of excellence in various arts, and could fortify a city with the same skill with which he produced a picture like the *Holy Family* of Francis I.; without ever hoping to attain such an eminence as the sculptor, Benvenuto Cellini, who carved a gem with the same hand that painted the Perseus, Benedict labored to acquire various kinds of knowledge, convinced that all arts and sciences tend to complete each other.

He never frittered away his time in idleness, as do so many artists, under pretence of seeking an inspiration, while they enervate themselves by the use of tobacco in every shape and form. He did not think it necessary to form exaggerated theories of art, and become, in consequence, the lion of a circle of petty admirers. He remained in his studio, and when he felt that his hand was not faithfully interpreting his thought, he did not try to force it, but turned to some useful and yet relaxing study. His friends were all of the best type. He did not care for conversation of such a kind as to disturb the harmony existing between his conceptions and his execution.

For, if gayety is a relaxation to the mind, licentiousness only troubles and disturbs it. So Benedict's friends belonged to the unhappily small class of literary men—journalists and artists—who resolutely set themselves against the too general immorality of the day. Closely united, they formed a brave little band, who depended upon each other for support and protection. Why does this sort of good-fellowship so seldom exist, except among those who are rather the brigands, the *bravi*, of art than its apostles? The followers of that camp opposed to such as Benedict are, in their individuality, protected, upheld, and sustained in a manner quite different from their adversaries.

The painter, poet, sculptor, or author, who is earnest, moral, and Christian, finds himself alone and isolated. Far from seeking each other out, assisting each other, and fraternizing, such men seem to lack either that fraternal feeling or the necessary attraction. They do not seem to realize that, if they wished, they could form themselves into a serried column as well as their antagonists.

Two powerful incentives kept Benedict firm in the way he had chosen: one was his faith, upon which the cold wind of doubt had never blown; the other was his attachment to Sabine. His gratitude to her father was somehow mingled and, as it were, diffused in the deep, pure affection with which he regarded Sabine. He entertained for her much the same species of respect and admiration which Dante felt for Beatrice, and Petrarch for Laura, and which gave to poetry "La Divina Commeddia" and the "Canziones." Without directly confessing that she was the end and aim of his efforts, the young sculptor had never dreamed of offering the fame or fortune he might achieve to any other than the merchant's daughter.

He told himself repeatedly that the rich heiress would no doubt despise the poor youth who owed his very livelihood to the charity of her father; but he consoled himself by the thought that M. Pomereul had himself known poverty, struggled with privation, and considered it his bounden duty to protect those who fought the battle of life bravely, without weakness or presumption.

On the day when he brought the statuette of Steinbach's Sabine to his master's house, Benedict felt that his fate was to be then and there decided. If the young girl, with her father's consent, accepted this long-cherished work of his, she would likewise consent to become his wife. Ah! how he had trembled for the result, and how great had been his joy when M. Pomereul held out a hand of welcome to him, and called him son.

Thenceforth he had believed his fate certain—his happiness secured. With Sabine for his wife he could never go astray, he could never fail. The thought of her had sustained him during the five laborious years of his early youth, and strengthened him in his manhood's riper age. She had been his hope and his conscience, and she was to be his model and his aim in life. If ever a man was happy it was Benedict on the night of his betrothal. His happiness seemed so pure, so complete, so certain! Only a few days must elapse till the girl, who raised her eyes so frankly to his face, would be his wife. He saw her, in anticipation, in the studio on the Boulevard de Clichy, seated beside him while he worked, praising or criticising by turns. He imagined them at evening forming part once more of the family circle, where Sulpice's gentle austerity never interfered with the general gayety.

What courage and what strength the title of husband would give Benedict! He would no longer have to think and act for himself alone. He would be responsible for the happiness of that dear one whose destiny M. Pomereul had confided to him with so noble a confidence, accepting industry and affection from him as his only wealth.

Yes, Benedict was happy that night. And when he

slept his dreams brought before him again loved faces, and the echo of their gladsome words.

A thunderbolt fell upon his hopes and his happiness. M. Pomereul's murder, in itself, was to him a source of the deepest grief. He had never known his own father, and his filial affection had centred upon this man who had been his benefactor. Hastening to the house of mourning, he had been given the farther intelligence which made his sorrow two-fold. Not only had the honored head of the family fallen by the hand of an assassin, but an accusation was made against the brother of the woman who was so soon to be his wife.

Benedict was well aware of Xavier's follies, but he never believed the accusation even for an instant. He trusted the wretched boy blindly, overwhelmed as he was by circumstances, and caught in the meshes of a net from which naught, as it seemed, could deliver him. He not only interested in his behalf his best friend, Léon Renaut, but he showed the prisoner a thousand little kindnesses and marks of affection which only the wretched can fully appreciate. He was very little in sympathy with the worthless life Xavier had been leading, and even felt a sort of dislike towards the frequenters of low theatres and other fashionable haunts of vice, and would never have dreamed of making him a companion. But since the blow had fallen, and poor Xavier was branded as a parricide, he felt only the deepest sorrow for him, beholding in him the hapless victim of circumstances, and a deeply afflicted son.

This was a greater test of his affection than ten years of ordinary devotion. Benedict felt that he owed Sabine this proof of his love for her, and that by devoting himself to Xavier's cause, he would show in a way more convincing than words the depth and sincerity of his attachment. Imagine, therefore, his grief and disappointment when Sabine refused to see him during the whole time of Xavier's trial. Of course, her mourning and her intense anxiety were sufficient reasons for her seclusion, and yet Benedict had won from Sabine herself, from M. Pomereul, and now from Sulpice, a sacred title, which should, he thought, have procured him access to her.

Was it just that he should be treated as a stranger in that house which was now in great part hers? He accused her in his heart of coldness and indifference. He persuaded himself that she could not have the same deep love for him he had for her; not discouraged, however, he determined to triumph over her indifference by increased devotion.

So, unable to see Sabine, he devoted himself entirely to Xavier. He saw him every day, bringing new courage to that dejected soul, and if he did not succeed in softening Xavier's hard, rebellious nature, he at least kept alive his faith in friendship. The sculptor's visits, and those of Renaut and Sabine, were the prisoner's only consolation. He rarely spoke of Sulpice, and when he did so it was almost with hatred.

Incapable of understanding his brother, he accused him of cruelty.

During the terrible scene at the court, the sculptor had not dared to approach Sabine, who sat as near as possible to Xavier, but when Xavier, having heard his sentence, gave that one last despairing cry, "I am innocent!" it was Benedict who held him in his arms and supported him, for the *gendarmes*, touched by the scene, allowed Xavier that moment's consolation.

Next evening Benedict went to see Léon Renaut.

"Do you think Xavier will appeal to another court?" he asked.

"No," said the lawyer, "he has positively refused."

"And yet another court might—" began Benedict.

"There is no use in hoping against hope, my friend," said the lawyer; "Xavier would have no chance before any jury."

"So the unhappy boy must go to the convict-prison till he is transported?"

"He is in such a state of health," replied Renaut, "that it will be possible, I think, to have him kept where he is at present. We will meanwhile work to obtain some further concession. Public opinion is divided in his regard, some believing him to be the victim of a judicial error. He has been sentenced, it is true, but the sentence may not be enforced."

"In the mean time, Léon," said Benedict, "I shall try to see Mlle. Sabine."

"Courage," said Léon gently and half sadly.

"Why, do you fear that she will refuse?" cried Benedict.

"She is an angel," said the lawyer, "and will, I fear, refuse to join your life to hers, or make you share her burden of sorrow."

"Ah!" said Benedict, "could she be so cruel?"

"But she will suffer as much as you in that case," said Léon.

"Your anxiety agrees but too well with my own misgivings," said Benedict; "but I must learn my fate at once. Good by, Léon; I will be here to-night, if the blow which has stricken Xavier has not also killed my hopes."

The sculptor went out and proceeded to the Pomereul homestead.

It was about eight o'clock in the evening.

The passers-by on the Chaussée d'Antin saw no lights in any of the windows; that rich and elegant home seemed like a deserted house. Benedict asked if Mlle. Pomereul was at home, and being answered in the affirmative, went up the first stairs. He was met by Baptiste; he asked him to let his young mistress know that he was there, and inquire if she would receive him; the old servant shook his head.

"I fear not, sir," said he; "Mlle. Sabine's way of acting frightens me. She neither speaks nor cries. She tries to keep up her strength, and meantime she seems frozen, going about the house like a spirit."

"I must see her, Baptiste, do you understand?" said Benedict, firmly.

The old man bowed, opened the drawing-room door for Benedict, and went to Sabine's apartments. He found her seated in a large arm-chair reading that book which is only less sublime than the Bible; she was seeking in the *Imitation* courage to bear her heavy cross. Dressed in black, her hair arranged with perfect neatness, but with no attempt at ornament, white as marble, and sad as the *Pieta*, Sabine seemed a living image of grief. When Benedict's name was mentioned, she put out her hand with a gesture as if imploring that he should be kept away, but with sudden resolution she rose quickly, murmuring, "It is better, much better."

To Baptiste she said aloud,

"I will see M. Fougerais presently in the drawing-room."

The servant disappeared. Left alone, Sabine went slowly over to the *prie-dieu* and knelt down.

"Thou who hast suffered in thine agony alone," she prayed, "give me strength to refuse the aid which is offered me. Like Simon of Cyrene he would share my cross. Grant, O Lord, that I may not accept this brotherly help! Thou, who readest all hearts, knowest that in mine is no secret for which I should blush. My feeling for him, increased by gratitude and respect, is so deep and lasting that it can never be effaced. I must feign indifference to save him who claims the right to share my misery and disgrace, and I fear to betray myself. My God! I am but a woman sorely tried; do Thou prove me worthy of the title of Christian, and lead me if it must be to suffer all things."

Burning tears gushed from her eyes. She wiped them hurriedly away, rose, and with a firm step went down to the drawing-room. Benedict was standing near the organ upon which Sabine had played that evening of their betrothal. He was recalling that tender and touching scene with a vividness which made it present. Alas! scarcely two months had elapsed since then, and how long ago, how far off it all seemed. So absorbed was he in these recollections that he did not hear Sabine's light step. When he raised his eyes she was standing before him with bowed head and clasped hands resting upon her heavy mourning dress.

"Sabine," said he, "dear Sabine."

A swift pang pierced her heart; fearing to betray herself she turned away, and taking a chair was silent a moment. When she spoke it was in a cold, calm voice.

"You wished to speak to me; well, I am ready to hear you."

"Did you not expect me, Sabine?" said he.

"If," said she with an effort, "I had expected you, I should have spared you the pain of this interview. I will now, however, do what I have heretofore neglected. As there is nothing farther to hope, I may as well put an end to farther illusions. Therefore, M. Fougerais, I release you from any tie which may bind you to me."

"You release me!" cried Benedict, warmly and indignantly. "And how have I deserved such treatment? How have I lost your confidence and affection? I understand: your idea is that you fear to associate me in the affliction which has most undeservedly come upon you. But the greater your trial, the greater my right to share it. You accepted me as your lover, your betrothed husband, when all your surroundings were happy and prosperous; you shall not cast me off now, when, as an orphan, you need an honorable man's support and protection."

"I have my brother," said Sabine, quietly.

"But the fact of his being a priest, and the duties thereby involved, separate you at almost every turn from the Abbé Sulpice. Besides, a brother's love, howsoever strong and enduring, is not always sufficient. Ah! you know me very little, Sabine, if you think that your affliction has not drawn me still nearer to you. I need not now repeat that, since I was old enough to dream of a future, it has always been with you and for you."

"I know," said Sabine, in a low voice; "but still I repeat that I release you from your promise."

"Do you fear that I hold you responsible for poor Xavier's faults—too dearly expiated, alas! by the sentence passed upon him? But you will not be left alone in your misfortune. To me and to society belongs the task of alleviating Xavier's condition, and working unceasingly to obtain your brother's release. Xavier is my adopted brother; I shall never desert him any more than you should desert me. And even if an unjust world involves you in Xavier's misfortune, what then? We will brave it together. Leaning on me you will breast the fury of the storm. My affection shall be so tender and considerate that it will pass by and you will scarcely heed it. Sabine, give me this greatest proof of your confidence, and accept me as your husband. I have come to beg of you to make good your father's promise."

Sabine did not speak for a moment, and there was silence, till Benedict said,

"Ah! your silence chills me."

"I am silent," replied Sabine, who seemed as if casting about for some mode of expression by which to crush Benedict's hopes at one blow, "because it is somewhat difficult for me to express what is in my mind, now that my father's wishes no longer weigh upon me."

"Weigh upon you!" cried Benedict. "Did he ever attempt to persuade you in any way?"

"Once only," said Sabine, blushing.

"What!" cried Benedict; "you mean to say that, on that day when I ventured to make known my secret hopes, and when they were encouraged in a manner so paternal, he did not leave you free?"

"I was not consulted," said Sabine, in a low voice.

"But still you did not refuse the husband whom he proposed to you?"

"Such a refusal would have distressed my father," said she.

"If left to yourself, I would not have been your own choice?" cried Benedict.

"No," said she, bowing her head.

"Ah, stop, mademoiselle!" cried Benedict; "you are torturing me. But still I ask myself if it may not be some mad feeling of heroism which accounts for your conduct to-day? Ah! do you not remember the evening of our betrothal? You accepted from me my mother's betrothal ring! You refused a dowry from your father, feeling certain that you could live by an artist's work. Were your courage and your happiness alike a cruel farce of which I was the dupe, because I believed my dream to be reality? Yet it seems to me that my heart could not have been deceived, and that I would neither have been so proud nor so happy. It seems to me that respect for your father's will could never have forced you to give me that proof of maidenly confidence. Let there be no deception on your part. I have worked for you; I have struggled for you. My whole ambition has been for you. You were my hope, and would be, I thought, my reward. I served Laban for the sake of Rachel. I kept myself free from all the follies and the temptations natural to my age that I might be worthy of you. I respected myself for the sake of your innocence and purity. If at times, seeing how easily my companions in art succeeded without real genius or industry, I felt tempted to do as they had done, arriving thus quickly at the goal of fame and fortune, your image arose before me, and I persevered in the thorny way wherein, if my feet were bleeding, at least I planted no flower whose odor was death. Sabine, if you desert me, if you cast me off, what is left to me?"

"Your conscience," answered she.

"May I not, in my despair, forget to hear its voice?" said Benedict.

"You think only of your own suffering, Benedict," said Sabine, "your regret for a young girl, your betrothed for a single day, your companion in an idle dream; but I have to mourn my murdered father, my brother condemned to penal servitude."

"I could wish you less strong, Sabine," said Benedict; "for then you might feel the need of consolation."

"The consolation which I crave cannot come from men," said she. "I expect it from God alone."

"Cruel child!" said Benedict; "but if that suffices for you, my heart has need of human sympathy."

"Be then my brother," said Sabine; "my brother like Sulpice and Xavier."

"And you will marry some one else?" said he.

"I will never marry," said she, extending her hand to him as she spoke.

"No!" said he; "I reject so false a friendship—a

worthless sentiment which in no wise responds to my aspirations, or the hope of my life. I accept my sentence: it is banishment; so be it! Perhaps at some future time I may find the key to the enigma which just now I cannot understand."

"Good by," said she, rising.

As she turned away, she repeated, in a lower voice,

"Good by forever."

As she was leaving the room the Abbé Sulpice entered. At one glance he saw what had occurred, and Sabine, throwing herself into his arms, murmured,

"I told an untruth, but it was to save him."

The young priest spoke in a tone of authority and even severity.

"You have done wrong," he said, "Sabine, very wrong. You do not know what harm you may have done to a man so noble, brave, and generous."

Sabine paid no heed to his words. For once she disregarded the advice of her brother. She only whispered, "Console him! console him!" and so saying hurried away.

Sulpice went straight to Benedict.

"Brother," said he, "for you will remain my brother, try to be brave. Summon all your strength and manhood. Who can tell whether Sabine may not—"

"Do not speak of her!" cried Benedict. "Her coldness and cruelty were the best proofs of what she said. In consenting to become my wife, she acted in obedience to her father's wishes. Thank you, Sulpice; thank you. I will come sometimes that we may talk over the time when I believed she would be a link between us. Good by. I am only a man, and I must be alone to think it all over."

He wrung Sulpice's hand, and hurried away. When he returned to his studio he felt as if it were a grave.

The room, furnished with such exquisite taste, the sanctuary of art which he had arranged with so much care and patience, that he might one day receive Sabine there, seemed now to him like a temple shorn of its holy images. His own works, which he had hoped she would have admired, seemed unworthy of any praise. He who had hitherto been so confident began suddenly to doubt of his own life and his own merit. He asked himself if he had not been a presumptuous fool to spend his youth at such arduous toil, which had led to so cruel a disenchantment.

He did not unite his weary soul with that of Christ, forsaken and suffering. His happiness, so suddenly overclouded, seemed to have carried away his faith in the universal shipwreck.

"Ah!" said he, in an outburst of self-pity and scorn, "my friends were right enough when they laughed at my wisdom, sneered at my cold statues, declaring that inspiration was not to be found where I persisted in seeking it. I wanted only Sabine, forsaken by the world, disgraced by her brother's sentence; but she has scorned and rejected me! At first I thought she would be my ruin, but, perhaps, in reality, she has saved me. I am free at last. I am young. I have talent. During all my twenty-five years of life I have never drunk of the cup of pleasure. In it I shall now find forgetfulness."

Suddenly he broke down, hid his face in his hands, and sobbed aloud.

CHAPTER XII.

An Artist Supper.

The war which France, with the greatest imprudence, had just declared against Prussia occupied every mind. Yet so great was the confidence in her own arms that no one doubted of ultimate success. Any one who expressed the least anxiety as to her glory would have been deemed wanting in patriotism. The war was regarded in the light of a brilliant military campaign, to end by an entrance into the hostile capital. There was no question of obstacles to be surmounted on the way thither, of delusive hopes, still less of defeat. At the moment of departure, the triumphant return was already hailed.

The Exposition of May, 1870, in spite of military and political movements, the rise and depression of stocks, and the excitement of the war, was followed with remarkable interest. The art critics pursued their *rôle* with a strong reinforcement of sounding phrases, much more interested in showing their skill as writers than in the progress of art, or in that of the painter or sculptor who served as the theme for their brilliant essays.

Still all the papers were unanimous in their praise of the work exhibited by Benedict Fougerais. It was not a work to attract the multitude, nor draw around it the admirers of the realistic school, but it was of such solid merit, and gave evidence of workmanship so scientific, that no one disputed its claim.

Benedict's group represented Religion trampling idols under foot; not idols of bronze, wood, or gold, which are called now Isis, now Jupiter, now Vishnu, or Brahma, but living idols, to which every one offers sacrifice: Wealth, Pleasure, Glory.

It was a grand and lofty idea, broad in its conception, sober in execution.

In it the artist had followed the traditions of the masters. The lines were severe, yet not stiff, the draperies supple and falling in graceful folds, while a scrupulous regard to anatomy was proof of long and patient study. The subject gave Benedict scope for great variety of form, expression, attitude. The love of gold was represented by an old decrepit man, whose skin hung loose and shrivelled upon his bones, and who held in his arms sacks of gold; whilst with one hand he clutched a purse. This figure, by its perfect workmanship, defied criticism.

Pleasure, under the form of a woman, had just thrown aside an empty cup, and was unstringing a necklace of precious stones. The expression of weariness and disgust upon the beautiful face, the drooping attitude, the draperies of the figure disordered by the sleep that follows drunkenness, proved the versatility of Benedict's chisel.

Glory was represented by a king, crowned and encompassed by crowns, trampling under foot the sceptres of other kings whom he had vanquished, and by the figure of a young man whose face bore the seal of inspiration, but whose lyre was suddenly and prematurely broken by death.

To complete the base of the group were sheaves of arms, vases of flowers, arranged artistically, so as to throw their branches over the pedestal, preventing the too sudden transition from the Carrara of which the group was composed to the black marble of the pedestal. Standing with one foot upon the reclining figure of the woman, her hand outstretched towards the old man,

AN ARTIST SUPPER.

as if condemning him to the torture of unassuaged desire, was Religion, her beautiful face raised to heaven as she displayed aloft the victorious Cross. It was a grand, pure face, the figure, somewhat larger than life, combining angelic sweetness with majesty.

This work showed the artist's real power, and at once placed Benedict in the rank of those from whom much was to be expected.

Benedict had been very happy while engaged upon this conception. Often did he exclaim, as he stepped back to contemplate an effect, "Sabine will be pleased." For he dedicated to her this work, into which a portion of his soul as well as his genius had passed. He had counted upon the profits of this group as a little capital upon which to begin housekeeping. He hoped that the government would purchase the group. To-day it had brought him fame; to-morrow it would bring fortune—not the fortune which most men covet, as a means of indulging in dangerous pleasures or wild dissipation which are equally enervating to genius, but wealth which, enjoyed sparingly and in moderation, brings with it repose. What greater happiness could there be than to behold Sabine happy in these peaceful surroundings, and to feel that this happiness was not purchased by yielding to subversive ideas, by worshipping gold for its own sake, or by servile homage paid to the degraded or frivolous taste of the multitude?

There was something great in having won a place among real artists, without being guilty of flattery, servility, or meanness. For who is totally exempt from meanness that is determined to succeed at any cost? Ah! it was in that hour of compensation for his laborious youth, that hour when success and happiness together smiled upon him, that sorrow had seized him as her prey, and rent his heart! She to whom his heart had so completely gone out, who had been his sole joy, now withdrew her hand cruelly from his, and declared that she had placed it there only in obedience to her father's will.

For three days Benedict remained shut up in his studio, as one suddenly stricken down. He no longer worked, nor even thought, for his thoughts ever strayed back to the young girl who had so coldly rejected him. Sometimes he tried to persuade himself that she had acted thus through a motive of self-sacrifice, and that she really suffered as much as he did from the separation which she believed was rendered inevitable by Xavier's condemnation.

He reminded himself how she had smiled upon him on the evening of their betrothal, and the innocent joy which had lit up her face. He heard again her clear, pure voice singing the hymn from Haydn; he found once more the woman whom he had once loved, cherished, venerated, and his heart beat high with joy. But hope was succeeded by profound despondency. Sulpice had said nothing to comfort him or give him hope. Did he, too, believe that his sister had never loved him? So the artist denied admittance to every one, and remained heart and soul absorbed in his sorrow. His strength failed with his hope. He who but the previous day had been ready for the accomplishment of great and noble work, felt himself suddenly incapable of anything. It seemed to him that his ambition had died with his happiness. Glory, the eagle flight of which his eyes had followed, now fell earthward with broken wings, and Benedict asked himself if the artist could survive the man's despair.

The statues in his studio remained in their covers of green serge; the clay grew hard in the tubs; the stools, upon which stood busts or statues just commenced, were strewn with fragments of dried earth. That room, so lately full of hope, life, strength, and industry, became, as it were, a sealed sepulchre, which Benedict did not care to reopen. At times he almost wished that death would seize him in his promising youth, and that the group he had sculptured might be his monument.

About a week after his interview with Sabine a large document, bearing the ministerial seal, was handed to him. He opened it absently. But in reading the enclosure his face changed and brightened. The minister informed him that the government desired to purchase his group, and asked his price; adding that, to encourage an artist who already gave promise of so brilliant a future, it had resolved to confide an important work to him. This was to be a group representing Hylas carried off by Nymphs, and was for the decoration of a monumental fountain.

"Aye," said Benedict, bitterly, "so it is; success, wealth, fame, when I have no one to whom I can offer them, when they are worthless."

He threw the letter aside, and resumed his gloomy train of thought. Presently he heard the bell. For a week past Beppo, his little Italian servant, who swept the studio, and served as model for lazzaroni and *pifferari*, and players on the *zampogne*, had orders to admit no one, saying that his master was unwell and unable to receive them. They usually left a card, promising to come again. But on this occasion the visitor was obstinate; he raised his voice threateningly, he even maltreated Beppo, who went so far as to place himself before the studio door in an attitude of defiance. The visitor took Beppo by the collar, threw him aside like a rubber ball, opened the door, and rushed in to Benedict.

"You are in to me," he cried, seizing the artist by both hands.

"Lionel!" cried Benedict. Then he added dejectedly, "But I am not myself."

"I know all about it," said the artist; "blighted affection, broken ties, illusions dispelled. You will get over all that. The trials of life come thick and fast upon us, but we must not sink under them. I expected this. Xavier Pomereul's trial put an end to all your plans. Of course you could not marry a girl whose brother was condemned to the galleys."

"You are mistaken, Lionel," said Benedict, "in my eyes Sabine was free from the slightest stain. I believe in Xavier's innocence, and I wanted his sister for my wife."

"After the trial?"

"Still more after such an affliction."

"That is heroic," said Lionel, "but foolish."

"Ah, but Sabine refused to marry me."

"By Jupiter!" said Lionel, "I call her a noble girl."

"But she broke her solemn promise."

"Mlle. Pomereul had promised to make you happy, but not to ruin you."

"She has succeeded in that by her cruel refusal. I worked for Sabine; my fame, if I can call it so, is her doing. With her, I could do anything; without her, I am fit for nothing."

"Oh, come, now," said Lionel, "you think so, but it is not the case."

"It is as true as my sorrow."

"Of course, but your sorrow will gradually grow less and less."

"I will never forget Sabine."

"Admitted. But neither can you ever forget art, which is the source of sublime pleasure. You will not forget sculpture, because it will be your support and consolation. You will find other Sabines in life, but you can never replace the art to which you have consecrated yourself."

As he spoke Lionel caught sight of the ministerial document with its red seal.

"That savors of the Minister of Fine Arts," he said.

"Read it," said Benedict, offering him the letter.

"Well," said the other, when he had finished reading, "you must ask thirty thousand francs for your group; it is worth more, but government invariably says it is not rich, and we must take its good will for the deed. The price being moderate, you may consider the purchase made. So you have thirty thousand francs in advance for the expenses of the fountain which is ordered."

"But I will not do the fountain."

"Now, there you are again with your notions. You will refuse government work?"

"Government work of that sort, at all events."

"Of that sort? What do you mean? The choice of a subject seems to me remarkably good for such a purpose. Have you a pencil here?"

As he spoke, he took a sheet of paper and a pencil, and began to sketch.

"A mass of rock will form the base. Hylas, who comes to slake his thirst at the fountain, will be upon one of them, bending towards the crystal wave, as a poet would say. Below, a nymph, carelessly reclining upon the golden sands of the fountain, seizes Hylas by the hand, gently drawing him downwards. Another kneels eager and trembling, gazing upon their prey, whilst a third glides about among the leaves and sedges, regarding the scene curiously, and waiting for the fall of Hylas, who is hastening to his death."

Lionel held out the paper upon which he had sketched the scene to Benedict.

"It is very natural," said Benedict, "but I am not in the least tempted to accept it."

"Why?"

"For a reason."

"An artist should never have any reason for refusing a government order."

"You are wrong there," said Benedict; "he must act according to his convictions."

"But what has 'Hylas and the Nymphs' to do with politics?"

"With politics? Nothing; but with my conscience."

"On my word, I am in the dark," said Lionel.

"Do you remember my group?"

"It made stir enough not to be easily forgotten," said Lionel. "The illustrated papers reproduced it; Cham made a caricature of it; nothing was wanting."

"Then you must see that I cannot be inconsistent."

"But I do not understand."

"I was brought up by a good man, M. Pomereul; taught by a saintly one, the Abbé Sulpice; betrothed to the purest and most innocent girl I have ever seen and admired. My studies, my laborious life, the atmosphere which I breathed, heart and soul, was totally apart from the usual ideas and habits of artists. My work was in accordance with my life. I admire the talents of such men as Pradier, Carpeaux, and Carrier-Belleuse, but I regret that it is wasted in producing dangerous if not indecent figures. I have sworn to pay homage to art by never executing, whatever the temptation, a figure at which any woman might blush. My studio is a sanctuary, not a harem."

"Then you are still thinking of marrying Sabine?" said Lionel.

"Why, because I did not marry her, am I to change all my plans?" said Benedict.

AN ARTIST SUPPER. 177

"You might modify them?" said Lionel.

"The beautiful must be always the beautiful," said Benedict.

"But the beautiful, like Hindoo gods," said Lionel, "may have a multiplicity of forms. Beauty lies not only in drapery, but in form. I admit that the 'Three Graces' of Germain Pilon is admirable, but none the less that of Canova is exquisite."

"I promised to follow that path."

"Whom did you promise? Your patron? His death released you from it. Sabine, who has refused you?"

"My conscience!" said Benedict.

"Ah, but then you must have two consciences—your conscience as a man, and your conscience as an artist—the one does not in the least interfere with the other. I understand and approve of your irreproachable life, but it has nothing to do with the marble figures which you represent."

"Hold there," said Benedict, "an artist's work is a reflex of himself. I could never again sculpture a group of Religion trampling Idols under foot, if those idols were my own, and if religion were not sacred in my eyes.'

"You could never do that, but you could do something else. Let me tell you your group is superb, but you will probably show your greatest strength in carrying out this government order. You will never persuade artists that it is as great a proof of genius to create a draped figure as an undraped one, or that it is not more difficult to model an Eve than a Lucretia. Whatever may have been the deserved success of your last group, it can never reach the same height that Hylas and the Nymphs will."

"Perhaps you are right," said Benedict; "but I will at least have the inward satisfaction of knowing that I have been faithful to the course I marked out for myself, and that I have never made art subservient to passion."

"Wait forty-eight hours before you give your reply about the fountain," said Lionel; "but do not lose a moment in fixing the price of your group. I am going in that direction and will deliver your letter."

Benedict began to write.

"By the way," said Lionel, "I am having a house-warming this evening. I came in fact to give you my new address. Of course I may count on you."

"You do not understand me, Lionel."

"I understand that you are despondent, and want cheering up."

"I need to be alone."

"You need plenty of company to make you laugh."

"I will never laugh much again. I feel as if my youth were over."

"Then you should only work for funeral decorations henceforth, my good fellow. Make a statue of Art with his torch extinguished, his compass, his lyre, and his chisel broken, and then have done with it. Make your will, and if you are too good a Christian to use a brace of pistols, set off for La Trappe and take the vows. But do not attempt to live in the world and not be of the world. Fra Angelico became a monk, and Fra Bartolomeo wore the cowl. One must be consistent, so unless you want to put a cloister grating between yourself and the world, you must do as it does, and howl with the wolves, only showing your teeth less and making less noise than the rest. What does this supper amount to after all? Sitting down to table with some friends who appreciate you."

"And who have not a single idea in common with me."

"Upon art perhaps not, but upon *paté aux truffes*

my dear boy, it is another story. You need not drink if wine does not agree with you; you need not sing if you do not feel inclined. You can sulk in a corner if you please; you can rail at our gayety from the heights of reason. You can represent, if you wish, the philosophers at Couture's "*Fête Romaine.*" There are concessions enough for you, I hope."

"Thank you, Lionel, but I cannot—"

"Refuse, you were going to say," said Lionel; "I believe you."

"No, accept," said Benedict; "my wound is too deep."

"The more reason for healing it."

"It will reopen."

"When the weather changes, perhaps. But try to keep the barometer at fair weather."

"No, Lionel, once more no."

"You are wrong, Benedict, and I am sorry to see it. If you nourish your grief in gloomy silence, it will become a disease. It will paralyze your brain and your hand. It will render you incapable of everything. You will be among those to whom the world says with an evil joy, *Væ victis!* You must not let yourself be conquered in this struggle. Rise the greater for misfortune. Forget Sabine, give the Muse the place once held in your life by that young girl, and, arrested in your course for an instant by an unforeseen obstacle, cross with one bound the barrier at the foot of which you had lain down to die."

"I have not strength for all this."

"Not of yourself alone, perhaps, but sustained by your friends, and I am a friend, Benedict."

"Then leave me to grieve."

"To grieve with me, yes. You shall tell me of your dreams of Sabine, of your perished happiness; and I shall speak in glowing terms of the Muse who presides over sculpture. I will paint for you the glory which you now disdain, and in a few months you will not only be contented, but happy."

"If I could believe this."

"You may believe me, Benedict, for what you are suffering I have suffered."

"But was the one you loved like Sabine?"

"Yes, but I found that art was better and higher still."

"I do not know whether you are my deliverer, or merely a tempting spirit," said Benedict; "but your visit has done me good."

"And an evening spent with us will completely restore you. Will you come?"

"I would be a melancholy guest," said Benedict.

"The philosopher of the *Fête Romaine*, it is agreed. We will expect you."

"At what hour is supper?"

"Nine o'clock."

"You can set a place for me, Lionel."

"And I will take your letter to the minister. *Au revoir*."

They shook hands and Lionel went out.

"Ah, *signor mio*, I shall be scolded," said Beppo to him.

"Get your master's clothes ready, you young vagabond," said Lionel, "and spend these five francs to my health."

Beppo showed every tooth in a broad grin. Benedict called him in a moment to take his orders.

"Lionel is about right," thought Benedict; "if sorrow is not strong enough to kill us at once, why should we let it do so by degrees? I will not enter into gayety or folly to-night. But contact with others may cheer me up."

Benedict made an unusually careful toilet, and at the appointed hour arrived at his friend's studio.

AN ARTIST SUPPER.

It was a large room with a very high ceiling on which draperies forming a sort of tent concealed all defects in the plastering. Brilliant pictures in large gilt frames claimed immediate attention. Lionel had truly an artist's temperament, and everything from his hand showed power and originality. Rare pieces of *faience*, curious coats-of-arms mounted in panoplies, statuary or terra-cotta figures, various knick-knacks, canvases by Beauvais with female figures, bunches of flowers or wings of birds peeping out from dark draperies, contributed to the charming effect of the whole. All the artist's apparatus had been pushed into corners, and the supper table was served in the centre of the room. It was in excellent taste, but in such sumptuous style as to remind one of the gorgeous feasts which Veronese loved to represent. Venetian crystals filled with flowers, silver and gold ornaments of German workmanship, goblets for champagne, pitchers of foaming ale, flasks of Italian wine, thickset decanters, bottles covered with straw, and long-necked ones of Rhine wine from the royal vineyards of Johannisberg, sparkling Moselle, Chiraz, with tops of rose-colored silk and seals of fragrant wax, made up an inviting whole.

Vases of flowers, pyramids of fruit, chandeliers of waxen tapers alternated with substantial dishes. Under the tablecloth was a rug of the thickness of two carpets, and the cloth itself was of the finest linen ornamented with lace and with a rich border. In the corners of the studio statues of Venetian negroes holding candelabra completed the ornamentation.

When Benedict entered, nearly all the guests were assembled. They were deep in conversation and his entrance was scarcely noticed. The late ones having arrived, the curtains were drawn and supper began. Benedict did not regret having come. He sat beside ac old brother artist, who indulged in many pleasant reminiscences, and the gayety was for some time within perfectly reasonable limits.

Some literary men, principally art critics, enlivened the occasion by excellent stories. The mirth was real and hearty. The drinking was done slowly. The night was long, and the windows, carefully curtained, did not permit day to penetrate too quickly into the studio. At length the company began to grow heated. Congratulations were exchanged on mutual success. Benedict received a great many compliments, and, as he omitted to mention the purchase of his group by the Minister of Arts, Lionel took care to announce it. Every hand was immediately stretched out to him, and this spontaneous sympathy did him good. He realized how hard it was to live in solitude, and depend on one's self, and he resolved to follow his friend's advice and dispel grief by the pursuit of pleasure. He slowly emptied his glass, touching it to that of an art critic, and his face began to light up; but it was not with the inspired light of old; it was rather with the flush of wine which quickly removed all traces of tears. Conversation became more animated; words flew about like arrows. Foolish stories were told; each one spoke of projected statues or paintings. In turn Benedict was questioned as to his.

"Ah!" said Lionel, "he has no choice—the subject is given him."

"By whom—a banker?" asked one.

"Better than that."

"A prince?"

"No; a king called Government."

"What is it?" asked a dozen voices.

"Hylas and the Nymphs."

"He is in luck!" cried they.

"You do not know him; he refuses."

AN ARTIST SUPPER. 183

"Bah!"

"He has sworn to make Madonnas in perpetuity."

"Take care, my good fellow," said one; "that is dangerous."

"In what way?" asked Benedict.

"To be too fond of draperies. It seems as if you find it easier to dress a lay figure than to reproduce nature."

"No," said Benedict, feeling bound to defend his convictions; "it is because I have too much respect for art to turn it to base uses."

"Bah! then you would suppress the best creations of Michael Angelo, and burn Raphael's "Triumph of Galatea." Art for art's sake, my boy. A fig for those who shield themselves under a pretence of morality. I could understand your scruples if you were about to marry; but as I hear that is all over, there will be no one to criticise your work, and you need not fear to offend the squeamish conscience of a pretty young girl. To refuse a government order! It is an unheard-of thing."

"Perhaps, sir," said a critic, "you have some idea of reforming society, and remodelling it according to your notion. You will never succeed. To keep the favor of the multitude, go with it. What harm would there be in modelling the Nymphs and the youth Hylas, as depicted in the fable? You have proved that religion has power to inspire you. Show us now what poetry, the theogony of Greece, can gain from your chisel."

"To the fountain of the Nymphs," said Lionel, raising his glass.

Benedict was silent. His neighbor filled his glass for him.

"Empty it in any case," said he. "You are free to do as you wish. They will call you a devotee."

Benedict touched glasses with his neighbor.

"To art!" cried he, "under whatsoever form it be
To art, whose love never deceives us, and who makes of
us what we are, and will make us immortal!"

Gildas now raised his glass, and sang some verses in a
ringing voice.

"Bravo, bravo!" cried the young men.

Lionel filled the poet's glass.

"The second verse," said he, and the poet improvised
a second.

"That is too melancholy," said a voice. And the poet
began a third and last stanza, treating of the sublimity
of art, and the immortality which it purchases.

This was followed by an outburst of enthusiasm. The
poet's hand was warmly shaken, and he was congratulated on his efforts.

Conversation then began to change its tone. Bottles
and decanters were emptied with astonishing rapidity;
the guests raised their voices, and some became very
much affected. The journalists registered in their notebooks the name of Préault, the ideal sculptor. The
mirth became boisterous; they all talked together in
different keys and on different subjects. An amateur,
seating himself at the piano, played the "Marche aux
Flambeaux," whilst the artists, half tipsy, took a dish,
a chandelier, or a lamp, and walked in procession
round the room. Others threw themselves down on
sofas to smoke, and the poet began a discourse on the
"Visions of Opium."

Heads grew muddled, words inaudible, and soon half
the company was asleep. Before they left the studio a
servant opened the shutters. It was broad daylight.
Each one rose, stretched himself, passed his hands
through his dishevelled hair, glanced at his disordered
clothing, at the remnants of the feast, and, lighting fresh
cigars, went away, thanking Lionel for his royal banquet

"Stay," said Lionel to Benedict.

The young sculptor paused.

"Are you tired?" said the painter.

"No," said the other.

"Do you feel better?"

"I have less contempt for others and less esteem for myself," said Benedict.

"That is not bad. Do you feel like working?"

"I? I have not an idea in my mind."

"So much the better. We will rest together. I will dispose of this evening."

"Where will you take me?"

"To the theatre."

"To hear some fashionable craze?"

"Exactly."

"So you want to kill my soul?"

"To kill the worm which is gnawing at it."

"Can you be certain, Lionel, that the soul will survive?"

"Its only use just now is to make you suffer."

"Just now—yes; but once it was all my joy and strength."

"Once is far off, Benedict."

"Yes; and Sabine will never be my wife. As you will, I will stay. Take me where you please."

For a week Lionel continued what he called his saving of Benedict. He hurried him from pleasure to pleasure, varying them and inventing new ones with a sort of genius. At first Benedict was wearied and disgusted; then he began to find the pleasures less repulsive, and, as they gave him forgetfulness, he ended by craving them.

One morning, however, he said to Lionel, whose apartments he now shared,

"Have you any modelling wax here?"

"I think so. Isidor began his group of Centaurs—a piece of idiocy. Use the Centaurs for whatever you want."

Benedict sat down at the table and began to model. Meanwhile Lionel painted on his Déjanire. Both were silent, each absorbed in his work. At length the waning day, with its darkness, warned them that their task had been already too far prolonged. Lionel threw aside his brush, and stepped back to judge of the effect of his work. He fixed a mirror in the proper position to show the canvas. Satisfied with his work, he said, rubbing his hands,

"The Déjanire is the excuse for the Centaur. That will come. And you?" turning to Benedict.

Benedict did not hear, but continued to model. Lionel leaned over the sculptor's shoulder and watched him. Benedict was just finishing the rough cast of the Fountain of Hylas and the Nymphs.

"Bravo!" said Lionel, with sincere admiration. "It is a great work, and will be the beginning of your real fame."

"Perhaps," said the sculptor; adding in a low voice, "something has died within me."

"What is that?"

"My conscience," answered Sabine's lover.

CHAPTER XIII.

The Golden Calf.

The fourth floor of the Pomereul mansion was occupied, as we have said, by the servants and by the Abbé Sulpice. His apartments were so arranged that the first served as antechamber to the second. The antechamber was furnished in straw, the walls covered with dark paper, and in the centre of the room stood a table of black wood loaded with papers. The second was like a monk's cell. A low bed formed the background; a *prie-dieu* was placed under a handsome crucifix which occupied one of the panels; the third was completely taken up by book-shelves, giving evidence of the abbé's taste for study. A desk full of deeds and manuscripts, a lamp, a sofa for visitors, and a straw chair for the abbé himself, completed the furniture.

The young priest rose at five o'clock, celebrated his morning mass at the Church de la Trinité, returned at half-past seven, took a frugal meal, and received visitors till ten o'clock. He then went down to his sister's apartments, and joined to some extent in the family life till it was time to set out for Charenton, where he superintended the education of the children, visited the sick, and consoled the suffering.

When he returned home, he devoted two hours to his correspondence, reading and answering letters. Then he again received those who wished to see him; afterwards made his calls, or went whither his ministry was required, returned, took a very simple meal in his own room, spent a little while with Sabine, and retired to take his much-needed rest.

There was no need of being announced at the abbé's door. It usually stood open, and every one who had a favor to ask, whether he were rich or poor, passed in by turns. The lady of rank stood side by side with the poor workwoman; the mechanic found himself in company with some influential functionary; and, if the Abbé Sulpice showed partiality to any one in the matter of admittance, it was to the most miserable, whose time was naturally most precious. People came from all parts of Paris to see him. Many of the highest rank were often to be met in the antechamber of the Abbé Sulpice, and dignitaries of the Church came to seek counsel of the young priest, whose saintly life placed him so high in public esteem.

Sulpice never felt vain of this influence which he exercised over so many souls. To the poor he simply said, "Suffer patiently." To the rich, "Give of your abundance, and, if you have the courage, even make sacrifices in order to give."

One morning the banker, André Nicois, presented himself in the anteroom. Whilst the Abbé Sulpice was busy within, consoling, fortifying, advising, the banker passed in review the hapless ones who had come to seek aid of the priest; for all were in some way poor or suffering. Some sought material bread, others food for the soul. Some asked for courage to bear some affliction. Mothers, holding pale and worn children to their famished breasts, asked for alms to keep them from starvation. Young men came for strength and guidance to resist the temptations of life.

The banker having come last was the last to enter the abbé's private room. When the young priest recognized him he held out both his hands with the greatest warmth.

"You come," he said, "as a living reminder of my dead father who loved you so much."

"Love fully returned by me," said Nicois; "and God is witness that you, your sister, and your unfortunate brother, are equally dear to me."

"What can I do for you?" asked the abbé.

"I come, in the first place, to make restitution. Thanks to your timely assistance, I passed through a financial crisis. I have come to return you the hundred thousand francs which you placed at my disposal."

"I have no right to refuse it," said the abbé, "as there are other heirs to my father's fortune; but I want you to promise that, if ever you are in any difficulty, you will apply to us."

"I readily promise," said the banker.

"So your affairs have really taken a favorable turn?" said the abbé.

"Yes," replied the banker; "and the present political movement is greatly to my advantage. The war, which has ruined a great many speculators, has thrown an operation in my way by means of which I realized three millions at one stroke."

"Three millions!" cried the abbé.

"Yes, three millions," said the banker.

"May I ask you a question?" said the abbé.

"Certainly."

"You are fond of money?"

"Very fond."

"But you are not avaricious?"

"No; for the avaricious love to hoard money. I love to spend it."

"Then you desire to amass a princely fortune by which you can outrival the most luxurious in luxury?"

"I love money," answered Nicois, "because it is the great power of our century; it founds newspapers, buys up the consciences of men, and governs everything."

"Except those who despise it," said the abbé.

"But they are rare," said the banker.

"It is strange," said the Abbé Sulpice, "but I seek in vain on your face for any traces of this idolatry of the golden calf. I can find none. I do not believe, if you will allow me to say so, that this thirst after riches is natural to you; it is an excrescence upon your character. The longer I look at you the more am I convinced that your disposition is generous."

"You may be right," said Nicois; "but, as you know, habit becomes a second nature. My father, who was born rich, was ruined by the failure of a correspondent I was then seventeen—just at the age when the goods of fortune seem most enviable—and I felt the loss of my father's money bitterly. He did not long survive his misfortunes, and his last advice to me, with his dying breath, was to give up all the pleasures of youth, and that enjoyment I so much craved, in order that I might make a second fortune. 'Listen,' said he; 'the Dufernois have a daughter, whose dowry will be a million. She is ten years old; you are seventeen. Our late reverses will not prevent Dufernois from giving you his daughter. I have arranged everything for your happiness. Therefore let all your dreams, hopes, and aspirations tend towards that one goal of wealth. The first million, I grant you, is always hard to make. When you get one from Dufernois the rest will come of itself. Repair what was not my fault but my misfortune. Take upon the Bourse the place which I once occupied. Sovereigns succeed each other upon the throne of France; the kings of finance alone retain their power.' I answered in a way which satisfied him, but when he insisted upon my marriage with Mlle. Dufernois I hesitated. He saw it, and fixed a piercing glance on me. I hung my head.

"'I am dying,' said he, 'and I want your promise.'

"I gave it. He died, feeling that my own and my mother's future was secured. I kept my word. Thenceforth I worked with redoubled ardor, not so much for love of money at first, but in obedience to my father's command. Yet at times I reproached myself, reproached myself bitterly."

Nicois paused, and seemed to hesitate.

The abbé took his hand.

"Speak," said he; "it will do you good to tell me the story of your life. I am a friend."

"But a friend who is rather too austere."

The abbé pointed to the crucifix.

"A confessor, if you will," said he.

"Not yet. But in whatever way you put it, I know I can depend on your discretion."

A slight pressure of the hand he held was the abbé's sole reply.

"I was young," said the banker, "full of youthful ardor and impetuosity. My mother was a good woman in every sense of the word, but indifferent about religion. She bore my father's name with honor, but she did not teach me what she had never known herself, the inviolable principles of duty which depend upon the keeping of God's commandments. Her advice was good, but never rose above social propriety or personal advantage. She wished me to be happy, but she thought I could be so without that faith which had been disregarded in her own education. I was young, ardent, fiery, impulsive, impatient of all restraint, and more ambitious of pleasure than of fortune. The entire liberty I enjoyed, the want of all religious belief, at my twenty years of age, necessarily led me into a dangerous path, and I followed it. Without consulting my mother, forgetful of the promise to my dying father, I became engaged to a beautiful young girl, but who, alas! was poor. She believed in me entirely; when it was time for me to settle in life, when I was twenty-five and Mlle. Dufernois eighteen, my mother reminded me of my father's wish. I asked for time. I had not courage to tell the confiding creature whom I loved that I had lied to her, and read her contempt for me in her honest eyes."

Nicois shuddered.

"It was hard, indeed," said the abbé, "but why did you not state the case to your mother?"

"She would have laughed at my scruples. Not judging my conduct from a religious standpoint, she would have thought my fault a very trifling one, and have had no hesitation in bidding me break the heart of the poor child whom I had asked to be my wife. On the other hand, the Dufernois family treated me already as a son-in-law. Mlle. Coralie had long regarded me as her betrothed. I found myself helpless between the obligations contracted for me by my father, my attitude in the house, and the intimacy between my mother and these friends. Doubtless, had I confessed the truth to Mlle. Coralie, she would through pride have advised me to marry the poor girl to whom I had solemnly pledged my faith. But I will tell the whole truth without reserve, and in spite of my shame disclose the entire workings of my miserable heart. I knew that Mlle. Dufernois, who had been brought up to consider herself as my future wife, bore me a tender affection, somewhat timid, it is true, but infinitely charming, graceful and attractive. She had never dreamt that any other man could be connected with her life. Her innocent soul rejoiced that she could so easily obey her family in the matter of choosing her husband. She treated me with touching deference, and did nothing without my advice; as the time for our marriage approached she became more affectionate, but still remained calm, smiling and dignified. Her beauty, and the elegance of her manner captivated me. I compared her, in her wealth and beauty, with the poor girl to whom I had dreamed of uniting my fate. Yet, if I had been free, I should never have hesitated. My heart imperiously inclined to my first love; but reason, society—all my surroundings urged me towards Mlle. Dufernois. I was forced to settle matters and to fix a date. I agreed to everything; in the first place for want of any sufficient reason to oppose to whatever was expected of me; when I found myself bound so that retreat was impossible, I asked myself what was to be done with the other one."

Again the banker stopped, overcome by these recollections. His eyes were fixed on vacancy, as though his words had evoked some phantom upon which he gazed.

"How far off it is, how far off," he repeated, "and yet, when I recall those days it seems but yesterday. When the time of my marriage was settled I made pretext of a journey to explain my absence, and told the poor forsaken one that I would be away a month from Paris. One week afterwards I married Mlle. Dufernois. She had every quality which could attract; from the day of our union I felt in a new world; I even persuaded myself it was my duty to act as I had done. I banished remorse by asking myself if some ambitious motive had not influenced the poor girl whom I no longer loved. Having betrayed her I calumniated her to myself, though she conquered me there. When she learned my marriage with Mlle. Dufernois, she wrote me a letter full of pity and forgiveness. She prayed that Heaven might pardon me, and concluded by saying: 'I am heart-stricken and I know that I shall not live long. A just God who punishes all our faults will demand expiation for the wrong you have done me. Alas! my greatest pain now is that all my love for you cannot avert this chastisement.'

"Very soon after I heard of her death."

"Poor child," murmured the Abbé Sulpice.

"Alas! even her death affected me little. I forgot my victim in the happiness of seeing a child at my fireside. This child became my joy, my hope, and my ambition. I consecrated my talents and my whole future—my very life to it. I felt myself a better man beside its cradle. The child was lovely, as fair as a lily, with sweet, pure, blue eyes. Its hair was of a peculiar tawny color, increasing the beauty of the spirituelle face. The mother was enraptured. Till then my desire for wealth had been moderate. My wife's dowry seemed sufficient, and I abandoned myself to the mere pleasure of living, promising later to launch out into speculations. Everything combined to make me perfectly happy. The recollection of the poor dead girl scarcely ever occurred to me, and when it did, made little impression upon me. Happiness inspires a singular confidence. But the prediction of punishment was verified, though delayed for four years."

The banker wiped the cold perspiration from his brow.

"Courage, courage," said the Abbé Sulpice.

"About that time," he resumed, "I was obliged to go to Austria; I expected to be away only three weeks, and did not think of taking my wife and son. While I was in Vienna I received a letter written in despair by my wife. It contained but these words,

"'Our child has been stolen.'

"If a thunderbolt had fallen upon my head I could not have felt more utterly crushed. Our child stolen! By whom, and why? I hastened to Paris. I questioned my wife; she had no clue. During my absence a strange servant was engaged; four days after the child went for a walk with her and disappeared. The servant, fearing the mother's anger, did not return. A complaint lodged against her at the police office caused her to be found.

She fell upon her knees weeping and sobbing. She was honest. It had happened in this way: Having taken the child to the Tuileries, at its request the nurse went into the Champs Élysées, where some puppets were being exhibited to a number of children. There was a great crowd around the stand; the child, enjoying the performance, raised the cloth, trying to discover the secrets of the wooden actors, and his nurse laughed with him in his glee. When the performance was over there was a sudden panic in the crowd; children cried, mothers became alarmed. The greatest confusion prevailed, and when the servant sought the child, it had disappeared. She ran to and fro questioning every one. No one could give her any information. Meantime the performers had taken up their stand, packed their puppets and departed, so that the girl did not even know the spot where my poor little Marc had disappeared. I advertised in every paper and offered immense rewards; I had placards posted everywhere, describing the child and his dress, but all in vain, he was never found. My wife, in her despair cried out,

"O my God, my God! why are we so afflicted! we have never injured any one."

"Then I remembered.

"The loss of my child was God's punishment on me."

"Did not this thought lead you to repentance?" asked the Abbé Sulpice.

"No," said Nicols; "my grief was fierce, wild, selfish. It hardened me instead of making me better."

"Alas!" murmured the priest.

"I blasphemed God, whom I said had punished an innocent woman and child for my crime. I would not even admit that I deserved punishment. I made use of all the sophistry by which young men excuse the criminal levity of their conduct. I compared my blighted life with the easy life of others, and I cried out that God was unjust. No other child came to supply the loss of our poor Marc. We remained alone with the bitter recollection of the lost child. Often did I follow a crowd of little beggar children, seeing a resemblance to my son in some of them, and drew the little vagrants into conversation, and whenever I saw jugglers dragging miserable children after them, I stopped and questioned them hoping for tidings of my child. I had moments of despair when I beat my breast and sobbed like a woman. More than once in my outbursts of grief I revealed at least a portion of the truth to my wife. She guessed the rest. Slowly and gradually she shrank away from me. I felt her growing estranged and detached from my life, as a flower from its sustaining stem. She seemed almost to hate me. In the depths of her soul I knew that she accused me of being the cause of her misfortune. Her love for our stolen child became stronger than her love for me. She began to remember my strange moods at the time of our marriage, the anxiety concerning which she had so often questioned me, and which she now understood, in spite of all attempt at dissimulation. Henceforth, I had neither companion nor friend in her. Madame Nicois, indeed, remained a model wife, whose conduct was beyond reproach; but, as far as I was concerned, merely a silent shadow, bound to my life indeed, but no longer sharing it. I made some efforts to win her back, but I failed. Pride forbade any farther attempts, and I was left alone, all alone."

"And did you not even then think of God ?" asked the priest.

"From that time," replied the banker, "dates my craving after wealth. Happiness being denied me, I remembered the advice of my father, forgotten during those happy years; I bitterly felt that all was false in this world, woman's love, the promise of childhood; that the love of gold alone fulfilled its promise. Gold brought influence, purchased honors which no man could win for himself, opened every door, surmounted all difficulties, subdued everything by its power; gold was itself fame, for in Paris luxury is celebrity. A banker who obtains a loan for the government is ennobled at his pleasure, and becomes allied to princely families. A man rich enough to own a newspaper is a power; the ministers flatter him, the court makes advances to him; authors compare him to Mæcenas, when they are about to publish their last novel. All the beautiful things which art creates, or the wildest fancy invents, are his, if he so desires. He builds mansions of marble in the heart of Paris, and finds flowers of every land and clime in his conservatory. To be rich in Paris is to hold the greatest of all power. Once understanding this, I said to myself, I will be rich. If I were rash in my enterprises, they were nevertheless crowned with success. If any transient difficulties embarrassed me, the ultimate result far surpassed my hopes. I fought innumerable battles, and never found my financial Waterloo. My name is side by side with the most distinguished financiers, and that gold which I so eagerly craved, I now possess in such profusion that I know not how to spend it."

"Do you find the expected happiness in its possession?" asked the abbé.

"I am weary of the mere gratification of being rich," said Nicois; "but not of the proud comparison which I can draw between myself and those who have nothing."

"Then you admit," said the priest, "that the love of gold has been baneful in its effects? Far better for you to have less wealth in your coffers and more pity in your heart for others."

"Pity for others?" repeated the banker.

"And why not, my friend?" said the priest.

"Because no one suffers what I have suffered."

"Have you forgotten," asked the priest, rising as he spoke, "the last bitter trial which has brought Sabine and me to the foot of the crucifix?"

"No," said Nicois; "certainly not, but think of my child, my child! you have only lost a brother."

"And with that brother, the victim of a deplorable act of folly, we have lost the honor of the family, which God knows we highly prized. Sabine has, moreover, given up the intended marriage which my father so lately blest, and I can only weep with her."

"What? Mlle. Sabine will not marry M. Fougerais?"

"She cannot," said the priest, "and I approve of what she has done. For it would be wrong to bring the dowry of unmerited disgrace to a worthy man so full of heart and of talent. I deplore it though, for I doubt if Benedict is strong enough to stand such a test. What must be our regret, if that noble intellect of his should lose the sentiment of the good, the beautiful, the true, now so strong? If Benedict once ceased to be the Christian artist whom we loved, he falls into an abyss, whence there is little hope of rescuing him."

"This is terrible," said Nicois; "and do you not curse the hand which has stricken you?"

"We adore it, even in its severity," said the priest.

"Have you any hope?" said Nicois.

"Yes; that light may be thrown upon it all," said the abbé.

"But if such should not be the case, if like Lesurques, your brother should die before his innocence is made manifest?"

"I shall look for justice there," said the priest, pointing upwards.

"There above us," said the banker, "is the air, the

ether peopled with countless stars, but that is all. I do not believe in another life."

"That is the very reason why you are inconsolable," said the priest; "believe me, there is no sorrow so great that faith cannot soften its bitterness. To the Christian a grave is a cradle. When we kneel beside a funeral pile, we venerate the remains of a being made to the image of God. Whilst our eyes follow it into the eternal world where all is pure and incorruptible, the certainty of its joy is the best solace for our grief. Ah! if, recognizing the hand which had stricken you, you had bowed down humble and contrite before the justice of Heaven, deploring your fault instead of blaspheming God, you would have suffered less I assure you. If, in the name of your lost child, you had relieved misery, assisted poor mothers, provided asylums for orphans, you might have appeased the anger of God, and obtained the recovery of your child. You believe your wretchedness is complete, but are you certain that Heaven has punished you sufficiently?"

"Spare me!" cried Nicois; "do not add to my misery."

"I would rather," said Sulpice, "apply thereto the sovereign remedy of resignation."

"Ah! if you could promise me that at any cost I should find my child."

"I do not work miracles," said Sulpice; "nor do I tempt the Lord, my God. I simply tell you of His law, and transmit to you His precepts. You have suffered a great deal, and hitherto found no alleviation for your grief. It is because He alone who inflicted the wound can heal it. All your wealth could not console you as much as one tear shed at the feet of God."

The banker shook his head.

"I have given up hopes of finding my son," said he,

"and I cannot suffer more than I have done. Thank you for hearing me with such patience. My heart still remains closed against that God whom you would fain make me to love. To find happiness in abnegation and self-sacrifice one must have known and loved that God from childhood."

"Then," said the priest, "there is nothing I can do for you?"

"Do not say so," said the banker. "I regard you as among my warmest friends, and friends are scarce. If I should ever have new cause of suffering I will confide it to you alone."

The banker shook hands warmly with the young priest and went away.

"My God!" cried the priest, when he was thus left alone, "wilt Thou permit that heart to suffer so, instead of drawing it to Thee?"

He remained some time prostrate in prayer for the man whom so many envied, and who was, nevertheless, so wretched. Then going down stairs, he found Sabine, who had just come in.

"You have been there?" he asked.

She answered by an affirmative nod.

"Tell me of him," said the priest.

"I found him more prostrated than ever by his misfortune. There is reason to fear for his health, which has been terribly shaken by all these shocks. He is in a high fever. He asks justice of men and forgets to ask pardon of God. If I did not hope that he would yet be acquitted, and that the real culprit would be found, I should ask God to take Xavier to Himself."

"There is every reason to hope, Sabine, even against hope. If the unhappy boy perseveres in these rebellious dispositions we can only pray and suffer for him and with him, that he may at length be brought to resignation. An occasion for further self-sacrifice may soon be offered us; even women may be called upon to fulfil a sublime mission, and in that case we will hope that our misfortunes have kindled in us a sacred and purifying flame."

"Ah!" said Sabine, "I understand. But for my utter loneliness and desolation you would have gone with the army. A soldier of the Cross, you would have faced death beside the soldiers of glory. When I see so many young and noble priests hastening to the scene of war, I have often thought that your place is with them; but my courage failed me when I would have advised you to follow them. I asked myself what would become of me, between the thought of my poor despairing brother and the memory of one whom I shall never see again."

"Then you still regret him?" said the priest. "You are grieving for him. Why not call him back?"

"Duty forbids it. Sorrow has its dignity, and I would rather he should think me cold and insensible than selfish and cowardly. If I cannot at once subdue an affection encouraged by my father and blessed by you, I can at least prove myself worthy a good man's love by wearing mourning like a widow."

Baptiste came in just then with the papers. The abbé tore them open with a hasty gesture, and glanced down the columns anxiously. Broken exclamations escaped him; his eyes grew dim; his heart beat high.

"Defeated!" cried he; "not in an equal combat, but overpowered by force of numbers. Reverses on all sides! And, though obscure soldiers are covering themselves with glory, and performing prodigies of valor, they cannot save the army, nor preserve France. Ah! will Heaven abandon the country of Charlemagne, of St. Louis, and of Joan d'Arc? Will this invasion, swelling like a threatening sea, at last engulf Paris? Alas!

there is no Genevieve's crook to oppose to Attila's battle-axe. It is heart-breaking to read of it. France betrayed, sold, delivered to its enemies by some new Judas. Such will be the verdict of posterity. Never again shall that sublime feeling of love of country fill all hearts. Never again shall France rise as a nation, indignant, wronged, but yet invincible. No nation could ever conquer her till she has once felt the shame of defeat. They spend the time for action in words. Plans are being made when the moment has come to take up arms, and meanwhile the Prussian army is encircling us in its folds, and will finally crush us."

"What!" cried Sabine. "Do you fear that France—"

"Will be conquered? Such is ever the fate of nations when, enervated by luxury, permeated to their very core by vice, they deserve a terrible awakening. How terrible it seems to me, as a priest, no less than as a Frenchman, that a Protestant soldiery should set foot upon Catholic France! And yet—"

"They dare not attack Paris!" cried Sabine.

"They will dare. It is their turn now."

"What will you do?" asked Sabine. "When I thought of your going away with the army to some distant place, and leaving me alone and desolate, my courage failed me. But if I can, as it were, fight by your side—take my share of the common burden, staunch wounds, console, and comfort—in a word, play my woman's part, count on me, Sulpice. The sister will be worthy of the brother. My weakness and hesitation shall be lost sight of in face of danger; and, rising above my own sorrows, I will do all for love of Him who has afflicted us."

Baptiste threw open the door of the room, and said, in a voice of deep emotion,

"Sir, a deputation from Charenton wants to see you."

"Show them in, and I will see them presently," said the priest.

"Bring them here," said Sabine; "they are, we might say, part of the family."

Baptiste went out for the workmen, and soon ushered in about twenty of them. They were men of various ages, all scrupulously neat in their personal appearance.

"Pardon us," said the spokesman, "for intruding upon you here, and, so to say, forcing your door; but our reason is important. Not a moment is to be lost in a matter which we have so much at heart. Terrible news is placarded on the walls; and, in spite of reassuring words from some of the papers, we suspect the fearful truth. We have come to you, our guide and counsellor, to ask your advice, and whether you are of opinion that France will be conquered in this war, and Paris besieged?"

"I still hope that France will repel the foe which has now set foot upon her territory; but Paris will be besieged."

"Then who will defend it? Our soldiers are on the frontiers."

"The Parisians," answered the abbé.

"We wanted but the word, sir," cried the man; "for we know that your advice will coincide with the dictates of honor. If the Parisians have to defend Paris, they must know how to hold a musket. Our comrades are frantic since yesterday's news; they long to fight like lions. This is our idea: since the beginning of the war labor is at a standstill. Let us stop all ornamental work for the present. The founders will find plenty to do; for cannon and artillery will be needed before long. They can serve their country by preparing engines of war; and the others—well, the others must learn to be soldiers as fast as they can. We will unite in forming an independent battalion. And we have come to ask you to be our chaplain."

"Brave men!" cried the priest, shaking hands with the foremost; "worthy sons of France! I accept with all my heart. You, arms in hand, and I with the crucifix, will do our duty before God and men."

"And I?" said Sabine, stepping forward. "And I, brother?"

"You will go to Charenton. Assist these brave men's wives. Tell them from me that their husbands shall receive their usual salary as long as the war lasts. Then, as we have to look forward to great trials and stern realities, you must choose the most intelligent women, and with them organize an ambulance in the factory. The wounded can be brought thither. Draw as largely as you please upon our coffers; for we shall be always rich if we always succeed in doing good."

"Ah, Mademoiselle," cried Blanc-Cadet, "we shall fight with tenfold courage, when we have the consolation of knowing that if a ball should strike one of us he shall be brought to our dear factory and cared for by you."

"We are only paying our father's debt, good friends," said Sabine; "the fortune which we now enjoy was made by you; it is just that it now be of assistance to you. You know that even before our recent afflictions we always had your welfare at heart. Your wives and daughters will henceforth be our sisters; I adopt your children. If any of you should fall upon the field of battle he will leave no orphans, they will belong thenceforth to the Pomereul family."

There were few dry eyes among the group when she had finished, but the Abbé Sulpice resumed:

"And it must be understood that I shall take upon myself the equipment of the men; any of you who have been soldiers can drill the others. This very day I will go to the archbishop and ask his approval. I shall not see you again to-day, as I have a great deal to do, but to-morrow I shall meet you without fail."

"To-morrow," repeated Sabine.

The workmen then withdrew, with renewed acknowledgments to Sulpice and Sabine, and the young priest almost immediately left his sister.

"My path is now marked out for me," said he; "let us be with God, and God will be with us."

Sabine spent the afternoon in arranging papers, and disposing of everything, as if for a long absence. At six o'clock her brother returned.

"On the eve of the gladiatorial combats," said he to his sister, "the martyrs always took their last meal together. I will share yours this evening."

"Ah, Sulpice, do you already think of death?"

"I want at least to be ready," said he. "But do not be downcast. For it seems to me that my mission will be long, and that I have yet to save Xavier."

Then he kissed her upon the forehead.

"It is, my dear sister," said he, "the brother's kiss and it is also the priest's benediction. And now hold out your arm."

She did so, and the Abbé Pomereul fastened thereupon the white shield bearing the Geneva Cross.

The young girl knelt down before him.

"My brother," said she, "and my father also, for you are my spiritual father, bless this life which will be exposed henceforth for my neighbor, and bless my death should God take me."

"Rise, Christian," said the priest when he had blessed her; "it is the will of God."

CHAPTER XIV.

THE WAR.

ON the night of the 1st October, 1870, a party of young men were gathered round a camp fire. It was very cold. And in spite of many armfuls of wood and logs thrown upon the embers, they could scarcely keep warm. They held their hands over the blaze which now rose into the air, and again, driven downwards by a blast of wind, almost scorched their faces. They were silent. At that crisis the thoughts of men, and especially of those who had taken up arms to defend the ramparts, were marked by a melancholy gravity. The beginning of that disastrous war had been remarkable for heroic efforts, for deeds of valor worthy the archives of glory; but, by a strange fatality, or by the incompetence of those who had usurped power on the 4th of September, all this courage, valor and enthusiasm were nullified. The National Guard, and the volunteers not being called to arms, were consumed with secret rage, thinking of the perils which threatened the capital on every side.

Each time that the call resounded in Paris they rose, sniffed the air, scenting the powder, and attaching the last green branches to their muskets, thus saluting in advance the victory which was to break up the brazen column that now threatened the besieged city with destruction. Every evening, alas! the remnants of heroic battalions returned from the slaughter blood-stained, weary, their numbers lessened, blaming their commanders, who had made them believe that the war would be a war of extermination, and who veiled their cowardice under an appearance of devoted patriotism.

That night the hearts of the young soldiers were bursting with indignation.

Ever and anon one of them raised his head with a threatening scowl upon his face, or another examined the condition of his arms, while a third wrote in a notebook his will in favor of those dear ones whom he could scarcely hope to see again. Ever and anon a young artist, who was among the little group of patriots, recited some martial verses from the poets, or sang one of those military airs which so often serve to revive drooping courage, and to thrill the soul with love of country.

This little group of men, who gathered grave and stern around their camp fire, chilled by the cold night air, were all artists, students, or men of letters. They had been carefully chosen, poets, painters, sculptors and novelists, undertaking with noble enthusiasm and generous valor the defence of their beloved Paris, destined to be so treacherously betrayed.

In truth since the very commencement of that succession of disasters, unparalleled in history, they had indulged in much lawful anger, and shed many tears; but once the word went forth to stand, they were found arms in hand, with courageous hearts, a resolute, brave and noble phalanx, waiting to be cut to pieces, less indeed by the enemy than by the misdeeds of those who should have sustained them, and whose only aim seems to have been to act the Judas.

"What a dreary vigil!" said the youngest of the watchers suddenly breaking silence; "far better the roar of cannon than this death-like stillness. When the sound of artillery strikes upon the ear, then, at least, we can fight, struggle, and take our chance of victory or a glorious death. But when all is quiet, and we feel that in

these nights of perfect calm we are wasting our lives
and consuming our provisions, on my word it drives one
mad."

"Yes, Gildas," said another, whose face as the fire-
light fell upon it was dark with despair, while his voice
sounded hoarse and unnatural, "yes, Gildas, better the
struggle than such repose as this. What say you, Benedict?" he added, turning to one of the group, who sat
with his face hidden in his hands.

"I say," answered the young sculptor, "that I pray
Heaven to be among the first killed upon the field of
battle when we are exposed to fire. I am weary of this
defence which is not a defence, of this marching and
never advancing; of victories which end in retreat, of the
day's orders which resound with the names of obscure
soldiers who must be forgotten to-morrow."

"It is true," said a dramatic author, who was taking
notes on a tablet. "We are spectators of a bloody tragedy, and when the flag goes down we cannot exclaim
with the ancient armies, even in their defeat, 'All is lost,
save honor.' The soldiers have indeed sustained their
former reputation. But what will the leaders, the members of that usurping and incompetent government, answer to France when it demands of them, 'What have
you done with my sons? They were willing to fight, to die,
through you it has ended in a bloody farce.' Ah! may
the shame at least fall upon them. I swear that if we
come forth defeated from this struggle I, at least, will
do my utmost to place the stigma of infamy where it is
due."

"Think of the long list of battles lost," cried Benedict
Fougerais in a tone of feverish excitement. "When we
remember with what ardor the soldiers marched to
battle, and witness the result of the struggle, it fills us
with shame, terror and amazement."

"How proud we were," continued Gildas, "when the first battle took place outside of Paris, on the 19th of September. At Chatillon, Clamart and Plessis-Piquetour troops made a brave but useless defence; and the Bretons rushed into the thickest of the fight, with the scapular on their breasts and a hymn on their lips, their venerable chaplain following them into battle, animating them, consoling when they fell, and praying over the grave which he dug for them. Such details brought tears to our eyes and filled us with enthusiasm; but when these brave men had won a position, they were recalled and hindered from pushing their victory farther."

"Ah, but it was worse next day," exclaimed Benedict. "Gildas you remember, and you, Lionel. The Prussians, from their ambush, kept up a furious fire upon the forts of Aubervilliers and Noisy. The order was given in Paris, and the Bretons set out like the brave men they are, singing and vowing to return as conquerors. How they did fight! with what wonderful daring they skirmished about Bondy before making the assault! And when they had not only made good their position, but would have pursued the enemy, they were as usual commanded to retreat, which they did in good order, according to the reports.

"Oh," he cried after a pause, "if they had but called out a hundred or two hundred thousand of the national guard, sharp-shooters, infantry, volunteers, all under different names united for the same end. Only the word would have been needed. 'Dig a trench,' and the trench would have been dug. But, instead, a few battalions are ordered out, and go to unavailing butchery. In the history of all great sieges every man took up arms and fought, and when there were no more men to guard the ramparts, the women sufficed to defend them, and God be praised! the women of Paris once roused have heroism enough for anything."

"You are right," said Gildas, "and that is why whenever I see one of those heroic creatures wearing upon her arm the Geneva Cross I take off my hat with profound respect. People rail against the Parisian woman for her levity, her coquetry, her love of dress and of luxury; but there remains in her something of that old valor which belonged to the peasant girl who led the Parisians to their defence against Attila, and braved the fury of the 'Scourge of God.'"

"When we consider," said an old man, raising his tall figure gradually from the ground, "that the occupation of the village of Vitry and of Moulin Saquet by the Mauduit division had no result, any more than when on the following day it took up a splendid position at Villejuif."

"And at the very same time," said Gildas, "Admiral Saisset did something brilliant in the way of reconnoitring, and finished his retreat by inches."

"Always retreat," cried Benedict. "Read the bulletins. 'The troops fell back in good order.' The permanent occupation of places taken not seeming advisable, a retreat is made with the most wonderful coolness. Well, I say, let us have done with it; let us have no more retreat, no more falling back; we have had enough of this child's play, at which the enemy must be laughing behind its bastions! Come now, Colonel, you are a veteran, and have fought on many fields, and I ask you is this what you understand by war?"

An old man with white moustachios and figure somewhat bent, whom Benedict addressed as colonel, though he wore none of the insignia of such a rank, shook his head and answered in a voice, husky at first, but which gradually became clear and ringing.

"No, gentlemen, I will tell my children, as I have already told my old soldiers. I was at Sebastopol, and

when we heard the order, 'To the assault!' no leader eve
dared to stop us on our way to victory. I have fough
in Africa against the Arabs, and the watch-word amongst
us was, 'Return as conquerors or not at all.' Why, the
Spartan mothers had more military genius than the generals of to-day. 'Above or below,' said they to their
sons, as they buckled on their shields. In Mexico—a bad
country it was—but every one did his duty. In Italy,
wherever, in fact, I have heard the roar of cannon or the
whistling of bullets, the order was 'Go forward,' and
none ever dared to say 'Fall back,' till the enemy were
defeated or put to flight. That is why, do you see, the
old Colonel, who was wont to lead his Zouaves to fire,
would rather serve like you as private soldiers, than command men who might one day cast upon him the stigma
of a shameful defeat. I would willingly have offered my
country my long experience of war, and such military
genius as is the result of sudden inspirations; but I might
have been cast into the shade, and the orders of incompetent superiors so enrage me that I would break my
old sword. I might perhaps have given bad example to
my men by blaming their leaders, so I became a soldier,
and when the time comes I will shed my blood for my
country."

"Ah! it is deplorable," cried Benedict. "Paris will be
taken, when if she had been otherwise governed she
might have been triumphant. People hearing me might
accuse me of want of patriotism. Yet God knows I love
France, but to defend a city leaders are wanted as well
as an army. A struggle to the death, but an intelligent
and reasonable one; blood must flow in profusion, but
let it at least bring forth the fruits of victory."

"Yes," continued the old Colonel, "who would count the
cost if victory could be won? But unhappily, as it now
stands, those who are not traitors or eager only for their

own ends, are incompetent. France, which once possessed such scores of famous leaders, has still many brave and devoted generals, but not one of that calibre who, appearing in a great national crisis, saves a country by the sole power of his genius. Loyalty is not always sufficient."

"I swear," cried Benedict, "that the moment they show us a given point of attack with the word 'Advance,' I will advance without troubling myself about counter orders. And if victory is not for us I shall continue to fight, even though I remain alone among the enemy, and fall to rise no more."

After a moment's pause, he resumed in a tone of deep bitterness,

"For after all why should we value our lives so much? We have left fragments of our hearts on so many brambles that they are in shreds. To survive our defeat would be the most terrible of all our misfortunes. Having no other idol, we have kept that of military glory. We smile with gratified pride at sight of our flag. A stranger detects the note of haughty joy in our voices when we say, 'We are Frenchmen.' If, then, we must renounce this noble pride, hang down our heads and descend from our rank among the nations with agony such as we alone can know, then I say better, far better, to lie buried in the open grave of our country."

"Wrong, Benedict," cried Gildas, "wrong; even should the military glory of France be forever tarnished—and of that we need not despair—her artistic glory will still remain."

At this moment a scout arrived.

"Give me place at the fire and a mouthful of cognac," said he.

Room was made for him, and a gourd offered him. When he had somewhat warmed his frozen limbs, he said, rubbing his hands,

"Good news, my lads, we fight to-morrow."

"For a certainty?"

"For a certainty!"

"Who told you?"

"An aide-de-camp of General Noël's."

"Where?"

"At Malmaison."

"Are we among those who are to fight?"

"Yes, all of us, Franchetti's Infantry, the Amis de la France, and every one has sworn to fight unto death."

"Provided," said the Colonel, "that the force be considerable."

"General Noël is decided upon that course."

"Yes, but those above General Noël?"

"Well," cried the new-comer, "if we are again ordered to desert a position once taken I will break my sword, for it will then be useless."

"No," cried the Colonel, "no one has a right to do that now."

"But if we are driven to despair?"

"We cannot despair of God nor of France."

The new-comer then proceeded to give an animated account of the plan of action.

The little group listened with feverish interest.

"The troops for the assault will be formed into three detachments," said he, "each having its own artillery. General Berthaut will command the first, marching at the head with 3400 infantry, sustained by a squadron of cavalry and twenty pieces of ordnance."

"What position does General Berthaut intend to occupy?" asked one of the listeners.

"He will lie between the St. Germain Railroad and the upper part of the village of Rueil."

"And the second detachment?" asked the Colonel.

"Will be commanded by General Noël," answered the scout.

"At last," cried Benedict "our turn has come."

"But there will be fewer men and less artillery on our side, comrades," continued the scout.

"We will supply the want of both by redoubled bravery," said the Colonel.

"Thirteen hundred and fifty men and ten cannon," said the scout.

"Where are we to be placed?" asked Benedict.

"We are to fill up the ravine stretching between St. Conflans and Bougival, and force the park of Malmaison."

"Then the intention is to dislodge the Prussians?"

"To the last one," answered the scout.

The Colonel shook his head.

"At the worst," he said, "we know how to die."

"The last detachment," continued the new-comer, "under the command of Colonel Cholleton, will consist of sixteen hundred infantry."

"That is very little," said Benedict.

"A squadron of cavalry will take up its position in front of the old mill above Rueil, and unite the right flank with the left."

"How many pieces of artillery?" asked the Colonel.

"Eighteen, I believe," answered the young man. "Moreover, there will be two reserve forces, one ranged to the left under General Martinot, and consisting of 2600 infantry; the others towards the centre with 2000 infantry, two squadrons of cavalry, and 46 cannon for the whole reserve."

"A total," said the Colonel, "of 10,950 men, 4 squadrons of cavalry and 94 cannon."

"What is your opinion, Colonel?" asked Benedict.

"That it would require," answered the Colonel, "four times the number to attain such a result. Ah! what a disastrous war."

"Yes," cried Benedict; "the great and chivalrous battles recorded in military annals were not such as this. There is no such thing as real fighting. We shoot from a hollow. We are killed by a distant enemy whom we do not even see, and fall without a struggle ingloriously. Bravery in the present meaning of the word is the going to some appointed place, and as our comrades fall closing up the ranks. But that does not stir the blood, Colonel, as of old when it meant to sustain, man to man, the enemy's charge, to defend the ground foot to foot, to take his life or give up your own, to feel, in a word, that frenzy of battle, that fever of the blood and of the brain which takes from our view all but the enemy, and leaves no sound but the voice which urges us 'Forward, forward.'"

"Brave boy!" cried the Colonel; "you feel as I felt when first I rushed to the field. My first battles were like festivals to me. I dreamed of glory—military glory in its most intoxicating form. No feat seemed impossible; if one step higher, an order or decoration repaid my daring. When I began as a humble soldier, my mind full of the glorious traditions of our martial past, I saw myself in anticipation a general or even a marshal of France. Had not names more obscure than mine arisen to popularity, and won such triumphs? But I had come too late. There was no more to be gained in conquered countries; war had had its day. Our rapid campaigns in Russia, China and Mexico did not even interest the provinces. Glory was all very well, but we had need of rest. People began to ask themselves why their blood was necessary to the ambition of two men. I scarcely believed another war possible, when the King of Prussia, invoking the God of armies to bless his arms, set foot upon our soil. In this unequal struggle a tremendous outburst of military ardor could alone save us; as it is, there is no hope for us. Ten thousand men come forward where a hundred thousand are required. We fight like lions and do not win. If we dislodge a Prussian troop from its position, the black adder of a new battalion replaces the first. The circle of fire and of iron must enclose us, and we shall be victims sacrificed to the short-sightedness and incompetence of our leaders. Meanwhile let us fight—struggle—prove that we value something else more than our fortune, and if Paris must perish, let it bury us in its ruins."

A sober silence followed the Colonel's words.

The tactics followed by the generals since the commencement of the war proved the justice of his reasoning. Silently and sadly the men gazed absently at the fire, the warm tints of which glowed upon their faces. No sound was heard save the measured tread of the sentries. Each one thought of all he held dearest, and from the depths of his soul bade farewell to those whom in all probability he would see no more.

"Boys," said the Colonel, "follow the last advice of an old trooper; wrap yourselves in your blankets, and sleep till the drums awake you at daybreak; a soldier should be in good condition on the morning of a battle."

Gildas, the young scout, and others of the party followed his advice. But Benedict did not move; he sat still regarding the dying light of the watch-fire till it was almost extinguished, when he rose to get some wood. The wood crackled and soon leaped into a flame. The young man, drawing a note-book from his pocket, wrote by the light of the fire for half an hour with feverish rapidity.

His last thought was for Sabine Pomereul.

In his heart's testament, drawn out thus on the eve of battle when his return was uncertain, he declared to her that, in despair at having lost her, he had been led away from the path she had traced out for him in those old happy days. He begged her to pardon his weakness, and concluded by saying, "I am going to fight for France, and if I die, the ball which kills me will do me less harm than your rejection."

As if soothed by her memory he followed the example of his companions, and wrapping himself in his greatcoat went to sleep. He awoke at the sound of drums in the distance.

All trace of despondency had vanished from the minds of Benedict and his companions. They were going to battle. It was one against three, but what did it matter? they never gave it a thought. They all could remember battles won against greater odds.

The enemy was intrenched at Malmaison. They had to carry the place by assault.

After all it was a hand-to-hand fight at the point of the bayonet; it was to shoot down with rifle balls, or break heads with the butt end of muskets; and this point gained, to descend like an avalanche upon the bulk of the enemy, to make a gap at any cost, and so break the iron chain which was enclosing Paris.

O brave, beautiful, heroic youth! When we behold those improvised soldiers already inured to the hardships of camp life, we can understand how culpable were the chiefs who did not profit by such valor. The Colonel himself was no longer the cold speculator of the evening previous, the judge of a party whose adversaries he measured, and whose strokes he counted in anticipation. The roll of drums, the clank of arms, the neighing of horses, the sight of muskets, and, above all, of the flag which they were to follow and to defend, reanimated the old hero of the Russian and African campaigns.

At some distance were seen the great vehicles, surmounted by the white flag marked with a red cross, indicating that the International Aid Society was ready to play its humane part. Priests passed through the ranks, grave and recollected, now giving to one soldier their blessing, to another some advice, or distributing medals and scapulars, the shields of faith which, if they did not guarantee against wounds, at least preserved the wearers from despair and unbelief. Occasionally a soldier was seen to call a priest aside to a deserted part of the camp, to kneel and receive absolution for his sins, and rise with a more sublime and resolute courage in his face. There was no singing or laughing, jokes attempted fell on unresponsive ears. They waited the signal for departure. General Noël appeared, passed the men rapidly in review, and cried "Forward!"

The wheels of the artillery sounded on the road, the flags were unfurled, the standards floated to the wind, and the soldiers marched with a buoyant tread inspired by their eagerness for battle.

This handful of men, for they were only 1300, had sworn to do marvels. During the march no word was exchanged save oaths of mutual protection in case of danger. None were strangers to each other in the hour of battle. Men became brothers as readily as if they were upon the brink of the grave. At length General Noël's troop arrived at the ravine of St. Conflans, in sight of the park of Malmaison. General Noël was soon joined by General Berthaut. It was about one in the afternoon. All at once the artillery opened a furious fire. The soldiers could distinguish nothing amid this hurricane of iron. The smell of powder invigorated them. But the infantry was forced to remain inactive, blinded by the smoke of the artillery, and unable to discern the position which they were to carry. Eagerly they awaited the cessation of firing to take part in the action. At length, at an order from General Noël, the infantry advanced, crawling upon the earth, concealing themselves in the undulations of the ground or behind the walls or shrubbery, their ears on the alert, their muskets loaded, till they had approached the object in view—Malmaison. The park was full of Prussians who had thrown up therein gigantic works. Groups of soldiers had taken shelter behind the crenelated walls. From every loophole death came swift and terrible upon the soldiers who were to storm the intrenchment. It is true the fire of artillery occupied the enemy, and covered the French whilst they carried out General Noël's plan. But at a given signal the artillery instantaneously ceased firing, and the troops advanced with admirable valor. Little time sufficed for them to gain the ravine which leads downwards from the stream of St. Cucufa to the American railroad intersecting Malmaison. The left flank under General Noël passed the ravine with wonderful impetuosity, and climbed the heights leading to La Jonchère. As they pursued their way a terrible volley of musketry burst from the woods and the houses. The Prussians had taken up position in spite of the fire of artillery, and it seemed impossible to brave that storm of balls and musketry.

"Well," cried Benedict, turning to his comrades, "are we to remain here?"

"How can we go on?" asked another.

"You see that even the General hesitates," said Gildas.

"But there is no hesitation for me, I swear," cried Benedict; "if they cry, Go back, I will go forward. I came to fight and fight I will. If I am afterwards accused of want of discipline, so be it. Who has a right to care for our lives if not ourselves?"

Benedict was not mistaken; the General, seeing that his troops would be cut to pieces by the enemy, gave the order to retreat; the soldiers hesitated, and would, perhaps, have obeyed, when the Colonel cried,

"Boys, let all who love me follow me. We will join the others above!"

An electric thrill was felt in the ranks; a hundred young soldiers sprang forward, and rushing through fire and smoke, disappeared from the gaze of their companions, going over the ground with incredible rapidity. Ten of them fell in this rapid ascent. Alas! none could stop to raise them. They were constantly under fire, and they could not pause a moment till they had effected a junction with the Zouaves of the brave commander Jacquot. It was a goodly sight to see him among those bronzed soldiers, brave as lions, rushing on to the combat, dashing against the crenelated walls of the park, like a tremendous wave dashing against the rock as if to uproot it.

The shots came, they could scarce perceive whence. Those who fell served as ladders to the others. It was a terrible but withal a beautiful sight.

The Zouaves, collected in the angle formed by the park of Malmaison, below La Jonchère, performed prodigies of valor, and notwithstanding the bristling breastworks, notwithstanding the cannon pointed through each embrasure, effected a breach and leaped resolutely into the park. A fearful conflict ensued. Hand to hand, tooth and nail, they fought; heads were used for battering rams, bayonets for poniards, the butt ends of muskets for battle-axes. The Prussians, ten times more numerous than the Zouaves, rushed upon the handful of valiant men who, intrenching themselves against the walls, fought a terrible, furious, desperate fight, strewing the ground with corpses. The fusillade had just ceased in the park when by the widening breach rushed in the troops of which Benedict, Gildas and the Colonel formed part. At last their desire was accomplished. The struggle was a personal one and terrible in the extreme; they measured themselves against the enemy; the fury of battle, the thirst for vengeance, and, above all, the heroic feeling of defending their native land, took from them all thought save that of victory, even though it was at the cost of their blood. Gildas forgot that he had written pages which gave promise that he would become a first-class writer; Benedict forgot his glory as a sculptor, and the Colonel his old bitterness. They had but one thought, that they were Frenchmen, brothers, heroes, exposing their lives as a last rampart against the blows of the enemy. Gildas, carried away by his valor, had become detached from his comrades, and was assailed by a score of Prussians, defending himself bravely at the point of the bayonet, or beating about him with the end of his musket, breaking heads and wrists alike, and dealing death about him. But vigorous as he was he became exhausted; several weapons were directed against him, and the young man fell, uttering one cry.

"Benedict, help!"

The appeal was answered.

"I am here, brother!"

With a bayonet in each hand and a third between his teeth Benedict sprang to his assistance, wounding right and left with his triangular weapon. Blood flowed freely; howls of pain mingled with threats of vengeance. The whole rage of the Prussians was turned against the sculptor. Gildas rose at first upon one knee, then upon both, and at last, getting upon his feet, hurried to Benedict's side, for he in his generous ardor had rushed into the very midst of his assailants.

That was not a battle, it was a massacre. Zouaves, infantry, volunteers, all performed prodigies of heroism, crushing the enemy against the walls of the park of which it had made a fortress. It was one of those incidental feats not mentioned by generals in their reports because not witnessed by them, but which remain in the memory of all who have followed the history of that epoch of patriotism.

The Prussians, despairing of being able to hold the position, abandoned it hastily. The Zouaves remained in possession. In the heat of the battle Benedict saw their commander Jacquot totter, struck by a ball. He rushed to his assistance, supported him, and at length succeeded in bringing him to a sheltered spot, where in a hollow of the ground he laid him. Benedict returned to the field. To him the victory seemed incomplete; it was not sufficient to have driven the enemy from their position, but to pursue them. Victory had declared for France, but the advantage must be preserved. As they looked around them how many of the comrades did they perceive dead and wounded before their eyes!

The order for departure was given.

What! abandon this formidable position which they had so hardly won! Their assault then was in vain, was but a gross insult to these brave men, a bloody mockery of noble sentiments. Again had men been sent to die, to rally the others, and to be ordered back to the city!

Benedict felt his blood boil at the very thought.

"My friends," said he to his companions, "this is shameful treachery; to return to Paris now is to break our oath. We are soldiers, it is true, but volunteer soldiers; the heroes of to-day and perchance the martyrs of to-morrow, not men from whom discipline has taken away all idea of thinking for themselves. We may be rash, perhaps, and insubordinate, but we will not go back."

"No, no," cried twenty voices.

The bugles sounded, the drums beat a retreat.

"Forward!" cried Benedict.

And with his group of friends he rushed in pursuit of
the Prussians. On went the latter heedless of death,
unconscious of wounds, scarce pausing to note those who
fell from fatigue, and whom they trampled under foot.
Their panic carried them across the park, and already
had they leaped the enclosure, when the arrival of a
large force of their own troops changed the whole aspect
of affairs. With this unlooked-for help their courage
revived. The little band of Frenchmen, carried away by
their ardor, waited for no help. Alone in the midst of
that immense park full of threatening shadows, believing
the victory already theirs, they suddenly found themselves not alone obliged to fight the battle over to ensure
victory, but to fight and to die without hope of deliver-
ance. The Colonel, Gildas, Benedict, and their companions found themselves in an instant surrounded by
Prussians. They bethought themselves then of that immortal battalion which, at Waterloo, held the English in
check till the last of the heroes had fallen, stricken unto
death; and with the promptitude which sprang from their
imminent peril, they formed a solid group and faced the
enemy, ready to die, but not unavenged.

So proud and warlike was their aspect that the Prussians saw at once the victory would not be an easy one.
They could no longer fight with the musket, so that the
sabre or bayonet was all that remained to these cham-
pions of death. Poor Gildas, wounded in the right arm,
fought with the left; a blow from a musket felled him to
the earth. Benedict with two of his comrades was fighting still, but he received a dangerous wound upon the
head, and fell in his turn upon a heap of dead.

That was the end of their heroic struggle. The Prussians disappeared during the night. Whilst they evacu-
ated the park two infantry men who were only slightly
wounded rose, and groping their way in the darkness,

summoned up all their strength, seeking egress from the park, and perhaps a place in an ambulance wagon. They hoped to have litters sent for such of their companions as were still alive. Doubtless there must be as many wounded as dead among the heaps of motionless forms upon the field. But, if these young men's courage was great, their exhaustion was great. Weary and bleeding freely profusely from wounds hastily staunched, they could scarcely keep upon their feet. The way was strewn with heaps of corpses, forming terrible furrows on the ground. Ever and anon from some hollow in the earth, or a heap of wounded, rose a plaintive moan: some unfortunate asking help, a dying soldier craving a drop of water to ease the sufferings which death was soon to end. The two men were losing hope both for themselves and their unfortunate comrades; not a lantern glimmered before them; far as the eye could reach all was darkness; nothing could be heard but the heavy tread of the retreating French forces who, more discouraged than ever, cursed in their hearts the infatuation or worse of those who had ordered a retreat.

The two soldiers felt that soon they themselves would have to lie down and die.

All at once they saw a glimmer of light in the distance.

A dark figure soon became dimly perceptible; it seemed to stoop every moment and rise again, no doubt examining the faces of the dead, who, with features distorted by agony, and their useless weapons still clenched in their stiffened hands, called Heaven, as it were, to witness their defeat. A simultaneous cry for help escaped from the two soldiers. Guided by their voices the figure and the light began to advance in their direction, slowly, indeed, for the heaps of dead constantly barred the passage; the man stumbled over corpses and his feet slipped in the blood, delaying his difficult progress. As he came near the others saw him distinctly by the light of the lantern. In its pale and tremulous rays he had somewhat the appearance of a supernatural being. A red scar showed with cruel distinctness on the marble white of his face, and gave a sort of sublimity to the incomparable sweetness of its expression. The whole figure resembled those of the martyrs, who, like their Divine Master, received a crown of thorns, or were seared with red hot irons. A black robe, caught up a little in the broad sash so as not to impede his motion, enveloped the tall figure. A crucifix hung at his wrist, and a Geneva Cross was distinctly visible upon the sleeve of his cassock.

"You are a priest," said one of the soldiers; "are you alone?"

"Yes!"

"Are there any ambulance wagons near by?"

"The ambulance wagons of the International Aid are crowded with the dying, and every litter is also in use. Where are the wounded whom you wish to succor?"

"Alas! we do not know," said they, "we can only hope that our comrades are not all dead."

"Come," said the priest, "I have two arms, and can at least save one poor fellow. Bring me to where I can be of use."

After a fatiguing walk they brought him into the park, now transformed into a vast cemetery. Those who had fallen in the first struggle were stiff and cold; the victims of the more recent one were still warm with life. It was a fearful task, this searching among the dead. The three men constantly paused and knelt upon the ground, seeking, by the wan light of the lantern, for the faintest motion of heart or pulse. Alas! all whom they thus examined were dead.

Among a heap of corpses, many of whom seemed by

their uniform to be foemen who had fallen by his hand, lay a young man, the heaving of whose chest showed that life was not yet extinct. His breast was torn open by a wound more ghastly than deep. His face was covered with a mask of blood flowing from a gash upon the forehead. He was breathing, indeed, but could they hope that he would survive being carried to a distance?

Another wounded man attracted their attention by his groans. At length he managed to raise himself, crying wildly, "A second retreat is commanded. Oh, the cowards, the traitors!"

It was the Colonel, who had taken up again his old grief and hatred with the breath of returning life.

He supported himself on his left arm, but when he attempted to use the other, he muttered, "My shoulder is broken."

One of the soldiers made a sling out of his handkerchief, and said to the veteran, "Can you stand?"

"I think so," answered the Colonel.

"Soldiers," said the priest, who had raised the other wounded man as tenderly as a mother lifts her child, "I will take charge of this one. Let us go. If possible we will return when we leave these two in a place of safety."

The weaker of the two infantry men went on before, carrying the lantern, the other supported the Colonel, the priest bringing up the rear with the wounded man, whose two arms fell heavily over the priest's shoulder, and whose rigid figure had every appearance of death. No one spoke. A sigh from the wounded man, or a groan from the Colonel alone broke the silence. Ever and anon the little group paused to take breath, and bravely resumed its march.

Providence came to their assistance. A wagon rolled by. They called out, and were answered; it was the ambulance belonging to the *Theatre Italien*. It received them all five. The two brave infantry men were almost as pale and exhausted as those they had rescued; but the flask offered to them revived them considerably.

"Where am I to leave these wounded men, sir?" said the head of the ambulance corps.

"In the Rue de la Chaussée d'Antin, No. 15," answered the priest.

It was about ten o'clock at night when the wagon stopped its burden at the place indicated by the priest. The doors of the house were immediately thrown open, and men came out carrying the wounded in with indescribable care and tenderness, and placing them in a large apartment on the ground floor. A young girl dressed in black, except for a white nurse's apron and a red cross on her arm, advanced pale and anxious.

"You have just come from the battle-field, brother?" said she.

"Yes," answered the priest; "and I have brought two wounded men, an old and a young one. The latter is quite irrecognizable on account of the blood."

He was instantly laid upon a bed, and the young girl approached with a fine sponge, warm water and soft linen bandages. His breathing was inaudible, and it almost seemed that his heart had ceased to beat. The young nurse gently bathed the wound upon the forehead, separated the hair, and washed away the dreadful clots of blood; the face was once more visible, though disfigured and pallid, and with closed eyes. The girl paused in her task and trembled, drew back with dilated eyes, and cried out in a tone of horror,

"Sulpice, Sulpice, it is Benedict whom you have brought to me dying!"

Her courage and her heart failed her at once. She was but a woman, and she forgot that she was just then the only nurse in the house. A word from Sulpice recalled her to her mission.

"God is witness," said he, "that I did not recognize him when I raised him in my arms on the field. He is a guest whom God has sent us. Sabine, forget everything else."

Sabine pressed her brother's hand.

"I will do my duty," said she, "and if our Lord thinks I have suffered enough He will save Benedict."

When the doctor came next morning to visit the wounded he declared the Colonel's wound to be slight, but pausing before Benedict shook his head.

"Take good care of him, Mademoiselle, but in any case the poor boy will look at you many a day before he sees you, and hear the sound of your voice for long before he understands. Do you know him?" asked the physician quickly.

"He was my father's pupil and my betrothed, Benedict Fougerais."

"Ah!" said the doctor, "art has done its share in this fatal war. Cavelier, the author of 'Penelope,' was killed; Leroux is mortally wounded; Vebert may never again handle the brush, and Benedict Fougerais can only be saved by a miracle."

So saying the doctor went away full of grief and emotion.

CHAPTER XV.

THE TWO BROTHERS.

SABINE's grief at sight of her betrothed exceeded her strength. She was as pale as Benedict himself. Her eyes were dimmed with tears; sobs shook her frame; her knees bent under her; she fell prostrate, her face hidden upon the bed.

Sulpice found her thus.

"Sabine," he said "the greater the duty the more need of courage. You should rather thank God that He permits you to nurse Benedict and perhaps save his life." These words roused the young girl from her lethargy; she recovered her composure, and with a hasty but fervent prayer for Benedict and herself set about her task. After a time the wounded man began to show signs of life; but though his eyes opened and fixed themselves upon Sabine, he knew her not. Fever had set in, and in his delirium he went over all the details of that terrible struggle. He was gentle and docile as an infant, however. He even smiled and seemed grateful for the care of which he vaguely felt he was the object, but he was not conscious of the presence of his betrothed, and in his wanderings spoke of some one whom he called Sabine, but so vaguely that it was difficult to distinguish whether he had his own Sabine in mind, or the daughter of Erwin de Steinbach. Days and nights passed and still Sabine performed her manifold duties, bravely setting aside her own consuming grief. As often as possible she found time to visit the hapless Xavier at the prison of Roquette. His heart was not yet softened by his captivity. The sentence which had fallen on him, despite his innocence, did not lead him contrite to the foot of the Cross. Cursing the injustice of men, he likewise cursed what he called the injustice of God.

The chaplain of the prison vainly tried to calm and console him. The very sight of a cassock aroused his anger. In his hatred for Sulpice he included all who wore the same dress, and spoke to him of the same Saviour. Too bad a Catholic to understand the dread mystery which enshrouds Confession, he would fain have had his brother betray its secret, forgetting that he had doubted a hundred times of the absolute secrecy of priests.

Sabine's visits calmed him for the moment, but these brief interludes were usually embittered by the recollection of Sulpice. He poured out all his venom and bitterness, and the poor girl felt powerless to console him. Far from calling religion to his aid, he dwelt forever on the recollections of a vanished past. Now he was at a gambling table with its heaps of banknotes or piles of glittering gold; again he was at some luxurious board, at a theatrical performance, or listening from his stall to the impassioned strains of Don Giovanni, Favorita or La Juive. Overcome by these memories, and contrasting the past with his present state, he began to think of suicide. He hesitated, however, not through any greatness of soul or faith in God, but for fear of physical suffering, of which he had an inordinate dread. Besides, there was no hurry. As long as they left him at Roquette life was endurable. But he resolved that the moment they spoke of New Caledonia he would manage to destroy himself, even if he had to dash out his brains against the wall. During the bloody reign of the Commune Xavier's condition was ameliorated. The new keepers were indulgent to criminals, and showed more consideration for murderers than for priests dragged from the churches. They felt that at need they could depend upon those whom the law had condemned. As they had nothing to lose, not even life, for it was under sentence, they would be naturally ready for any atrocity, and in Ferré, d'Urbain and their accomplices were found the last refuge of cut-throats. It is true that Xavier, low as he had fallen, and hardened as his judges had made him appear, would have shrunk from crime of any sort; but in times of anarchy there is always hope, and the young man saw liberty in bloodshed, excess and sacrilege.

Sabine told him all that had occurred on the night of the battle of Buzenval; described Benedict Fougerais brought in covered with blood and dying, and herself approaching his bed like a Sister of Charity.

"It is all your own fault," said Xavier; "if you had married him he would not have gone."

"Yes, he would," said Sabine. "I would have been the first to urge him to take up arms in defence of his country. The only difference would have been that he would have had a wife whose family was disgraced."

"Ah!" said Xavier, "so you are another victim of Sulpice's silence."

"Do not speak so," said Sabine firmly; "you have too little idea of holy things to understand them aright. I would sacrifice my life to give you freedom, and I would rather sacrifice my own happiness than see Sulpice false to his oath. Yes, we are both victims, but of a sublime law called duty; but I much prefer to suffer than to be forced to despise Sulpice. I love Benedict with my whole heart. From childhood upwards I remember him almost as part of the family, and at last my father chose him for me as a husband. Yet I found the courage to give him up. If you knew, Xavier, what comfort there is in faith, you would fall on your knees, were it only for consolation's sake."

But Sabine could make no impression on her brother

and this was another thorn in her sorely tortured heart. Soon, however, she had the consolation of seeing a favorable change in Benedict's condition. The wound in the breast was closed, and that upon the forehead, though taking longer to heal, caused them no anxiety.

Sometimes he had intervals of consciousness. There had been, in fact, no concussion of the brain. The delirium of pain, the excitement of the life he had recently led, the great mental shocks of the various phases of the war, the superhuman struggle at Buzenval, had all a much greater share in paralyzing his faculties than even his terrible wounds. Thought returned slowly, but when he understood what was passing about him, and knew that he was with Sabine and Sulpice, his happiness contributed to his cure. The doctor warned Sabine not to deprive him of hope, declaring that a violent shock might be his death, and Benedict, finding her so kind and gentle, began to hope everything for the future. Sulpice himself brought Benedict as soon as he was able home to his studio on the Boulevard de Clichy. Beppo being scarcely sufficient to provide for his master's wants, Sulpice found as nurse for him a widow whose husband had fallen at Montrelont. Having thus attended to the welfare of his friend, the priest began to devote himself again to his work at the factory of Charenton. The rich must give the example. The people had suffered and bled, their wounds must be staunched. But it was the people themselves who would not accept the offered help. The cannons of Montmartre were seized; the muskets destined for the defence of the country were used in a general revolt.

The cannon still boomed and fights were fought, but it was no longer soldiers and noble volunteers defending the sacred soil of their country. An army was, indeed encamped outside of Paris, besieged for the second time but Paris, mutilated and bleeding, had scarcely time to count her ruins; they were increasing every day.

The mob who fought in Paris, and defended the capital against the regular army, were the members of the Commune, their banner, a red rag, inciting them to sacrilege and murder. Churches were sacked; ruffians openly preached their doctrine of free love in the sacred places. Wretches abolished all religious law, decreed the suppression of worship, and tore the divine Figure from the crucifix. Women wearing red sashes, their hair falling in a loose net upon their back, and a leathern bag slung at their side, ran about among the half-drunken populace, vomiting out terrible blasphemies. Often great wagons stopped at the doors of churches, and presently officers of the Commune, in costumes bedizened with gold, and escorted by a band of pillagers, were seen to emerge laden with their spoils. They had ransacked sanctuary and sacristy, emptied the cupboards and seized a rich booty.

The reign of liberty began by proscriptions. Blood flowed on the streets. Generals were shot in the corners of obscure gardens. Men who had written volumes against capital punishment to screen miscreants from the consequences of their crime unrelentingly put to death whomsoever they suspected of being opposed to their desires or their vengeance. Many were forced into the service of these brigands. Night and day the *Vengeurs* of the Commune searched houses and dragged thence young men and old, forcing them at the bayonet's point to serve in their ranks. The Rouge journals invented a language consisting of oaths and blasphemy. Terror was mingled with disgust, and horror surpassed even terror. Street boys carried about hideous pictures, accompanied with indecent songs or dialogues, in which the dead whose remains had been profaned were made to bear a part. The convents were thrown open, under pretence of liberating the nuns, and the holy mystery, enshrouding their austerities and discipline, exposed to the vulgar view. Novices and professed sisters were alike driven into the streets, at the same time that civil marriage was proclaimed sufficient, and divorce made legal.

Yet all these horrors, these blasphemies, these profanations, these legalized thefts, this persecution, and the insane ravings of the wretched rags they called their newspapers, did not suffice for the Communists. The hatred of religion produced hatred of its representatives. Blood could not flow fast enough for their desires. They would fain have had speedier and more frequent executions. Hostages were taken who were chosen principally from amongst the clergy and magistrates. Priests, both secular and religious, were brought before the tribunal of the Commune. To the great honor of the Parisian clergy it must be said that they rose at once to the height of persecution and martyrdom. They remained at their post, they continued to celebrate the divine office, and to expose themselves to death at the foot of those altars profaned by the ruffian soldiers of the Commune. They continued to visit the sick, teach the children, and every priest in Paris, deeming himself no greater than his Master, hourly expected to share the fate of the archbishop, then a prisoner at Mazas.

Sabine had not a moment's rest. She was in constant fear for Sulpice's life or liberty, for the young priest would not even yield so far to the Commune as to wear secular clothes. He continued as usual to officiate at the church, and deeming himself unworthy the grace of martyrdom, was ready to meet it if necessary. Late one evening, as he was passing a Communist post, a drunken sentry suddenly barred his passage.

"Citizen," said he, "your passport."

"I am a resident of Paris," said Sulpice, mildly.

"That's nothing. I want your papers, your passport."

"If you come with me to the Rue Chaussée d'Antin I will give you all the papers you require."

"So you do not carry them about you," said the wretch. "All right, I will sign your passport."

Drawing a revolver from his pocket he pointed it at Sulpice, when an officer interposed.

"Have no fear," he said; "but it is better for you to come with me to the guard-room than to remain at the mercy of this drunken fellow."

The abbé thanked the officer and followed him. After half an hour's walk through streets bristling with barricades he was ushered into a sort of hall, at the door of which stood a sentry. Eight or ten others, some of whom belonged to the International Aid Society, were brought in shortly after.

For two hours Sulpice was kept in this room, which was fairly reeking with tobacco, and ringing with the licentious songs of the half-drunken soldiery. They were all drinking and smoking, save those who had rolled drunk under the table. Meanwhile Sulpice's name was taken and his case referred to the head of that detachment. The latter gave orders that the priest should be brought to the Prefecture. It was about six in the evening when he reached there. He was immediately brought before the commandant.

"Where's the accuser?" asked he of one of the soldiers.

"Accuser? there is none. All that is a farce. He's a *calotin**—a priest. A patriot has a right to condemn the oppressors of the people. However, the captain is coming."

---

* A derisive epithet in allusion to the skull-cap sometimes worn by priests.

The captain said a few words in a low voice to the commandant; the latter gave the signal, and the priest was surrounded, seized and thrown into a cell, whence they had that morning released a criminal. Three days passed before his examination took place. At the end of that time the Abbé Pomereul was taken out, jeered at, insulted and mocked by a crowd of ruffians wearing the red sash, and led through various corridors till he came to the tribunal of so-called justice. Rigaut raised his head, hearing a knock at the door, and gave orders that the prisoner should be brought in.

It would be hard for any one that had not seen this wretch, who held in his hand the lives of the hostages, to form any idea of his face; the sharp features, the vulture-like profile, the thin lips parting over the white teeth, the cruel and tiger-like expression, made up a repulsive whole, which once seen was not easily forgotten. His very countenance breathed that gall, venom, and bitterness which made him condemn the just to death in mere hatred of virtue.

When Sulpice was thrust into the presence of Raoul Rigaut, the latter asked:

"Your name and age?"

"My name, Sulpice Pomereul; my age, twenty-eight."

"Your profession?"

"That of priest."

"That is to say," sneered Rigaut, "peddler of indulgences, masses and absolutions, whose office it is to oppress and deceive the people."

"Rather to bring them to respect divine law first and human law afterwards," said Sulpice.

"Bah! you teach them to execrate us who represent the law."

"No," cried Sulpice, "for you represent neither law, because you lack the necessary strength, nor justice, because you have not the right."

"So you teach them to despise the Republic?"

"The Commune represents neither government nor authority, nor even the popular voice," said Sulpice; "it is an emissary of disorder, bloodshed and anarchy."

"Do you know where such words must lead you?" asked Rigaut.

"To La Roquette, where you have imprisoned our archbishop," said Sulpice.

"And from La Roquette?"

"To the place of execution," answered the Abbé Pomereul, composedly.

"Do you want to save your life?" asked Rigaut.

"I have no right to throw it away," said Sulpice.

"Then fling your cassock to the dogs," said Rigaut; "take a musket and fight with the people for the sacred cause of liberty."

"The liberty I seek is not of this world," said Sulpice; "do as you like with me."

Rigaut's face lit up with savage joy as he gave the order,

"To La Roquette with the rest."

Sulpice's face never changed, and he said not a word, though there was a pang at his heart. He thought of Sabine left alone, all alone in the world.

It was about seven o'clock.

Through streets crowded with National Guard soldiers, infantry of the Commune, and *Vengeurs de Flourens*, his escort dragged him, a target for the insults of the crowd. Women spit upon him; his shoulders were bruised with blows, and some even struck him in the face. But he made no complaint and walked on firmly, with head erect, praying inwardly for his persecutors. They forced him to make a real Way of the Cross, for they stopped at every barricade and tavern, fraternizing with other ruffians, and drinking to the safety of the Republic, till, becoming more and more intoxicated, they grew more and more brutal to their hapless prisoner. He had eaten nothing since morning. His head swam and his limbs trembled, but he concealed every sign of this involuntary weakness from his captors, lest they should attribute it to cowardice. At length they reached the gloomy entrance to La Roquette. Sulpice, beholding its high walls, offered up his life in advance. He was kept in the waiting-room for an hour, and meanwhile the list was called to make sure of the identity of each prisoner.

"Where are they to be put?" asked the head turnkey.

The governor shook his head.

"We have no place," said he.

However, after a whispered consultation with the head turnkey, he ordered them to be conveyed to the fourth division.

"And," said he, "to give this bird of ill omen an opportunity of plying his craft, put him in cell No. 8. Its tenant is so fond of priests he will eat him up."

"Always fond of your joke," said the turnkey, smiling complacently at the governor.

The under turnkey rattled his keys and bade Sulpice follow him. It had grown dark, there was no light in the halls; the keeper lit a small lamp and led Sulpice through long corridors, regularly divided into cells. Pausing at No. 8 the turnkey selected a large key from the bunch, and opening the door, cried out in a hoarse voice,

"Comrade, here's company for you. If you're troubled with remorse you can unburden your conscience."

With a malicious laugh he shut Sulpice in.

Sulpice remained just inside the cell, which was completely dark. He could only catch a glimpse of a straw pallet whereon was stretched a motionless figure. The tenant of the cell rose as the door closed, and sitting on the side of the bed, tried to distinguish the face of his companion in captivity.

"From what the keeper said," he began, "I suppose you to be one of the hostages. Let me hope, sir, that you will have the good taste to leave me in peace during the time you share my apartment. Half of this couch is intended for you. I will readily place the whole of it at your disposal. I only ask to be left to my own thoughts, and that no one will disturb my last moments."

At the first sound of his voice Sulpice trembled. He rushed over to the pallet, seized the prisoner's two hands, and in a voice of mingled joy and tenderness cried,

"Xavier, my brother!"

"Sulpice!" cried the prisoner in amazement. Then he added bitterly,

"I understand. Your apostolic duty required that you should come here and force me to hear the exhortations which you must know by heart by this time. You must needs have the soul of that brother whose life you have sacrificed. You want to offer it as another trophy to your God. But you forget that your Master abhors human sacrifices, while you offer me up to a chimera of duty."

"You are mistaken," said Sulpice, gently. "I did not force myself upon you even for the sake of your soul. I am a prisoner like yourself."

"A prisoner! Why what fault could you have committed?" cried Xavier.

"The same as the archbishop, the curé of the Madeleine, and all who represent religion and justice."

"But you will get out of here?"

"Yes, to die," said Sulpice.

"It is horrible!" cried Xavier.

"No; I swear to you, my brother," said Sulpice, "I would meet death willingly, if only I could first reconcile you with God and teach you resignation."

"Resignation," cried Xavier, " when I am innocent!"

"Of what crime have I been guilty?" asked Sulpice. Xavier was silent. A struggle was going on in his mind.

While his brother was at liberty he had cherished a sullen hatred against him. But seeing him now a prisoner, condemned to almost certain and speedy death, his resentment melted away.

"Take heed of what I say, brother," said Sulpice; " be assured whatever the Lord does is well done, and I adore His hand in the punishment no less than in the recompense. Just now you can only see the horrors of your fate; death frightens you, your flesh trembles at the thought, you curse men and blaspheme God. Yet if for one moment you could understand the ways of mercy, you would be resigned as I am. Xavier, we have no longer time to look back to regret departed joys. Our eyes must become accustomed to the darkness of the tomb; our minds must learn to fathom the mysteries of eternity. If ever you believed that I exaggerated my duty to God, to you or to myself, if you accuse me of cruelty or harshness towards you, I beseech you in this hour, when we are face to face with death, to believe that I could neither be false to God, to you nor to myself. I offered my life in exchange for yours, and I will bless God if He deign to accept it as the price of your liberty."

"My liberty?" cried Xavier.

"Yes; a chance of liberty may be nearer than you think. The wretches who hinder the priest in the discharge of his duties will shortly have need of all those who are outlawed by society. Very soon, now, in a few days, I believe, they will throw open the prison doors."

"For what purpose?"

"That you may all be made docile instruments in the accomplishment of new crimes."

Just then the shuffling of feet and the clanking of

swords mingled with oaths and imprecations were heard in the corridor without, and the list was called of a certain number of the condemned.

Doors were opened and closed, there was a sound of footsteps descending the stairs, and all was still again. Xavier shuddered and Sulpice fell upon his knees.

In a few minutes a sharp, irregular volley of musketry resounded in the courtyard below, two or three pistol shots, and a shout of " Vive la Republique !"

"Xavier," said Sulpice, seizing his brother again by both hands, "martyrs have just fallen, our turn may soon come. I swear to you by our dead mother, by my vows, by my own soul, that we must prepare to die, and to die as Christians. Xavier, I know you would find it hard to lay bare your conscience to a strange priest. But to me, poor boy, what can you tell that I do not already know, and am not already prepared to excuse? It is not alone the minister of God who questions you, but your friend, your brother, who upon the verge of the grave asks if you have ever known real happiness?"

"No," said Xavier, shaking his head.

"For each imperfect joy did you not find a hundred vexations? The cup of revelry contained its drops of gall, the sinful pleasures produced weariness and satiety. In vain you sought new excitement for heart and mind. The void remained in the heart, and the weariness in the spirit."

"It is true," murmured Xavier.

"You offered incense before every idol that the world adores. You sought for love, but, knowing not that beauty ever ancient and ever new of which St. Augustine speaks, you did not find even its pale reflection. You pitied me because I lived in poverty, fasted and crucified my flesh; yet, amid all these privations, my heart often leaped for joy, and I praised God with hymns of thanksgiving."

"Ah!" cried Xavier, clasping his hands and resting them upon his knees.

"Oh, do you not regret having turned your mind and body to evil uses?" said Sulpice.

"Yes," said Xavier, "but now my soul seems dead within me."

"Men, judging you by your faults," continued Sulpice, "have loaded you with shame and obloquy, and the Lord has permitted it, because wealth and prosperity kept you away from Him. Now He calls you. He knows how severe is your trial. He himself, though innocent, submitted to the false judgments of men. If you will only raise supplicating hands to Him He will save you, and grant you for inconceivable time the happiness which the world promises indeed, but is powerless to give."

Again there was a clamor in the hall, and Xavier could distinguish the words,

"Paris is in flames! The buildings of the Minister of Finance, the Legion of Honor, and the whole of the Rue de Lille and the Tuileries are burning."

"O God!" cried Sulpice, "have you forsaken us?"

Innumerable voices took up the refrain.

"The Versaillists must find Paris a heap of ashes. To work, all good patriots! Let us put a bullet in the hostages, and set free all who will take up arms for the cause of the people."

The rattling of keys was heard and shouts of joy from the prisoners. Presently a crew of thieves, murderers and ruffians of every description were let loose to take their part in the human sacrifices, and revenge themselves upon society which had so lately condemned them. Xavier's door, like the rest, was thrown open and a keeper offered him a musket.

"Come, here's a chance for you," he said. "It's better to get a bullet put through you than to wait for Charlot's knife. The Versaillists have taken the half of Paris; they are upon our track, but we are not conquered yet. We will defend the Republic to the death, so here's a chance for you to escape."

The young man sprang forward eagerly. But Sulpice was before him. Seizing the weapon which the man was offering his brother, he bent it across his knees with astonishing strength, broke it, and threw the fragments to a distance.

"Why did you do that?" cried Xavier.

"To save you," answered the priest, calmly.

"Miserable *calotin!*" cried the keeper, "not content with preaching lies, you want to hinder those who are about to take up arms for the Commune."

"I want to prevent Frenchmen from fighting with Frenchmen," said the abbé.

"Your fellow prisoner should take the knife to you,' said the keeper. "Do you think the pretty boy is a paschal lamb? He killed his father, and you want to prevent him fighting the Versaillists. It's not just."

Far from adding to Xavier's desire for liberty, so strong a moment before, these words filled him with horror.

"My boy," said Sulpice, "if you go down into the street and fight behind one of those barricades, no one will believe in your innocence. There remains a means of proving it to the world: prefer death to dishonor and even your accusers can no longer deem you capable of such a crime. Your rehabilitation is in your own hands. Stay with me. Let us die together. Better such a death than a life of dishonor. Besides, you may be certain, Xavier, that God, who never leaves a good action unrewarded, will permit that if your life be not saved, at least your memory will be cleared of the terrible stain that rests upon you. In this supreme hour draw near to the brother and the priest. I must be firm, for God is in my heart, and if you waver I will be here to support you. Stay; such a death will be martyrdom! It will efface every fault, and by the baptism of blood you will be restored to your primal innocence. Stay, Xavier, for the expiation of past sins to purchase heaven."

Sulpice knelt at his brother's feet. With streaming eyes and voice choked with emotion he implored him thus. He offered to God his future sufferings as the price of this soul doubly dear and doubly sacred in his eyes, and so ardent was his prayer, so eloquent his tears that Xavier's hardened heart was softened, and kneeling in his turn he raised his brother's crucifix to his lips. Thenceforth he heard neither musketry, nor the groans of the condemned, nor the shouts of the soldiers. Absorbed in his new thoughts, occupied with the remembrance of the speedy death that awaited them, he threw himself with one great sob into the arms of the brother whom he had so cruelly misunderstood.

The night was spent by the two brothers in discussing their approaching death. Ever and anon keepers rushing through the passages cried out that the Rue Royale had been completely destroyed by fire, that the public granaries and the theatre at St. Martin's Gate were in flames.

"Alas!" thought the brothers, "our deliverers, the soldiers of the army, will come too late."

The night passed in prayer, repentance and interchange of affection.

Xavier had made the sacrifice. Becoming truly Christian he was resigned. A portion of his brother's sublime courage passed into his soul. From that time forth he judged his past life with rigorous severity. His awakened conscience showed him all his faults. The bitterness of his remorse might, indeed, have made him despair had not Sulpice, crucifix in hand, reminded him of the mercy of God. That was a holy vigil of tears and prayers, during which those who were soon to die forgot themselves in prayers for their afflicted country.

In the morning Sulpice got paper and pen. He wrote a long letter to Sabine, the martyrs' grave and tender farewell to that beloved sister. Having encouraged her to bear this new trial bravely, he advised her to become Benedict Fougerais' wife. These last thoughts given to earth the priest turned entirely to God. Without the tumult increased every moment. The Square de la Roquette was filled with a howling multitude. They announced the progress made by the Versaillists, cursing them the while. The brethren had taken shelter about the guillotine and in cemeteries; driven from the last barricades they could find no other asylum than Père la Chaise.

The populace, which had witnessed the murder of the archbishop, cried out for new blood like the wild beasts in a menagerie. In the humiliation of their ignominious defeat the leaders of the Commune resolved that blood should flow as long as their moment of power lasted.

Some were killed in the last struggle, falling among the heaps of corpses which they had made; others assumed female garments, hoping in this disguise to escape in the general disorder that was certain to follow the taking of the capital by the Versaillists. Whilst one portion of Paris hailed the tri-colored flag as the symbol of order and security, the red flag of the Commune still waved over other parts of the city. The oppression of which the Communists accused their foes was practised a hundredfold by themselves. Incendiary fires and a final list of crimes marked the fall of a power which had only existed to commit murders. For the second time that day the turnkeys came up, accompanied by an officer of the Commune, who read out the list of condemned prisoners. As they pronounced each name its owner advanced, saying, "Present."

They were all priests or gendarmes. The one saw the approach of their fate with holy enthusiasm, the other with manly fortitude. The soldiers hurriedly whispered a confession of their chief faults; the priests gave them absolution and embraced them. Sulpice and Xavier appeared arm in arm. A murmur of astonishment and pity passed through the group of the condemned.

The Abbé Sulpice, pale as marble, his brow still marked by the red scar, seemed ripe for martyrdom. Many of the spectators had reason to know his generosity and benevolence. Even among the Communists some few felt a sort of painful surprise at his condemnation, but the greater number were filled with savage joy, and clapped their hands in triumph. At this moment a breathless, panting girl rushed through the crowd, and threw her arms about Sulpice. It was Sabine, who, seeing that her brother did not appear, and aware that the arrests were still continuing, had rushed from prison to prison till she came to La Roquette. She vainly begged to see her brothers, and, brutally refused, had spent the night, spite of terror and fatigue, outside an adjoining shop. She never lost sight of the prison door, so that if her brothers were brought out she must see them once more. In the morning, she questioned every passer-by. They were all in expectation of a new execution, and Sabine felt hope die in her breast. Only one comfort remained: to receive Sulpice's last blessing as he passed to the place of execution. She was forced by the crowd up against the wall, where she awaited the appearance of the condemned. When the prison door grated on its hinges her heart almost ceased to beat. She made a violent effort, raised herself on tiptoe to see, and with a cry of joy threw herself into the arms of Sulpice. The Communists would have repulsed her brutally, but a woman interposed, and the hapless girl remained clasped for a moment to that generous and noble heart which so soon must cease to beat.

"I followed you, Sulpice, I followed you," she cried frantically; "if they murder priests, surely they will murder Christian women. If you die I cannot live."

The Abbé Sulpice pressed Xavier's hand.

"Yesterday," he said, hastily, "I said die, to-day I say, live. Save yourself, profit by the tumult; you cannot help me by staying here. Take Sabine away from this scene of horror."

The soldiers and spectators, surprised and even touched for an instant by Sabine's appearance, soon discovered that these family affairs were interfering with the justice of the people.

The word of command was given, the band of Communists began to move. Sabine, rudely snatched from her brother's arms, fell upon the ground. The abbé bent towards Xavier.

"Save her," he cried, "I command you!"

Xavier hastily seized the prostrate form, and disappeared in the crowd, while the Communists with their victims passed on towards the Boulevard des Amandiers.

CHAPTER XVI.

Jean Machû.

It had seized its prey at last, that ferocious beast called "the people of Paris," which during eighty years has made such violent efforts to become supreme master of France. It howled, it fairly shrieked for joy, to see in its power the two classes of men whose lives are spent in maintaining peace and good order: the priest, who educates children to virtue, and the *gendarme*, belonging to that picked body of soldiers, sworn to carry out the law even at the expense of their lives.

Truly, witnessing the unreasonable hatred evinced by these wretches against men whose only crime was the defence of justice against injustice, the preservation of the rights of property, and even of human life, it was plain that their sole object was impunity to commit every possible misdeed, and more especially those worthy of capital punishment.

Calm and dignified the prisoners walked among that furious crew. They, the soldiers of duty, who had upheld the honor of the French flag on many a hard-fought field, and won their crosses and medals by many a wound. Yet they were not insensible to their fate. Bitter anguish filled the hearts of these bronzed and bearded *gendarmes*, at thought of their wives and children left unprovided for and unprotected, and whom they were never to see again. Besides, this was being led to execution like cattle to the slaughter; death would have had no terror for them on the field; even yet their hearts would have leaped for joy at the sounds of battle. But to die at a street corner, to be shot down at the hands of ruffians, seemed to them too terrible. They asked themselves what crime they had committed to merit so terrible a chastisement.

"If I were alone in the world," said a *gendarme* to the Abbé Sulpice, "it would be all one to me. I am a soldier, that means I have courage to face death. I am a Breton, therefore I have the faith; but my wife is ill, and my poor little ones are not even walking yet. Who will take care of the widow and the orphans? They will be obliged to beg, and if the news of my death should likewise kill the mother, public charity will have to take the children as beggars, pariahs. It is terrible, so terrible that I am tempted to ask, now when about to appear before my Judge, whether I can expect justice?"

"Yes, comrade, and more than justice, for, if possible, mercy seems among the divine attributes, to precede all others. Your death will be repaid to your children. You speak of justice. It will be done. We fall to-day, but our murderers have more to fear than we. Martyrs in a holy cause, we are sure of an eternity purchased by our death, but what have these poor wretches to expect? Covered with the blood they have shed, tracked like wild beasts, despair in their hearts, and blasphemy on their lips, they will die cursing their fellow beings; or they who survive will dearly expiate by a life of anguish the murders of to-day. As to your children, be assured there are many noble souls who will be touched by their helpless state, and in the name of the Master I serve, I dare to promise you protection for them."

Whilst they spoke thus their little group had passed on to the Boulevard des Amandiers, through the Rue de Paris, and along the Boulevard des Couronnes.

Meanwhile the drums and clarionets performed a sort of triumphal march, often drowned by the singing of the Marseillaise and the frenzied shrieks of the populace. The Communists, irritated by the calm recollection of the doomed men, sought to disturb the peace of their last hours by furious words, and even blows. Ever and anon their progress was interrupted by an accession of curious people. Women, who might have served to personate the furies, wearing red cockades and flaming red sashes, heaped insults upon the priests, who prayed aloud. One of these miserable creatures seized her child, and tossing it on her shoulder, cried out in a coarse voice, "See the oppressors and murderers of the people are passing by. They are going to be shot. When you are big, you must show your hatred for them as your father does."

The child, with its pretty, rosy face, looked with innocent amazement at the poor prisoners, and recognizing its father among the Communists, held out its little arms to him. The wretch took the child and kissed it twice. As he did so he heard a sob just behind him, and turning saw the big tears rolling down the bronzed face of a soldier.

"My children, my poor children!" cried the *gendarme*.

"See!" said the child, "that poor man is crying. Why is he crying, papa?"

"Because he is going to be shot in the name of the Commune!" answered the father.

The child, not understanding, made a movement as if to wipe away the tears from the man's eyes. But the mother, seizing the child roughly, was soon lost in the crowd. Meanwhile the bystanders laughed and jested upon the probable demeanor of the accused when they were really face to face with death. An old priest fell down. He was dragged up brutally, amid a shower of blows; but, accepting the arm of a soldier, he went on bravely, fearing to appear irresolute.

The sad procession proceeded along the Rue de Paris, where it is crossed to the right by the Rue Haxo. The spot appointed for the massacre was the Cité Vincennes, the entrance to which was at No. 83, Rue Haxo. They reached this place, which was well known to malefactors of all sorts, by crossing a small kitchen garden, and a large courtyard, stretching out in front of a large detached building, dingy in appearance, where the insurgents had established their headquarters. Somewhat to the left was a second enclosure, which before the war had been intended to be used as a hall for *bal champêtres*. A basement, around which the vine-clad trellis-work of this despoiled pleasure-ground was to have run, rose breast-high before one of the walls. Between this wall and the basement was a sort of trench, some ten to eighteen feet broad. A moderately large air hole opened into a cellar, which occupied the centre.

When the hostages reached the Cité Vincennes they expected to be shot at once. But the leaders who were to assist at the murder were not to be found. Or perhaps they simply desired to prolong the martyrs' agony. One of the Communists suggested that they should be temporarily shut up in the cellar. This motion was received with general approbation.

The insurgents hurried the condemned through a gloomy hall, down a noisome staircase, and into a large cellar, which received light and air from a vent hole opening on the street. They had not even a wisp of straw upon which they could stretch themselves while awaiting the supreme moment. The priests knelt down and began to recite the Psalms. This brought a hideous crowd to the air hole. Men and women thrust their faces against the iron bars, seeking by the most horrible language to distract, torment or disturb the prisoners' dying moments. Their sublime fortitude awakened in them a sort of admiration, even as it roused their hatred to fury. But neither taunt nor insult had power to trouble the ears of those who were so soon to die. Heaven seemed too near; they forgot the vileness of earth. The more their bodies suffered, the higher rose their souls, victorious over fear and sorrow, till they found their God. Among those who crowded the streets and rejoiced at the bloody tragedy, enjoyed in anticipation, were many of Methusalem's frequenters. Not that they had forsaken the Rue Git-le-Cœur, but the Naine, its maid of all work, willing to do her share for the public weal, had established a canteen on the Rue Haxo. Upon her counter were displayed black coffee, brandy and other invigorating beverages, even to vitriol, and all suited to the various tastes of her customers. This monstrous being, eager to display her convictions, had assumed a flaring red apron, reaching from her chin to the shoes which covered her misshapen feet. She laughed, she sang, she danced, repeating phrases from the "Père Duchesne," predicting the triumph of the Rouge, and inciting the last defenders of the Commune to blow up Paris.

"Are you afraid, boys," she said, "or is material wanting? Will you wait till those sneaks of Versaillists have you in their claws? You needn't expect much mercy then! But it's not ten or twenty of these dogs of *calotins* you should shoot, but crowds of them. Fire a bomb, and then fire another, till the last of these devil's preachers are lying there to rot. What's the use of turning churches into barracks if you don't do away with God? You promised you would. Down with the rich, with soldiers and priests! We want republicans. No time like the present. Roll your powder barrels into the gutter, put a match to them, and then for a dance. Who loves a dance as much as I?"

"Never tired joking, Naine," said a man in the uniform of the *Vengeurs* of the Commune.

"Oh, it's you is it, Jean Machû?" said the Naine; "what will you take?"

"Something strong, as strong as you have it," said he.

The Naine poured him out a tumbler of brandy.

"To your health, Naine," said he; "but come, keep me company."

"Your treat?" asked she.

"To be sure," said Machû; "you sell your wares, but you don't consume them."

The Naine filled a second glass, clinking it against that of the felon.

"To your speedy marriage, Naine," said Machû.

The Naine laid down the glass.

"It's no jesting matter, Jean," said she; "there's none would have Methusalem's servant."

"You think so?"

"I'm sure of it."

"You're not so sure, though, but there's one you'd like to have," said Machû, grinning.

A flush passed over the hideous face.

"What put that into your head?" said she.

"Oh," said the Commander of the *Vengeurs* of the Commune, "never you mind; but I met one the other day that you're very fond of."

"Methusalem?"

"No, you are his servant, but you're not in love with him for all that."

"Well, who do you mean?"

"Fleur d'Echafaud!"

"You saw *him!*" she cried, bending over the counter eagerly.

"Yes."

"Where?"

"At the prefecture. He's in the *Vengeurs*."

"Oh, if the Versaillists catch him," she cried.

"He will scarcely have time to marry you, Naine!"

"It's no joking matter," she said almost fiercely; "if they take him they'll kill him."

"The very notion that he's in danger makes you show your teeth and claws," said Machû, laughing. "I told you so."

"And you're a fool for your pains," said she, sullenly. "I don't want him to be taken, it's true. But I am the only one, do you hear, Jean Machû, the only one that knows why his life's precious to me."

"You ought to have more confidence in your friends," said Machû, still jesting.

"Do you know where he is now?" she said, quickly.

"How can we know from day to day what becomes of people?" said he. "The gun does its work quickly. You and I, Naine, may be dead to-morrow."

"Once I've seen the end of those gibbering fools that are braying their litanies in the cellar," said she, "I'll just be off to Methusalem's. If Fleur d'Echafaud wants a hiding-place send him to me. I know one. You are welcome to it, too, Rat-de-Cave."

"That's not my stamp, Naine," said Rat-de-Cave, with sudden gravity. "I'll never hide. I'll be behind the last barricades with the last *Vengeurs* of the Commune, and I swear the Versaillists'll never get me alive. I'll defend my skin all I can; but once the game's up, I'll make an end of myself."

Just then there was a stir in the crowd to make way for a young man in a dazzling uniform glittering with gold lace. He belonged to Bergeret's *Enfants Perdus*. Jean Machû looked round to see what was going on, and the Naine mounted among the bottles and glasses on her counter. Her eyes hastily scanned the crowd, and all at once lit up with a sort of fierce exultation as she muttered,

"Fleur d'Echafaud."

Hastily descending, she resumed her place at the counter.

Jean Machû meanwhile advanced to shake hands with the new-comer.

"Well, Marc Mauduit," said he, "what's going on down yonder?"

"The Versaillists are taking barricade after barricade," said Mauduit; "our soldiers are being defeated at every point."

"Did you come here to fight?"

"I came to look about me," said Mauduit, "and to make sure of some hiding-place."

"You came to the right spot this time," said Machû. "Some one was speaking of you just now."

"Who's that?"

"The Naine. She knows a hiding-place."

"That will be good for to-morrow," said Fleur d'Echafaud.

"I think you might have the grace to thank her," said Machû.

So the brilliant young man approached the counter, and accepted a cup of coffee from the Naine.

"To-morrow," said he, "I shall need you."

"Ah!" said she, "you will need—"

"Any disguise you like and a safe shelter."

"The disguise will be ready in an hour, and the hiding-place—Git-le-Cœur."

"But Methusalem might betray me?"

"He would if he dared," said she, "but he dares not."

"Who will prevent him?"

"I will."

"You!" said Fleur d'Echafaud, laughing heartily.

"Yes, I," said the Naine. "Because I watched over you like a mother you think me only capable of love, and that I could not hate. You are wrong, boy, you are wrong. My hatred is terrible. I brood and brood over it till it bursts out."

"It's so very droll," said Fleur d'Echafaud, laughing still more immoderately.

"Droll!" cried she; "you think my hatred a thing to laugh at."

"Yes," said he, "because everything about you is ridiculous, my poor Fantoche. You are not a woman and cannot have a woman's feelings. Nature made you a monster, and a monster you will always be."

She fixed such a glance on him as would have terrified any one else.

"Well," said she, slowly, "never incur the hatred of Fantoche, for you would find it terrible."

A solemn, mournful sound just then reached their ears. It was the prisoners singing the *Miserere*. This cry for mercy, coming as it did from the bowels of the earth, in the voices of men hourly awaiting execution, had so peculiar a grandeur that the bloodthirsty, drunken populace involuntarily shuddered. Surely the victims were stronger than their persecutors. A Communist soldier seized his gun, pointed the barrel of it through the bars, and fired into the cellar, saying,

"That will make them shut up."

A groan was heard; one of the condemned had fallen. But this cowardly act only seemed to revive their courage, and the last versicles of the psalm arose more solemn and imploring than ever. It was literally out of the depths, that cry unto the Lord of "Miserere! Miserere!"

As day waned the crowd instead of diminishing grew

greater The combatants of the barricades and fugitives of all sorts flocked thither, where there were still arms to load, houses to burn, crimes to commit. Many of them, tracked from street to street, and from house to house, asked only a corner of ground where they could die, crying "Vive la Commune!" The intoxication of anger or strong drink lent courage to the one half, while the other trembled at the fate which awaited them. The first paraded such of their quarters as were threatened but not yet invaded, while the second hastily cut their hair or beard, assumed various disguises, tore the red stripe from their trousers, and broke the arms which would have doubly compromised them, first because they were stolen, second because they were stained with blood.

When it was night the Naine carried her table, bottles and her stove into an empty shop close by, and without even thinking of sleep, continued dealing out her wares, and seasoning her sales with the sinister language of the knitting-women of the Commune. The spacious apartment was soon filled with the birds of ill omen who prowl about at night, thieves by profession, young men more carefully dressed, the pillars of smoking-rooms and public balls, half-drunken Communist soldiers, hiccoughing out mutual exhortations to die for the Commune, and borrowing from each other in the name of sacred equality.

The distant growling of the cannon was as an undertone to all this. In proportion as its sound drew nearer, they knew that the regular army was gaining Paris inch by inch. At length, spite of anger, hatred and fear, sleep overcame some of the motley gathering in the Naine's shop. She herself nodded over the counter, whilst Fleur d'Echafaud and Rat-de-Cave spoke together of their near future.

"Ah, well," said Fleur d'Echafaud, "I have had enough of the Commune and the rights of the people.

It's all very fine, but dangerous. It sounds well at the club or in the newspapers to advance such ideas, but to sustain them with helmet on head and revolver in hand is another thing. I have only twenty-four hours more to wear my uniform, so covered with gold lace that it took half the money from the Pomereul safe to pay for it. Once to-morrow's drama is played I will make tracks, and turn up again after some time as Marc Mauduit, the model secretary. What about you?"

"My way is different," said Rat-de-Cave, brusquely. "Cannons have been put in Père la Chaise. I'll serve the last of them."

"Why not try to save yourself?" asked Mauduit.

"What use? What would I do afterwards?" said the felon.

"What you have always done," said Mauduit.

"Steal and murder?" said Machû.

"I don't think you are destined for an embassy, it's true," said Mauduit, sneeringly.

"To steal, to kill," said Jean Machû, gloomily. "Always the same thing; besides, they leave thoughts sometimes that are like—"

"What can your thoughts be like?" said Fleur d'Echafaud.

"Remorse," said Jean Machû, in a hollow voice.

"You know remorse? You?" cried Mauduit.

"Call it what you like," said Machû. "I know what it is to pass sleepless nights, and always to see the face of a man accusing you. I know what it is to say, 'The air I breathe is stolen, my liberty is stolen, and another is paying the debt I owe to Justice.'"

"Amen!" said Fleur d'Echafaud.

He leaned both hands upon the table, as if weary of the subject, and buried his face. But the Naine, in her sleep, uttered a name:

"Louise, my dear Louise."

Her sleep seemed troubled. Again she spoke:

"You shall be avenged, Louise; you shall be avenged!"

Fleur d'Echafaud raised his head and looked at her. She was hideous; there was foam about her lips, her nostrils were dilating, her brow furrowed with wrinkles. Fleur d'Echafaud almost fancied that she pronounced the name of André Nicois, but he thought himself mistaken. What link could exist between the rich banker and the deformed creature, who had begun by being the attraction of country fairs, and now served the kitchen of Methusalem?

Night passed. At dawn the voices of the priests, somewhat more feeble, were heard again. All night long they had prayed the prayers for the dying. Priests and *gendarmes* alike, awaiting the carrying out of their terrible sentence, were of one mind and one heart. They had but one hope. The condemned soldiers knelt before the priests, who, exercising their divine ministry, prepared them more and more for death. The hostages had been left entirely without food, and hunger was added to their other torments. Morning brought again to the air hole those who impatiently awaited the hour of the sacrifice. They felt that the progress of the army gave them scarcely time for this last crime, and that they had need of haste. However, whether because of the anxiety caused by the resolute advance of the Versaillists who were taking Paris, street by street, house by house, or from some other cause, the fatal order was delayed.

Nearly another day passed in suspense.

At last a young man wearing the red scarf of a delegate of the Commune came to the headquarters at the Cité Vincennes, with instructions for detachments of Communists belonging to a battalion of the Eleventh

District, and a battalion of the Fifth District. Immediately after some of Bergeret's *Enfants Perdus* went down into the cellar, and ordered the prisoners to come up. They obeyed without thought of resistance. Faith shed its ineffable calm over them, and the priests gave a final benediction to the soldiers, who walked to death as firmly as to battle.

At sight of the prisoners cheers of savage joy were heard, and the soldiers could scarcely keep back the crowd. Not that they cared to protect the victims, but they feared lest in the tumult some should escape. The enclosure whither they were hurried was already occupied by the staff of different battalions. The fifty hostages and their executioners filled what was left of that narrow space. A portion of the crowd found it impossible to assist at this last act of barbarity. The hostages were placed against the wall, and a squad of soldiers, with loaded muskets, stood ready to fire on the word of command.

Sulpice embraced his brother priests, exchanging with them what was indeed the kiss of peace of the primitive Church, which at the conclusion of the love-feasts was given those about to die.

Just as the Abbé Pomereul turned from the embrace of an old priest who had clasped him in his arms, two men covered with gold lace and bearing swords pushed their way resolutely through the crowd to obtain a position in the front rank of spectators.

"The Commandant Machû and Colonel Marc Mauduit," whispered the crowd, making way for them respectfully.

Scarcely had Machû come face to face with those who were about to be shot, and scanned their faces with a rapid glance, when he sprang forward with the agility of a tiger, and covered one of them with his own body.

The soldiers who had just raised their muskets paused,

and the officer in command advancing to Machû, who was interrupting the justice of the people in a manner so extraordinary, said,

"Commandant, the moment of execution is come."

The Abbé Sulpice's defender turning quickly faced the crowd, saying to the officers and soldiers who drew near with irrepressible curiosity,

"I must have this man's life. I must have it!"

"You must have a fearful score to settle with him, Commandant," said a soldier, "if the justice of the people won't answer you."

Sulpice in amazement recognized the man who had come between him and death.

"Jean Machû!" he cried, involuntarily.

"Yes; I want his life," pursued Jean Machû, the felon.

"You want to let a priest, a deceiver of the people, escape from justice? Never!" cried the crowd.

"He saved me," said Jean Machû, hoarsely. "I'll not be in his debt."

"Shoot the *calotin!*" cried a child.

Fleur d'Echafaud whispered in his comrade's ear,

"Are you mad? Once he dies we're safe."

"Death to him! death to him!" cried the crowd.

"Comrades," said Machû, "you know me. I showed my patriotism well. I set fire to the Finance buildings, when the telegram came from Ferré. I was there when we shot the archbishop. I've been all the week from one barricade to another. The friends of the people Delescluze and Milliere, were my friends. I'm ready to fire the last gun with you, but for my services I want this man's life."

"So that he can sell you later on, and get you shot by the Versaillists."

"If he promises not to betray me," said Machû, "he'll keep his promise."

"He, a Jesuit, a *calotin!*"

"You don't know what his word's worth," said Machû. "I am a Communist, and a ruffian, and a robber besides."

"You flatter yourself, Commandant," said a voice.

"I pillaged Notre Dame de Lorette," pursued he. "I helped to put a blaze to the old cathedral. I have robbed God and men. This priest knew all about it, and he never said a word."

"He was afraid of revenge," said some one in the crowd.

"Not he," said Machû. "You see he does not tremble even now before you."

There were cries of "Back, Commandant!" "Clear the way!" "Machû is a traitor!"

"Machû's not afraid of any of you," said the Commandant of the *Vengeurs* of the Commune. "The first who makes a step forward is a dead man."

The felon cocked his pistol and waited. No one stirred.

"His life," said Machû. "Will you give me his life?"

"Never!" cried they.

"Well, I'll tell you the whole story," said Machû. "Just now it doesn't much matter having one or two things more or less on our conscience. We may all be dead to-morrow. I not only committed crimes for the general good, but I robbed this man's father. I took a hundred thousand francs out of his safe."

"Bravo!" cried several voices.

"He knew it, and never let up on me."

A murmur passed through the crowd as Jean Machû continued, still screening Sulpice with his own body:

"I killed his father, and he didn't give me up."

A murmur of incredulity was now heard in the various groups.

"No," said Machû; "he didn't give me up, because the secret of confession sealed his lips. You cry out against priests, but I respect them. I've done many a bad deed in my day, but I want to save this man to show my gratitude. You must either kill both of us or neither. Once he's in safety I'll come back to die with you."

The Abbé Sulpice tried to detach himself from the felon's grasp.

"Leave me to die," he said; "martyrdom is the noblest death for which I can ever hope. God in His mercy will take account of the efforts you have made to save me. Do not force me to desert my brethren. You have spoken some dangerous words, but they will be forgotten if you leave me to the hatred of my enemies."

"No," said Machû; "if they're obstinate about it we'll die together. But they daren't fire."

As if to contradict this assertion the officer cried out, "Present arms!"

Once more Sulpice tried to escape from his deliverer and rejoin his friends.

The soldiers of the Eleventh battalion made a rush forward, like a tumultuous wave flowing in on the strand.

Machû felt his coat pulled; he looked down: it was the Naine. She made a mysterious sign to him, and held out a plain dark cloak, and as she, with a group of furious women eager to see the last act in the bloody drama, pushed into the front row, Machû wrapped the abbé in the cloak and drew him aside, whispering hastily,

"Think of your sister."

These words went to his heart, and Machû, profiting by his momentary irresolution, and aided by the diversion which the Naine had purposely created, dragged Sulpice into the old cemetery, thence into a squalid-looking house and up the stairs. They had just reached the top, when a discharge of musketry proved that the people of Paris had committed the most iniquitous act of their reign.

Though sheltered in the house, the priest and Jean Machû were by no means in safety. Going into an empty room they found some workmen's clothes hanging on the wall. The felon seized them, throwing them to the priest, and crying,

"Quick, quick! these brutes will follow us."

At the same time he took a handful of gold from his pocket and threw it down, adding,

"That's for the owner of the clothes."

Sulpice at length decided to accept the safety which Providence seemed to impose on him. He hastily donned the blue blouse and overalls, and putting a cap on his head, was so completely disguised that no one could have recognized him.

"Come," said Machû.

They went down cautiously. The house had two exits. With the keen scent of a thief, and the agility of a burglar, Machû opened a door, climbed a little wall, and assisted the Abbé Pomereul to do the same.

All this had been accomplished so quickly that the savage crew without had scarcely yet discovered what had transpired. They were still gloating over the writhing forms of their victims.

Meanwhile the Abbé Sulpice and Machû had reached a deserted part of Paris, where the Commune no longer had sway.

"Go," said the *Vengeur* of the Commune. "The Versaillists are there to protect you. After this you can think of me without cursing me."

"Ah!" said the abbé, "if you would only come with me and amend your life."

"It's too late," said Machû. "I'm going to play the last act."

With a sort of despairing energy he wrung the merciful hand held out to him, and ran off.

CHAPTER XVII.

The Barricades of Death.

The bloody tragedy was ended.

The bodies of the priests and *gendarmes* were thrown into a trench, and the populace, intoxicated with blood, rushed from the fatal spot, thronging the Rue Haxo, Rue de Paris, and the Boulevard des Amandiers.

Jean Machû's daring act would no doubt have drawn upon him the accusation of treason and the swift vengeance of the multitude had he not, immediately on returning to the Communists, begun with indomitable energy and lightning-like resolve to sketch out the plan of action for the final struggle. Their base of operations became more limited as the liberation of Paris was gradually being accomplished. They could no longer construct barricades by tearing up the pavement; on the contrary, they had to find barricades ready made, and a space sufficient to contain the proper number of combatants, disposed in such fashion as to maintain a desperate struggle. The streets were being swept by the cannon, cleared by charges of cavalry, and carried by the infantry. The Communists were looking around helplessly for a position in which to intrench themselves, when Jean Machû reappeared in their midst.

A hoarse murmur of reproach was heard at sight of him.

"I know what you have to say," he cried. "I saved a priest. But it was my own affair, and the first one who accuses me of treason to the Commune I'll blow out his brains with my revolver. If any of you like the prospect, step out."

Machû's resolute air awed the most daring, and the felon continued,

"You're disheartened; the more shame for you! You hear the guns and know that your turn's coming. For people like us the trial will be short; they'll thrust us against a wall and bang. Serve us right, too; but there are some of us prefer another sort of thing. Death is death. But it's better to defend ourselves, and give ball for ball, stroke for stroke. We are conquered, but let us die as good patriots and true Communists. We must fight; not in order of battle, for that would end too quick, but like poachers in the woods, or sharp-shooters in the hedges, and the scene of our last combat I have chosen. Will you follow me there?"

"Yes, yes!" cried a hundred voices.

"To Père la Chaise, boys. The tombstones will do us for barricades."

"To Père la Chaise," repeated the crowd like an echo.

Machû's idea was hailed as the inspiration of genius. In an hour's time a band of Communists, one and all resolved to meet death stoically, had possession of the cemetery; the last guns of the Commune were set up there, and preparations made to defend this last stronghold of the rebels unto death. After the many sacrileges they had committed, the Communists consummated a final one in bringing their fratricidal struggle to the city of death. The scene was more terrible than any that had preceded it. The soldiers soon carried the place by assault, and the *melée* became general. It was rather a massacre than a battle. The Communists, expecting no quarter, fought furiously, and the soldiers, exasperated by their losses, enraged at having to fight against such ruffians, marked their advance by the heaps of dead strewn among the tombs. Every chapel was a fortress. The

THE BARRICADES OF DEATH. 267

bullets flew fast and furious through the windows. When guns were broken the revolvers were used and daggers drawn. The blood-stained ground was slippery to the feet of victor and vanquished alike. Some of the wretches at length gave themselves up, but others put pistols to their heads to escape being made prisoners. A band of Communists, hard pressed, surrounded, and unable longer to defend themselves, surrendered; the terror of immediate death seemed worse than the more remote punishment of their crimes. Ammunition failed, the cannon were silent, and those who served them had fallen dead among the empty powder casks. A single group remained, consisting of some twenty men, headed by Jean Machû. As long as he had a cartridge he fired; when he had no more he seized his revolver by the barrel and used it as a club. A soldier snatched it from him, but Machû, picking up a knife from the ground, rushed upon his assailant. He hoped to gain at least this one last victory; struck by a ball in the right arm, he still fought with his left, but a blow from the butt end of a musket took him in the chest, blood gushed from his mouth, his teeth were already broken, and he fell upon a heap of dead, wherein soldiers and Communists were indiscriminately mingled. Four of his companions took to flight, vainly hoping to escape; others opened their coats and rushed forward to meet the balls. A volley of artillery swept the last of them away. In a few minutes all was still in the cemetery; the prisoners, with scowls of hatred and defiance on their faces, and blasphemies on their lips, were led away by the soldiers. Somewhat later litters were brought for the wounded.

It was dark night when Jean Machû recovered consciousness. Bruised in every limb, a sabre gash upon his forehead and his chest crushed in by the last blow, the poor wretch felt that death was inevitable. Nor did he dread it, for he knew that life could give him nothing more, and abhorrence of the past arose now predominant over every other sentiment. To his enfeebled mind came the recollections of his past life like visions. He would fain have shut them out from his sight and closed his ears against them. But no, he was doomed to hear and see, and this illusion of the senses, arising from the fever of his wounds, occasioned him mental suffering much more terrible than all his physical pain.

He was a child again, sporting in a great mossy wood thickly peopled with birds, which his mother tamed. His mother! he saw *her*, too, a pretty peasant woman, active and industrious, who, in the midst of her own poverty, had always a kind word for the afflicted and a crust of bread for beggars. His father was a wood-cutter of the forest, a rude trade, but one which had many compensations. It was good to see how Michel Machû threw by his axe at noonday, when his young wife brought him his meal, sitting on the trunk of a tree and opening her basket, wherein were hot soup, tempting meat, ripe fruits and wine. Together they took their repast, while the child sported under the trees and sang with the oriole. The father, seizing the child, tossed him in the air, or sought birds' nests for him, or caught him a live squirrel. When the mother was not too busy in the house she brought her sewing out of doors, while the husband worked and the child laughed for glee. At nightfall they all went home under the waving branches; the bell on the village church rang out the Angelus, the father raised his hat, the mother blessed herself, and the child grew grave seeing the gravity of his elders. Yes, those were halcyon days in the shadow of the woods, when the wood-cutter earned their bread with his axe. Suddenly the scene changed. One day the mother and child were in their little house, the former singing one of the ballads of the country over her washtub. All at once two neighbors came rushing in, with pale faces and eyes red with tears. They took the woman's hand, saying,

"Poor Mathurine! Poor Mathurine!"

"Something has happened to Michel," she said, instinctively.

"Yes, something terrible," they answered.

One of the women then took Jean in her arms, murmuring, "Poor orphan."

"My man is dead?" cried Mathurine, dazed and bewildered.

"Almost. You will scarcely have time for a last word," said the neighbors.

"Where is he?" cried Mathurine, "where is he?"

"They are bringing him home," said one of the women, throwing the door open as she spoke. Four men entered; they carried a stretcher; upon it was a motionless figure covered with a blood-stained cloth. A tree which he had been felling killed him in its fall.

Mathurine threw herself upon her husband, strained him to her heart, and vainly sought one word, one look, one sigh. He seemed already dead. They laid him on the bed and presently he opened his eyes. Seeing the terrible woe on Mathurine's face, and the tears in her eyes, he closed his own again, as if too weak to bear the sight of her sorrow. At length he made an effort to speak some parting words to those dear ones whom he was about to leave. He beckoned his wife to draw nearer to him, saying,

"Do not weep. I am dying. You have been a faithful, kind and gentle wife. You made my life easy and helped me to bear its troubles. I was too happy, Mathurine; I must leave it and you." He kissed his wife, drew her to his breast for an instant, then took Jean, whom his wife held up to him. He pressed him close to his heart, saying,

"You will never see me again, little Jean. Would that I might have lived to see you grow up, to teach you to be honest and industrious, as your mother will teach you to be pious. God does not will it, and I must be resigned. Remember my last words, Jean. Be a good son and an honest man."

Just then the curé of the neighboring village came in. Michel's face brightened. He was a simple and devout Christian, who had led a life as pure as the dawn which he saw every morning rising above his head. His confession was not long, and he died in peace and hope.

Here there was a gap in Machû's memories. He remembered his mother in a black dress crying over him; crying for her good husband, and for the future of her child. Jean still loved the woods; but he did not work in open day like his father. He haunted them at night like the wolves. He had forgotten his father's dying exhortation, and was deaf to the advice of his mother, who was almost heartbroken. A hard, fierce, rebellious nature was his; he laughed alike at the dying words of the one and the tears of the other. In vain did Mathurine, when all else failed, strive to terrify him by threats and predictions of evil. He laughed at *gendarmes*, as he did at saints and angels, and continued his evil way of life. Hidden in the brushwood, he waited for the game, laid snares, spread nets, and even if occasion demanded, shot goats. The gamekeeper, a worthy man, warned Mathurine repeatedly that he would have to bring action against Jean for trespass, poaching and dishonesty. The mother could do nothing with her son. She could only weep and pray. One night she heard the sound of footsteps and the clanking of sabres in the wood without. A loud knock came to the door of the hut, and the poor widow saw Jean, her idolized Jean, with handcuffs on his wrists and a scowl of defiance on his face. Caught in the act of poaching, he had resisted the *gendarmes*, and wounded one of them in the hand with his knife.

"Mercy, mercy, good gentlemen!" cried the mother, falling on her knees.

"Mathurine," said the wounded *gendarme*, "if I were alone concerned I would release this vagabond, but I have my duty to do, and he must come with us. I have brought him to say good by to you, because you are an honest woman, and Michel Machû left a good name in the neighborhood."

"Oh, where are you taking him?" asked Mathurine.

"To prison," answered he.

"My child in prison!" she wailed out.

"You must own he deserves it," said the man, "spite of all your goodness to him."

"How long will they keep him?" she asked.

"That," said the officer, "is the judge's affair, not mine, but I think they will put him in the House of Correction."

"Jean," said the hapless mother, sinking into a chair, "you have killed me."

When Mathurine recovered consciousness the whole terrible vision had passed away, but in her ears still sounded the clanking of sabres and of the handcuffs upon Jean's hands.

How well Jean remembered that night, the first step in the path of crime, sentence, punishment which he had ever since pursued. Precocious criminal of fifteen as he was, he did not reflect that the law gave him every chance of becoming an honest man. He never dreamed of repairing the faults of his youth by sincere repentance. On the contrary, he vowed vengeance against society, which he had so early outraged, and began a deadly struggle against its laws. Time passed slowly in the House of Correction. One day some one came and told him his mother was dead. Bad as he was the blow was a heavy one. He felt it to the core of his heart. But his companions soon dispelled whatever salutary impression it might have made on him. They stirred him up by so many anecdotes of tricks played upon the authorities, and plans for the future, that he began to long for the hour of his liberation. It came, and he was free. He had a little money in his pocket. He knew a trade, and might have earned an honest living; but he preferred idleness to work, and at any rate resolved to spend his money first. He met some companions. They brought him to wretched lodgings, and introduced him to some of the lowest dens in Paris. In a week's time his vague idea of going to work had vanished. He resolved to live without employment and exercise vagrancy as his only trade. He did not disdain to open carriages, pick up the butt ends of cigars, sell letter paper, or tapers for smokers, but whoever penetrated the garret where he lived would have been amazed at the curious collection of articles it contained—hams, new pairs of shoes, pieces of stuffs, balls of wool, ready-made garments, boxes of blacking, all lying in the most picturesque disorder, till Methusalem, the broker of the Rue Git-le-Cœur, came to bring order out of chaos, and to carry the whole lot off in exchange for some pieces of money.

One night Machû and a companion had been on a drinking bout. When they were about returning home, the weather being rainy, and their strength unequal to crawling along by the wall, they hailed a coachman, and gave him an address which made him toss his head.

Coming to a suspicious-looking house, they called out to him to stop, and alighting, began as it were to fumble in their pockets for his fare. Of course they had nothing. Jean Machû jogged his companion's elbow, and the driver having got down to open the door and receive the money, Machû by a rapid movement gagged him, while his comrade stunned him with a blow upon the chest, took his purse from his pocket, pushed Machû into the carriage, got upon the box and whipped up the horses. Next day the confederates made good cheer with the horses and the money. But shortly after the police, making a descent upon a notorious haunt, took Jean Machû. It was a more serious matter this time. A trial in a criminal court, the chain and ball, the departure with the chain-gang, and the galleys. Thenceforth Machû had only one thought, that of escape. And he accomplished his design by a series of adventures more extraordinary than half the wondrous tales that beguile the tediousness of the mess or guard-room. Having climbed a wall by means of his knife, he hung suspended over an abyss by a frail cord. Pursued by the keepers, and driven ashore by a furious storm, he rushed panting and exhausted into a hut, to which he was admitted by a young man of angelic countenance.

"The Abbé Sulpice, the Abbé Sulpice," muttered the wounded wretch.

Oh, how the circumstances of that night forced themselves upon his memory. How carefully the priest had warmed his stiffened limbs; with what more than brotherly love he had supplied him with all things necessary for his escape. More than this, in that little hut, at the door of which the *gendarmes* might any moment knock demanding the convict, the priest had spoken of hope, repentance, an honorable life to the felon, the outlaw of society. Nor had he stopped there. A letter of recommendation gave Jean Machû a chance to lead an honest life. His future might yet have been happy. A new name, an honest trade, would forever have disguised the escaped galley-slave of Brest, so that henceforth he would be unrecognizable. Touched and subdued by the priest's words and manner, Jean Machû had promised, and even made an effort to keep his word. He had gone to the manufactory, the proprietor of which had received him on the recommendation of the priest. But a robber whom he met, and whom he had known in other times, recognized him, deprived him of his savings, and threatened to denounce him, if he did not supply all his wants. In despair Jean Machû fled from the place, lest his real name might become known. Still weak from his wounds he remained irresolute, and at the close of day sat on the edge of a ditch by the roadside, asking himself what he was to do. Better throw himself at once into the furnace, and go to Paris. Once there his first visit was to Methusalem.

The latter received him with the honor due to a man who had escaped the galleys, and brought him into contact with some of the most noted thieves. Thenceforth his crimes changed, not in their nature, but in the manner of perpetration. Mere murders seemed very paltry enterprises, and the stage-coach having been rendered obsolete by the railroad, there was nothing to be done in that line, and so they sought some new path to renown. Theft arose to the dignity of a profession, a society regularly commanded. Its members were carefully organized, recruited from every portion of the city; they despised no auxiliary, and sometimes burst in with the news that they had just gained at one haul a band, lieutenants and captain, all ready to obey that scrupulously respected hierarchy.

Jean Machû was enrolled in a company composed of the most heterogeneous elements. He had under his orders classical scholars, clerks of government ministers, who, beginning by stealing paper and pens from the desk, had reached to this refinement of villainy. Machû had first met Fleur d'Echafaud at Methusalem's table, for the *Pension Bourgeoise* was the resort of all who were involved in dangerous enterprises. It was Marc Mauduit who had planned the Pomereul robbery, on account of the perfect facilities afforded him for knowing the house by his office of secretary.

Ah, what a night that was! The scenes of his double crime came before his wandering mind like the various acts of a drama. They go in, Fleur d'Echafaud and himself. The door of the safe is open, displaying piles of banknotes. While they are busy emptying it a man comes in. He must be killed. In a moment Jean Machû's fingers are on the old man's throat, a brute, a senseless being, interferes; he falls, stricken by Fleur d'Echafaud's dagger. The murderers fly in haste, leaving the murdered man, already rigid in death, and the chimpanzee writhing in agony. As they go down the stairs a noise is heard, some one enters and comes up towards them. 'Tis the Abbé Sulpice.

The name seemed to bring back consciousness. He found himself alone in that vast cemetery, transformed into a general grave, and the paths of which were strewn with dead. He had just passed in review his whole life, a life of shame, of crime, of utter depravity and wickedness. Around him was darkness, afar off through the gloom the red embers of the soldiers' bivouac. Jean Machû recalled in one brief moment his father's dying words, the sound of the village bells, the exhortations of the Abbé Pomereul on that night when the murderer, abusing the power given to the penitent by the religious law, had sealed the lips of the son upon the murder of the father.

Did Jean Machû really believe in the depths of his soul that there was no future life? That future life in which the Abbé Sulpice must so firmly believe, or he would never have kept faithfully the secret of confession.

In the wretch's soul one good thought found place.

"If I could prove his brother's innocence," he thought.

This idea took such complete possession of him that he cast about for any means of putting it into execution.

But to accomplish this he would have to escape from the cemetery, and pass through the detachments of soldiers stationed at all points.

"If I could change my clothes," thought Jean Machû. He slipped off his coat, bound his arm with his handkerchief, and began to grope in the darkness. He recognized by the touch the uniform of a soldier of the line. Slowly, very slowly, for his wounds were painful, and he was very weak, Machû took the dead soldier's clothes. Still more slowly he hid his own; but when he had succeeded in putting on the uniform, which he soiled by his touch, the cold sweat of exhaustion covered his brow, and he fell back, muttering,

"I can never do it."

He made another effort, however, and with indescribable exertion managed to get upon his feet. By grasping the marble railings, steps, or crosses, and pausing ever and anon to rest, he reached one of the alleys of the cemetery. A little farther on the light of a campfire guided him. His limbs failed, he sank down, but he crept along the ground, slowly, slowly, till he was near enough to cry out in a faint voice. A soldier heard him, hastened to his assistance, and brought him to the fire. Some drops of brandy revived him, but, from the pain of his wounds and terror at his situation, he fell into a sleep so profound that it was almost like a trance. When he opened his eyes the friendly voices encouraged him. He turned away his face from those honest ones which were bending over him, and feebly articulated,

"Comrades! Chaussée d'Antin! The Abbé Pomereul!"

"I see," said one of the soldiers, "you want to be brought there?"

Machû made an affirmative sign.

"Well, as the hospitals are all full, it is the best place for you. The first litter will take you there."

In a few minutes, Jean Machu, laid upon a stretcher, and so weak that he wondered whether he should be able to carry out his plan, was being carried by two men to the Rue de la Chaussée d'Antin.

With a new feeling of shame he had put his arm over his face, and as he passed many an honest citizen, believing him to be a soldier of that heroic army, uncovered with respect.

Sulpice, Xavier and Sabine were together in a room on the first floor of the house when the *concierge* ran up stairs quite breathless to Baptiste, who brought the message to his master.

"What do you want?" said the Abbé Pomereul.

"They have brought a wounded man here," said he.

"A wounded man?" repeated the priest.

"Yes, sir, a soldier!" said Baptiste.

"So, Sabine, your work is not done," said he to his sister, adding to Baptiste. "Bring him here, till a bed can be got ready."

Presently the litter-bearers carried their burden into what had been M. Pomereul's study. They withdrew at once, fully repaid for their pains by Sulpice, and the wounded man immediately raised himself to a sitting posture. Sabine and her two brothers were at his side;

but all at once Sulpice turned deadly pale, while a strange fire came into the convict's eyes.

"Here," he said, "they have brought me here. I remember the place well. The open safe, the door by which he came in. And there, there, the spot where I killed him."

"What is he saying?" asked Xavier.

"His mind is wandering," said the priest. "Leave me alone with him. I must save this soul. God owes it to me."

Sulpice said these words with such fervor that various expressions chased each other over the convict's face.

"Yes," said he; "I came to bring it to you. I am conquered. Mademoiselle, give me writing materials, I beg of you. And you, sir," to Xavier, "stay. I want your pardon, too."

Without knowing what it all meant, Sabine brought what he had asked, and knelt with them beside the dying man.

The Abbé Sulpice held him in his arms. Jean Machû wrote four lines in a scrawling hand, rendered almost illegible by weakness, and fell back exhausted. Sabine made a movement as if to raise him, and he gave her such a look of mingled shame, terror and gratitude that it went to her heart.

"I have not signed it yet," he gasped.

His fingers still held the pen. He traced some letters which were barely recognizable as the signature of Jean Machû. He motioned to Xavier to take the paper. The latter took it mechanically, but at one glance his face lit up with joy, and he fell at his brother's feet, saying,

"Pardon me, that I could not rise to your heights."

Sulpice hastily pressed his brother's hand, and turned to devote his whole attention to the dying convict. He held the crucifix to the cold lips, saying,

"Die in peace, in the name of the God who died to save the world. Die in peace, and may the shedding of your blood suffice to wash away your sins."

"No, not mine," cried Jean Machû, with sudden energy. "My whole life has been a long course of wickedness. My death cannot expiate such a life. Even you bear on your forehead a scar caused by me. Oh, why do you not curse me?"

"But remember the heroic actions of this day," said Sulpice. "Oh, I pardon you what is past from my heart."

"But your father, your father?" gasped the felon.

"The elect of God are merciful," said Sulpice.

"Your brother and sister?"

"We are Christians," said Sulpice.

With admirable patience, sublime charity and fervor, the abbé gradually calmed the convict's terrors. He took in his priestly hands that soul covered with so many sins and washed it in the Blood of the Lamb. By that miracle of inestimable power which is operated in confession the sins of Jean Machû, scarlet though they were, were washed away. His soul was filled with the plenitude of grace, conveyed by those solemn words falling from an apostle's lips.

Surely the Lord had awaited that supreme moment to reward the sublime faith of Sulpice, for scarcely had the words of absolution fallen upon that sinful soul when Jean Machû heaved a deep sigh and with that sigh passed away.

CHAPTER XVIII.

Lipp-Lapp.

Many guests still came to Methusalem's *table d'hôte* in the Rue Git-le-Cœur, but these assemblies were quieter than of yore, the mirth was not so boisterous, and even the second-hand dealer himself had a shade of anxiety on his face. He got rid as quickly as possible of his merchandise, and the Naine often passed whole nights in removing the markings from fine linen, upon which the embroidered coronet betrayed the source whence it had come. Moreover, a stove was placed in the Naine's kitchen, where Methusalem melted up silver, making ingots, of which he hastily disposed. Yet, far from diminishing, the number of his customers was constantly on the increase. Methusalem was obliged to establish for their accommodation a dormitory or lodging-room, as he had before established a *table d'hôte*. Most of his customers preferred remaining in this wretched hole to taking furnished lodgings which might compromise them. New arrests were being made every day. Methusalem's boarders were already well represented in the prisons of the Versaillists, and those who were still at large were by no means reassured as to their future. The most anxious of all was Fleur d'Echafaud. The rank he had held in the army of the Commune, his undeniable share in the murder of the hostages, in the sacking of the Legion of Honor and the Tuileries, in the burning of the Department of Finance and the houses of the Rue de Lille, made him prefer the tedious and obscure life of the Rue Git-le-Cœur to the more brilliant and noisy one he was wont to lead among a circle of which he was the oracle. His dress had undergone much the same transformation as his habits. Instead of the fashionable overcoat and cravat, he wore a blue blouse, open at the neck, showing the collar of the shirt and a bright-colored foulard loosely knotted. A black wig concealed his own peculiar shade of hair. With his cap jauntily set on one side, a cigar in his mouth, and his hands in his pockets, he looked like a young tradesman taking a holiday. Though it is true that every day was a holiday for him. Fleur d'Echafaud had also taken care to change his quarters. Methusalem's neighborhood seemed more desirable just then than the great thoroughfares. Before recommencing operations, he was waiting till the political situation should be once more clearly defined, till the law had done with the members of the Commune, and the crowd of hapless wretches who had followed in its bloody track. Moreover, he had never been so carefully watched and guarded by the Naine as since the moment when he had placed himself, so to say, at her discretion. Seeing her eager gaze so constantly fixed upon him, and she herself so solicitous for his comfort and welfare, Methusalem's guests were wont to indulge in many a rude jest, in which Fleur d'Echafaud himself took part.

"Naine," said they, "you must marry the handsome Marc."

"Yes," said the Naine one day, in a gloomy voice, "I will marry him, and in the church, too."

"Then you believe in God?"

A hideous laugh distorted her face.

"At the Abbey of Monte-a-Regret," she answered.

But this time Fleur d'Echafaud did not laugh. A cold shudder passed through him. What link bound him to the Naine? As far as his memory could reach, he remembered this deformed being seizing him in her disproportioned arms and carrying him hither and thither with inconceivable rapidity. He could recall the booth of the mountebank who had trained him, so that he was qualified to gain a livelihood on the rope or the trapeze, with the permission of the Mayor. The Naine, however, took him away and put him at a boarding-school, where she forbade him, under the most terrible penalties, to mention the profession he had followed for five years. Pride, however, would have suggested this precaution to Marc, even had the Naine never insisted upon it. When he finished school she seemed to abandon him, and he supposed she had left Paris. He found her again as servant to Methusalem, but he was by that time in Methusalem's gang, and an intimate associate of Jean Machû.

"Can this wretch have some secret design?" he said to himself, "and is she true?"

He could not answer, but a vague fear thenceforth took possession of him, and he resolved to quit Methusalem's hospitable roof as soon as he could create a new identity for himself, and pass into a new state of being. The burning of the Hotel de Ville, by destroying all registers of birth, facilitated such a plan, and the day would come when Fleur d'Echafaud would go on this errand to the Abbé Sulpice. His share of the hundred thousand francs, as well as the proceeds of the late pillage, had given Fleur d'Echafaud an income of six thousand francs. He could, therefore, choose between the peaceful life of a citizen, or the fluctuating career of an adventurer. It seemed to him safer to slip into an honest man's shoes. If later he chose to take part in such affairs, it would be on a grand scale. He would seek to ally himself with some industrial society, under the patronage of great names, he would speculate at the Bourse, become an unlicensed broker, and succeed at length, perhaps, in acquiring a large fortune.

But this fair picture, which he cherished by night and by day, had its dark and terrible reverse side. If there is a tenacious friendship it is that of the dishonest. They do not attach themselves to any one, they cling. They never allow one of their number to attain an enviable situation, except in the hope of future profit. They become the leeches of those who, starting at the lowest peg, finally reach the highest step of the ladder. Easier is it to escape the searching gaze of a detective than the affectionate remembrance of a felon. The latter is ever the better physiognomist. Jean Machû's death had been a great relief to his former comrade. In dying, the convict, overcome by the Abbé Sulpice's sublime generosity, had confessed his crime, and signed his last confession with expiring hand.

Under those circumstances there had been little difficulty in restoring Xavier Pomereul's good name, and securing his liberty. Fleur d'Echafaud was therefore easy on that score. Jean Machû dead, the secret of the robbery and murder of the Chaussée d'Antin was safe.

Some months passed. France was once more at peace, though the turmoil of politics prevented any great impetus from being given to trade. Every one was busy counting his losses, healing his wounds, mourning the departed, or calculating the decrease of his income through the rise of taxes or the losses sustained through war, incendiarism, and the Commune. The factory at Charenton still went on. It is true that upon the thresholds of the pretty homesteads built for his workmen by Antoine Pomereul was to be seen many a young mother wearing mourning, and holding her orphaned child in her arms. Touching sight! where the one had forgotten how to smile, and the other had not yet learned.

There was, however, no want among these working

people. The widows received a pension, because their husbands had fallen in defence of their country. If France forgot these improvised soldiers, the Abbé Sulpice remembered the heroes of Champigny, Buzenval and Montretout, and he paid their country's debt to them, with a generosity the more admirable that it was promptly and simply accomplished. The school took the children; apprentices, the labor of whom was always suited to their years, worked with ardor. Their main object was to please Sulpice, and in this they fully succeeded.

Xavier definitely left the home in the Chaussée d'Antin. The day after his sentence had been reversed and justice done him, he called his brother and sister.

"I am saved," he said, "but my conscience is not so easily rehabilitated. It is proved that I did not kill my father, but my life was such as to give rise to the accusation. I am only twenty-six, and have yet time to reform. It was a terrible lesson, but I will profit by it. My debts, which you so generously paid, Sulpice, must not come out of your inheritance, nor that of Sabine."

"Xavier," said Sabine, reproachfully, "are you too proud to owe that to us?"

"No, my dear child," said he; "but I have some sense of justice, and a great deal of affection. Besides, you know what use I have hitherto made of money; it is better not to trust me with any more. I am only convalescent as yet, and might have a relapse. Calculating everything—and you will see that I am a ready accountant, Sulpice—I have left myself a capital of 30,000 francs, that is to say, an income of 1500. I am going to live on that."

"You?" cried Sulpice.

"Why, it is impossible!" said Sabine.

"But you do not take into account what I can earn," said Xavier, and turning to Sulpice he asked,

"What do you give your cashier?"

"Six thousand francs."

"Poor Dubois is dying, is he not? Will you give me his place?"

"I cannot, my dear boy," said the Abbé Pomereul.

"Ah, I understand! My past record."

"God forbid that I should doubt your repentance," said the priest, in a voice of deep emotion; "but to fill that situation you must know book-keeping."

"Is that all?" asked Xavier.

"Of course."

"Then it is settled, for I know book-keeping," said Xavier.

"How long have you known it?"

"For nearly a year."

"Who taught you?"

"Dubois himself," said Xavier; "and the poor old fellow almost cried with joy to see what progress I made."

"That is wonderful," said Sabine.

"There are many wonderful things accomplished by the same power," said Xavier; "and that power is the grace of God."

"Well, well!" said the Abbé Pomereul.

"For the past year," said Xavier, "you have seen me going out every day, and have, no doubt, believed that I had returned to what I used to call my pleasures."

"No, dear boy, no, never!" said the abbé.

"I admit you had every reason to suspect me. My faults were so great that my conversion needed to be proved by facts. I promised you that I would give proof of it. One morning I went to Dubois's office. He was there with his daughter Louise, a pretty, gentle creature. They were both writing, the young girl at her father's dictation. Recognizing me, Dubois rose at once, out of respect for the family of his master; but he did not offer me his hand, as he would have done to you, Sulpice."

"He hardly knows you, Xavier," said Sulpice.

"The distinction, slight as it was, did not escape me," continued Xavier; "but it was just. I accepted it as such. This man owed me neither esteem nor regard. Such as he esteem only the truly deserving, and though the unjust sentence which had sent me to prison was reversed, I was none the less the worthless and ungrateful son, who had opened his father's safe."

"Why recall these painful memories?" said Sabine gently.

"I have no right to forget them," said Xavier. "Your very kindness impresses them forever on my mind."

"And Dubois?" said Sulpice.

"Dubois closed his books, and made a sign to his daughter. Louise was about to leave the room. I begged her to remain."

"'Sir,' said I, addressing that living example of honor and honesty, 'might I ask why you require Mademoiselle's services?'

"The old man reddened.

"'My sight is failing,' said he, 'and my strength declining. I have need of young eyes and ready hands. Louise helps me with the accounts.'

"He paused a moment, and continued with touching dignity,

"'The Abbé Pomereul is aware of this, sir; perhaps I should have given in my resignation, when I found myself incapable of filling the office, which has been mine for forty years. But I love this place, this factory. The workmen regard me almost as a father. However, sir, if you have any objection, speak.'

"'With a man like you,' I said, 'it is better to be perfectly frank. You are teaching Mademoiselle bookkeeping, will you also teach me?'

"'You, sir!' said Dubois, rising in his amazement.

"I gently forced him back into his chair, and went on.

"'My faults and misfortunes,' I said, 'have attained such publicity that I owe an equally public reparation to my own people and society at large. Repentance does not consist in words; it must be proved by deeds. I was an idler, I will learn to work; fond of dissipation, I will live with all possible regularity; I did nothing, I will now do good. Sulpice sowed the good seed, do you help me to foster it. Let me be your pupil, and while you teach me book-keeping, the heads of the different departments will initiate me, each one into their several employments. I know that the prodigal son will not find much favor with these hard-working men. But I will bear anything. A time will come when I shall reap the fruits of my perseverance, and when even the rudest workman will offer me his hand. Believe me, I shall value such a recompense.'

"Dubois looked at me in silence, but I saw tears in his daughter's eyes.

"I resumed.

"'You loved my father, M. Dubois, so did I; spite of all my faults, I loved him dearly. His death made him even dearer to me. Yet though I have repented, I dare not yet pray beside his grave. I am sorry for my faults, but I have not yet expiated them. I shall only have a right to go there when I am able to obey his last command, and take control of the house he founded.'

"Dubois was still silent.

"'Oh,' cried I, 'will you refuse to help me? Surely you cannot.'

"He spoke then in a voice of deep emotion.

"'You appeal to my affection for your father, sir; that suffices. When will you take your first lesson?'

"'Now,' I answered.

"I was there for three hours. When I left his manner towards me no less than his words delighted me. I had not learned much yet, it is true, but I felt my heart grow light; at least I had spent my time well. The same day I got books, and began to study patiently yet ardently. Dubois was astonished at my progress. In a month he brought me to the workshop, where he had probably related what had passed between us, for every face was friendly. They did not make any advances to me, but they did not repulse me.

"Poor Dubois sank rapidly, and sometimes his daughter gave me my lesson in his place. She explained things in a sweet grave voice, clearly and precisely. I never saw such serenity on any woman's face before."

"Really!" said Sabine, with a mischievous smile.

"You are malicious," said Xavier, smiling too.

"Go on," said Sulpice; "do not heed her malice."

"It is ever thus," she said to Sulpice; "they see, they hear, they love."

"Where was I?" continued Xavier. "Well, a few days ago, when I went there, instead of finding M. Dubois in his office, I found Louise, who was looking very pale, and who said at once, 'Would you be so kind, sir, as to come up into my father's room?'

"'Certainly,' I answered.

"I followed her trembling.

"Poor Dubois was in bed. When he saw me he tried to raise himself, and held out his hand. My heart leaped for joy. I took his offered hand gratefully, for he had been the friend of my noble father. He saw my emotion. He asked me to sit down.

"'Come, come,' said he, 'you are a true Pomereul.

Your conduct leaves me less regret now that I must go.'

"'But you must not go,' I said.

"'They are calling me up there, sir,' he said, 'but my last labors have been successful. You know I was named the model cashier. My books are in order. My accounts ready. There are as few errors on the pages of my registers as faults upon my conscience. You now know as much as I do; you must henceforth take my place.'

"I heard a heart-rending sob. It was from Louise, whose face was hidden on her father's bed.

"'Alone! I must leave her alone!' murmured the old man.

"'No,' said I; 'Sabine will befriend her.'

"Thanks, dear brother," said Sabine; "you anticipated me."

"I stayed longer than usual that day at Charenton," resumed Xavier. "I did not sleep much all night, for ' was weighing the great responsibility that I was about to assume. May I take Dubois's place, dear Sulpice?"

"Xavier," said the Abbé Sulpice, "you do not know what consolation you give me. Yes, brother, with all my heart. Repair your faults, work, make new progress every day, pray."

"And love," said Sabine in a low voice.

"Do not speak of that," said Xavier. "I am not worthy of such happiness yet."

"To-morrow," resumed Sulpice, "we will go together to Charenton. I want to install you myself in your new place."

"And I to make an agreement with Louise," said Sabine.

"Ever the best of sisters," said Xavier.

"It is sweet to contribute to the happiness of others," said she.

"Will you never think of your own?" said he.

Sabine shook her head.

"My happiness was a dream, Xavier," she said. "He who should have kept the shrine and the figure it contained inviolate has offered sacrifice to false gods."

"You are too severe, Sabine."

"I am just."

"But it was your rejection drove Benedict to despair."

"One who does not know how to suffer," said she, "is not worthy to be happy. Besides, brother, the man whom I loved was the Christian artist, despising the easy success which is a disgrace to the chisel and a stain upon a character. The papers are loud in his praise just now, I know; he is doing a work which will give him a high place amongst our sculptors, 'Hylas and the Nymphs,' but a work which would make me blush. No, this devotee of pagan art is not the man from whom I accepted the statuette, to whom I gave my hand, and from whom I received a betrothal ring."

There were tears in her eyes, though she spoke calmly and her face was pale.

"You are suffering, Sabine," cried Xavier, "you are suffering."

"Yes, I do not deny it," said she, "but I will be firm. God can console every sorrow, and will calm this as well. Virtue, Xavier, is often like the bitter draught given to the patient, the honey of sacrifice is at the bottom of the cup. I weep not so much for Benedict as for my old faith in him. I weep for the noble and disinterested man, who refused a dowry from my father; the good and honest man, who led a life of strict integrity and practical piety; the artist, who despised the approbation of the vulgar, and had Christ too clearly before his eyes to ever set up base idols in opposition."

Xavier kissed his sister.

"You are a noble girl," said he.

"Do not pity me, Xavier," said she, "if I lose the world I will gain heaven; and we can each have our little martyrdom, though we do not bear, like Sulpice, the aureola upon our foreheads."

Next day, according to promise, Sulpice accompanied Xavier and Sabine to Charenton. They went first to see Dubois. At sight of Sulpice his face lit up.

"I wanted to see you, sir," he said.

The priest sat down at the bedside, and the rest retired. While Sabine conversed in a low voice with Louise, Xavier regarded the two girls attentively. They formed a charming contrast. Sabine, fair, delicate, and slender; Louise, a perfect brunette. Louise was crying bitterly, and Sabine consoling her with many affectionate words. It was nearly an hour before Sulpice called them back to the sick-room. Dubois drew his daughter to his breast.

"I am dying," said he, "but the Lord in His mercy has granted me a last grace; He never forsakes those who put their trust in Him. You will not be alone in the world. The Pomereul family will adopt you. To them I leave you."

Louise only answered by her tears. The father drew his daughter's face closer to his own, and whispered some words which the others did not hear. They seemed to disturb her, for she blushed and trembled.

"It is my last wish," said her father.

"Father, oh father!" cried she.

"A sacred request," said he.

Louise might have objected further, but her father took her hand from before her face, and said,

"Promise, till I bless you."

"I promise," said she, kissing the hand which was about to bless her.

Sabine stayed all night with Louise. Sulpice went back with Xavier to Paris. The latter seemed greatly dejected; he hardly spoke to his brother, and Sulpice saw tears in his eyes. He did not ask the secret of this poignant regret, for did not Xavier know that it was the priest's mission to share all sufferings and console all pain? Next day they went again to Charenton, and, having seen Dubois and Louise, Xavier was installed in his new position. Thenceforth he entered upon its duties. When Sulpice saw him through the glass doors of the office, surrounded by papers and books tipped with brass, writing busily and wholly absorbed in his work, he could not restrain an exclamation of joy. Xavier showed him the books.

"What do you say to that writing," said he, "and my figures? I have made progress since I used to scrawl my morning notes."

"Indeed you have," said Sulpice; "I am more than satisfied with you."

For a week Dubois struggled with that terrible conqueror Death. Not that he feared it, for he had lived well; but the earthly tenement still sought to retain its tenant, the soul. He died in his daughter's arms, pressing the crucifix which Sulpice held to his lips.

The news of the honest cashier's death brought general grief to the factory. The workshops were closed, and the workmen all went to pray beside his mortal remains. Sulpice and Xavier paid the expenses of the funeral, and the faithful clerk was buried with the greatest honor. But besides the richness of the funeral draperies, there was a great concourse of people. When a stranger stopped, surprised at the display, to ask who was being buried, the Charenton men replied proudly:

"An employé of the house of Pomereul."

Dubois had asked that a cross might be placed over his grave. So a cross rose among flowers upon his funeral mound. When the grave-digger had finished his dismal task, Louise drew near the monument, holding two wreaths in her hand. She hung one upon an arm of the cross, and Xavier, seeing that she kept the other, said,

"You are forgetting this one."

"No," said she, "it is for our benefactor."

And in fact the coachman had evidently received orders, for on leaving Charenton, instead of going towards home, he drove to Montmartre. Xavier was silent, but his emotion was deep. He dared not question his brother, and Sabine, who had her arm about Louise, avoided meeting his eye. Never, since M. Pomereul's death, had Xavier accompanied them to the grave of the father whose life he had embittered. It seemed that Sulpice was now bringing him there, as if to say,

"Repentance has effaced your faults. Be restored to your rights; in the name of our dead father, I pardon you."

The carriage stopped at the gate of the cemetery. They all alighted. Louise would have fallen, but Xavier silently offered her his arm.

It was a melancholy autumn day, the dreariness of which was the more perceptible that it was among the first; the dead leaves crackled under foot, gray clouds scudded across the sky, driven by a chilly wind. The roses were all dead, and the late chrysanthemums reared their purple heads, already touched by the frost. Sulpice walked first, and Sabine and he were soon kneeling before a marble tomb. A sort of awe kept Xavier back, but Sulpice, turning, said simply, "Come."

And Louise, offering him the wreath, said, "Go."

Xavier took it, raised it to his lips, and fell prostrate on the marble slab, sobbing aloud. Through his sobs one word could be distinguished: "Pardon! pardon!"

Sulpice whispered to his sister,

"Take Louise away, and leave me with Xavier."

The young girl obeyed.

And the two brothers remained alone in the vast cemetery, already overhung with shadows.

Sulpice knelt beside Xavier, and said,

"You have asked our father's pardon. Now ask pardon of God."

"You wish—" said Xavier, bewildered.

"That, prostrating yourself here in this place of mourning, you should arise purified from every stain."

"But how can I? I am not prepared," said Xavier.

"To open your heart to the priest?" said Sulpice. "To go to confession? Why, your amendment of life for the past year and your present tears are preparation enough. The suffering soul is always well prepared to receive grace, salvation, mercy. And can I not assist you? Can any other heart as well as mine console yours? My tears will be united with yours, and if the sacrifice of a life, the holocaust of a heart be necessary, I am a voluntary victim, offering up the merits of a God to obtain mercy for you."

What passed after that was known to God alone.

The ardor of the apostle, the eloquence of the preacher, the piety of the priest, and the affection of a brother, all combined to soften and touch that still rebellious heart; and when the words of absolution had fallen on Xavier, Sulpice clasped his hands with indescribable joy.

'Father," said he, "your lost son is found; the dead has come to life."

Tears of mingled joy and sorrow, the outpourings of a heart ennobled by its priestly office, the repentance, the firm purpose of amendment, and the sweetness of reconciliation with God, were all experienced by the two brothers; they knew the joy which God reserves for those who love Him. It grew dark, and Sulpice took his brother away. They hired a cab, and were soon speeding towards the Chaussée d'Antin.

As far up as the Rue de la Victoire, an immense crowd impeded the driver's progress. Carriages were all drawn up, and horses pawed the ground impatiently. Shouts of laughter, which seemed contagious, could be heard in the distance, and repeated through the crowd, with cries of:

"He'll catch him." "No, he won't catch him."

"Let us get out," said Xavier; "we may be kept an hour here, and we can make our way through the crowd."

They paid the man his fare, and attempted to force a passage for themselves. But it was useless. They had to wait. They got on a few steps, when a sudden movement of the crowd thrust them back farther than ever.

"What is it all about?" asked Xavier of a spectator.

"I hardly know, sir; but it's something about a monkey."

"Just like Jocko, the monkey of Brazil," said a boy. "I saw that at the Ambigu for fifteen sous."

"A monkey?" repeated Xavier.

"Just imagine, citizen," said the boy in a shrill voice, "about ten minutes ago this great devil of an ape was sitting upon a balcony, watching the passers-by with a melancholy face. He must belong to some people who have *chic*, for his dress, which would be a Mardi Gras for us, looks like the big pictures in the Louvre. There he lay, like the Pacha of Egypt, on silk cushions, looking about him. I was looking about, too, and seeing the ape, began to make faces at him, which he returned—an exchange of civilities. But all of a sudden he got on his feet—I wouldn't say claws to a man of the woods so well dressed that *la Belle Jardinière* has nothing to equal him. He leaned over the balcony and looked down, growling all the time to himself. I looked in the same direction, and saw a fine young man in a blue blouse. He seemed like a printer, for you see, citizen, I always think that printers—"

"What next, what next?" cried Xavier impatiently.

"You are interested? All right, I'll go on. The fine young man with the black hair and red foulard necktie was going along gayly, swinging a stick. I believe the monkeys are about tired of sticks; they got too much of them among the negroes."

"Go on, go on!" cried Xavier excitedly.

"Decidedly, I am a success. I must learn to recite the '*Je te ramène*' that I heard at the Comédie Française, with an old gentleman's ticket. To return to the ape. The young man was spreading himself like a chap that's got chink in his pockets, when all of a sudden the monkey jumped over the balcony and rushed at him. He was frightened, and yelled like anything; off he ran, and the monkey after him. Everybody laughed, shouted, and cried out, 'He'll catch him,' 'No, he won't.' It's all very fine, though, but I'm taking proofs to an author, and this has delayed me exactly thirty-five minutes. But I'll tell him all about it; he can make it into copy, and I'll ask a share in the copyright."

"Here's for your story," said Xavier, putting his hand in his pocket and drawing out a twenty-franc piece, which he gave to the boy.

"You must be a prince in disguise," said the boy. "I'll catch the monkey, if you like, for the same price."

"Do, if you can," said Xavier.

"We think alike," said Sulpice, "it is Lipp-Lapp."

But the crowd all at once changed its tone, and exclamations of horror and anxiety were heard on all sides.

"The man's lost," cried they.

"Will no one kill the cursed beast?" cried one.

"How fiercely he growls over his prey!" cried another; "it's horrible!"

Xavier and Sulpice threw themselves blindly into the crowd, and soon reached the scene of horror. For such it really was. He whom the boy had described as a fine young man was now pale, haggard, badly bitten, his throat encircled by the bony fingers of the ape, gasping for breath and writhing in agony. No one dared to approach the terrible beast; they waited for the appearance of the police. At last a policeman came, sword in hand, and was about to attack the ape, when Xavier interposed.

"The ape is mine; you must not kill it," he said.

"But the animal is mad, sir," remonstrated the officer.

"Do you observe," said Xavier, holding the policeman back, "the chimpanzee has just torn off the black wig and disclosed the man's real hair, which is of a peculiar red?"

Looking at the wretch closely, a light flashed on Xavier's mind.

"Marc Mauduit!" he cried.

And fairly bruising the officer's arm in his nervous grasp, he said,

"On my soul, sir, Lipp-Lapp has just arrested the accomplice of Jean Machû, who murdered my father!"

The policeman immediately seized Marc Mauduit, as Xavier called off Lipp-Lapp. The latter seemed to understand that it was all right. He showed his teeth in a broad grin, and opening his brocade gown, pointed to a large white mark on his breast. It was the scar of the wound which Fleur d'Echafaud had given him. Then waving triumphantly the tuft of red hair which he held in his clenched hand, he offered it to Xavier. Just as the ape had garroted Marc Mauduit, and Xavier and Sulpice had witnessed the sudden *dénouement* of the bloody tragedy which had begun by the murder of their father, a deformed creature suddenly appeared emerging from the Rue de Provence.

Fleur d'Echafaud recognized her.

"Naine!" cried he, "oh Naine!"

The physical monster looked into the face of the moral monster, and an expression of sardonic joy lit up her eyes, as, clapping her hands in savage glee, she cried,

"André Nicois, it is our turn now!"

CHAPTER XIX.

THE DWARF'S SECRET.

THE Naine ran at full speed through the streets, jostling the passers-by, upsetting flower-stands, deaf to invectives or taunts. She only stopped when, as she was about to cross the great court-yard of the banker's dwelling, a tall lackey in gorgeous livery seized her by one of her long arms, and dragged her almost from under the horses' feet. The two splendid horses were attached to a carriage just then entering the yard. In this magnificent equipage sat a lady still young and sumptuously attired, upon whose features, beneath their mask of pride, was the imprint of some consuming sorrow. The Naine looked at her with an expression of such intense hatred that the banker's wife was startled. Leaning out of the carriage, she said imperiously,

"You know very well I allow no beggars here."

The Naine gave a fierce laugh.

"I do not come to beg," she said. "I come to sell."

The horses and carriage passed on, and the lackey was about to obey his mistress's injunction and drive the Naine from the yard, but she pushed him aside with astonishing strength, and said to the footman at the door,

"Your master is in. I must see him."

Her tone was such that the man hesitated.

"Do you happen to think, you living curiosity," said he at last, "that my master receives people of your sort? Be thankful if he throws you some sous."

"Did you hear what I said to his wife?" cried the Naine. "I don't ask for anything, I bring something.

Listen! The millionaire banker does not often give audiences, but I promise you he will turn you away to-morrow if you do not let me in. I want to speak to him, and I will see him, if I have to crouch like a dog at his door till he comes out."

"Out of this!" said the lackey, pushing her with his foot, "or I'll call the police."

The Naine shrugged her shoulders, and began to fumble in her pocket, producing at length an old paper and a placard yellow and falling to pieces with age.

"Can you read?" she said to the lackey.

"I don't want to see your papers," said he.

"Run your eye over that," said she; "it will make your fortune, perhaps."

The lackey read a few lines, stopped in astonishment, and looking at the Naine, said, "Well?"

"Take those to the banker, and say that a person who brings him news is waiting."

The lackey suddenly changed his mind about the dwarf, and, anxious to display his great zeal, refused to transmit the commission to M. Nicois' valet, but ran up-stairs himself, and asked to speak to the banker. The banker, in surprise, told them to admit the man. The latter, whose name was Lamourel, bent double and said, in a voice of well-feigned emotion,

"You will pardon my unusual conduct, sir, in consideration of my motive."

"What is your motive, and what do you want, Lamourel?" said Nicois.

"I thought there was no use letting the whole house into your secrets, sir," said Lamourel mysteriously.

"I have no secrets. What do you mean?" cried Nicois.

"I do not venture to pry into my master's affairs," said the servant; "I only wished to save him a great shock."

"Say what you have to say, Lamourel, and be done with it. I am busy," said Nicois impatiently.

"Do you recognize this, sir?" said the lackey, laying the paper open on the banker's desk, and taking care to point out the paragraph indicated by the Naine.

The banker scarcely suppressed a cry of pain.

"Where did you get this?" he cried. "What do you want? Why do you revive—"

"There is a woman below."

"A woman? Go on."

"She brings you some news."

"And she gave you this placard and this paper?"

"Yes, sir."

"Why did you not bring her here at once? Run down for her, Lamourel!"

"Because she is poor, deformed, hideous."

"What does that matter? She may possess the happiness of my whole life."

Lamourel hastened out.

André Nicois, a prey to conflicting emotions, read over every line of the paragraph in the paper which the Naine had so carefully preserved. In the column of casualties, were the lines:

"A terrible misfortune has befallen a highly respected family. A child belonging to M. André Nicois was stolen while walking with its nurse. The unfortunate girl, feeling that she had neglected her charge, would have drowned herself but for the intervention of the police. Every effort has been made to find the banker's son, but hitherto with no success. Fears are entertained that the mother will lose her reason."

"How well I remember! How well I remember," gasped Nicois, "my beautiful boy, my idolized Marc! Shall I at last find the key to this enigma? Will he be restored to me after twenty years? How much he may have suffered! What has he become? What is he doing? His misfortunes will only make him dearer to me. Oh! why does not this woman come? What is keeping her?"

As he spoke, the Naine entered the room. Prepared as he had been to behold a wretched object, the banker was surprised. He scarcely restrained a gesture of disgust and abhorrence; but overcoming his repugnance, he held out the paper to the Naine.

"You brought this, saying you had some revelation to make," said the banker.

"Yes," answered the Naine brusquely.

"Well, speak out, tell me all, and be assured I shall not be ungrateful."

"I also brought you a placard," said the Naine.

"Yes, relating to the same occurrence. Tell me what you know."

"I want you first to re-read the placard," said the Naine.

André Nicois read in a low voice:

"A reward of 25,000 francs is offered for whoever will discover and bring back to A. Nicois, banker, his stolen child—"

"That's enough," said the Naine; "have you the 25,000 francs?"

"Yes, and I am ready to pay them. I will double the sum. I will sacrifice half my fortune."

"The sum mentioned will do," said the Naine; "only it must be paid in advance."

"Do you doubt me?" said the banker.

"It is my habit," answered the Naine.

"But should your information be insufficient?"

"It is such as will enable you to see your son to-morrow, if you wish."

"You have proofs and documents?"

"Proofs and memories, proofs and documents," she repeated.

"Are you aware," said André Nicois, "that you are acting in a very suspicious manner? I could have you arrested."

"Have me arrested," said the Naine; "what can you say against me? What can you prove? I am poor, deformed, and ugly, but I work as a servant now, and used to be exhibited at country fairs as a deformity. Yet hitherto I have not done anything that comes within the province of the police. Drive me out or have me arrested, whichever you please, but I will not speak till I have got the 25,000 francs."

Nicois opened a drawer and counted out the money, handing it to the Naine.

"I am waiting," he said simply.

"Will you give orders that no one interrupts us?" said the Naine; "what I have to say will be long."

The banker rang; his valet appeared.

"Firmin," said he, "I am not at home to any one."

"Good," said the Naine, thrusting the bank-notes into her pocket; "now we can talk. You asked for proofs. Here."

The strange being drew from her breast a greasy portfolio swollen with letters, passports, and parchments of all sorts—scraps of paper covered with various handwritings, most of them scrawling and illegible—and threw them all into her lap, to use at need.

"You are growing old now, M. Nicois," began she; "but you were young once, and in youth the heart beats spite of everything. A man becomes a banker, but does not become all at once a miser. At twenty you did not care so much for heaping up gold, and you enjoyed your youth. Do you remember Louise Michau?"

The banker shivered.

"I see you remember," resumed the Naine; "she was the daughter of respectable people, though she had no other fortune than her two strong arms. Her dowry was her beauty; they called her Louise the Blonde."

"Why recall these things?" said Nicois; "it is of my son I want to hear."

"Do not interrupt me," said the Naine; "I speak slowly, and sometimes unconnectedly; it is just as I can. My mind is as dull as my body is deformed. If I once lose the thread of my thoughts, I may never recover it."

The banker threw himself back in his chair with forced and painful resignation, saying,

"I am listening."

"Louise was as good as she was pretty, and as confiding as good. She did not know how to lie herself, and she never dreamt that any one could deceive her. A man told her that he loved her, spoke of marriage, and of a brilliant future. Louise saw in such a union the happiness of her family, an affection equal on both sides, and all the joy of an alliance contracted in the sight of God and men, and—"

The Naine sprang to her feet, pointing her outstretched arm at the banker, as she continued:

"That man lied. A rich heiress crossed his path; he forgot his first love, who was poor. André Nicois, you were a brutal and selfish coward!"

The banker did not resent the insult which this monstrous being flung in his face. The remembrance of his fault, which he had avowed to the Abbé Sulpice, still tormented him at times. He bowed his head, while the woman went on, in a voice husky with emotion:

"I said that the family of this girl was respectable. Shame had never come upon them. Louise, smarting under the sense of desertion, fled from the home wherein she had passed her childhood. One creature alone knew her whole melancholy story. André Nicois you were her murderer!"

The Naine paused a moment, and went on:

"One morning the body of Louise was found in the river; her dress had caught on a branch, and her corpse was floating among the sedges. If you had seen her then, livid and ghastly, her eyes glassy, her lips purple, the sight would have touched even your brazen heart. But you had other things to think of. You were married to a rich heiress, and you were beginning to lay the foundation of your fortune."

The Naine drew out a package of letters, tied with a black ribbon, from amongst the papers in her lap.

"Here are your letters to Louise," she said. "Do you recognize them?"

"Yes," said the banker in a low voice.

"Do what you like with them now," said the Naine; "the armful of proofs which I possess will be of no use after this."

"But, my son! my son!" cried the banker.

"You did not know, perhaps," said the Naine, taking no heed of the banker's impatience, "that Louise had a sister. There is a story about the pretty daughter of a merchant, called Beauty, and a monster, who was called the Beast. In Louise's home lived, or rather vegetated, a shameful, hideous creature, a spectacle of ugliness, a curse and an affliction, at sight of whom children cried. Her mother and sister bore with her patiently; but no one else loved her.

"Now, this monstrous being took it into her head that, as men shunned her, she would spend her time among beasts, with whom she was more on an equality. She longed to have a farm stocked with all kinds of animals, and away off on the borders of a wood. As the city cast her off, she craved the desert.

"The day when Louise had been asked in marriage and believed herself loved by a rich man, she led this monster into the little garden, and, taking both her ugly hands in her own soft white ones, said,

"'Rose,' for the dwarf was named Rose, 'I am very happy. I am going to marry André Nicois. Do not shake your head, he has given me this engagement ring. Now, you have often admired the farm of the Huchettes. Well, that will be my wedding present. You will live there quietly, well off, and I hope as happy as you can be in this world.'

"Rose threw her arms around her sister's neck, overcome with joy. How deeply was she interested in this marriage; with what eager curiosity did she question Louise thereupon! No doubt she was glad of her sister's good fortune; but Rose had a selfish, evil side to her character, engendered by the contempt, unkindness, and aversion of every one.

"The monster, from whom her own mother sometimes turned away in disgust, had henceforth only one thought:

"'My sister's marriage will make me rich in my turn.'

"Every day she went to the farm, and, standing outside the paling, calculated the extent of the fields, counted on her fingers the number of trees; and, seating herself joyously on the ground, fixed her eyes on the blue slates of the roof as they glittered in the sunlight, repeating like a clock, tick-tack, tick-tack, the words that expressed all her hopes: "'The Huchettes will be mine.'

"This was a wild ambitious dream that haunted the half-demented brain of the Beast, who bore the name of Christian and kept a woman's heart under her hideous covering. She could not sleep at night, and when her eyes were closed she saw a great flower-strewn field, with the farm standing in the middle of it, and great meadows and running brooks. How she questioned

Louise: 'What did your lover say yesterday? Is the marriage day fixed? Why not confide all to your mother, and get your certificate of baptism?'

"'He wants me to wait awhile, answered Louise submissively, 'so I wait.'"

The Naine sought out another paper from her lap, and placed a printed announcement of marriage on the desk before the banker. Then she went on:

"So Louise waited till André Nicois, who had promised to marry her in the village church, became the husband of Mdlle. Dupernois. When she ceased to wait, she very soon ceased to live. You have the announcement of your marriage there; here is the report of the policeman, testifying to having found Louise's body in the river."

André Nicois crumpled the two papers in his hand, and remained a moment with his eyes closed, overcome by these memories. When he opened them, the Naine was standing in front of him, watching him with the ferocity of a wild beast.

"You are Rose!" exclaimed he.

"Yes," said she, "Rose, the sister of the dead girl, whose fate I swore to avenge, avenging myself at the same time."

"What had I done to you?" said Nicois; "I never even saw you."

"What had you done to me?" she screamed. "Do you forget my dreams of fortune, my farm, the future Louise meant to make for me, if you had kept your promise? I do not pretend to be more loving than I am. I was sorry for Louise, because she was always kind and sympathizing, but I was more sorry for the fortune of which you had robbed me. My double sorrow filled me with rage and hatred against you. My rage was that of a beast deprived of its prey. For months I was half crazed, going from the Huchettes to the river, and from the river to the cemetery. Sometimes I wept for my sister, oftener yet I cast about for means of revenge. I thought of taking an axe or a stick and killing you, some dark night, at the street corner. But I remembered that your sufferings then would be too short, and I sought another means. Dying would be only one struggle, a little blood spilt, and that's all. Louise had only suffered for a short time, but I was never, never to realize my hopes. Beings like me, deformed in mind and body, are slow and sluggish. At last, one day I heard you required a nurse. I knew you had a child. My vengeance was at hand. That day I uttered shrieks of joy and danced like a madwoman. At last I could punish you; at last avenge my sister on your wife and child."

"I see it all! I see it all!" cried the banker.

"The Beast became as cunning as a fox. She gained every approach to your house. She flattered the servants, and made them believe she could tell their fortunes from their palms. She made friends with the dog by bringing bones to his kennel. She did not hurry. Her work was like that of the snail. She proceeded slowly but surely. You remember going to Austria?"

"I remember. Oh! I remember," said the banker.

"Your family was in Paris at the time. I watched your house, followed your child, spied upon the servants, and one day, taking advantage of a crowd of children who had collected to see some show in the Champs Elysées, I carried off your son through the crowd, took him in my arms and ran. He laughed at first, thinking I was playing. When he began to cry, I brought him to my garret, took off his rich clothes, dressed him in rags, and started for the country.

"I ran, ran, breathless and panting. The child, tired of crying, had fallen asleep. When he woke, we were far from the city. I left him with some peasants, and went home. They thought I had been taking a long walk, and did not question me as to my absence. Your wife, half crazed with sorrow, wrote to you, and you came back. You put up placards, offering a reward of 25,000 francs for the recovery of your son. I hesitated. With that amount I could purchase the Huchettes. But on reflection I saw that the event was too recent. Suspicion would have turned upon me, and before paying me the price I should have been questioned. I would have got months or years in prison for the return of your son. Besides, I not only wanted to enrich myself, but to revenge my sister. So Marc never returned to you. I often wondered what I should do with him. It was impossible to leave him long where he was. But while I was in this state of uncertainty, an incident decided both our lives. A company of mountebanks passed through the country at the time of the Patronal Feast. They had a two-headed woman, the Northern Hercules, and a five-footed calf. Attracted by the spectacle, I mingled with the crowd outside the door.

"'Come in gratis,' said the two-headed woman; 'among professional people—'

"I went in, and as the spectacle was about ending, the clown made a sign to me from behind the curtain of the booth:

"'The manager wants to speak to you,' said he.

"'What for?' said I.

"'He wants you to make an engagement with him.'

"I did not quite understand what he meant, but I followed the clown.

"The manager, a big, red-faced, coarse-looking man, looked at me and laughed, showing every tooth in his head.

"'Upon my word,' said he, 'I haven't one like you in

my whole collection. What will you take by the year to exhibit yourself at fairs? Your picture will be on the placards, and you will rank with foreign artists.'

"'What will I take?' stammered I.

"'Yes. A hundred francs a year,' continued Guigolfo. 'costume supplied, expenses paid, food fit for a princess, and brandy at discretion.'

"'That will answer,' said I, enchanted with the prospect. 'But the child?'

"'You have a child?' he asked.

"'There is one that must go with me,' said I.

"'What age?'

"'Three years.'

"'Pretty, easy to train?'

"'Fair, rosy, and slender.'

"'Twenty francs a year for the child, and we will sign an agreement for four years.'

"'When do you leave?'

"'To-night.'

"'Where will you be to-morrow?'

"'At Melun.'

"'Wait for me there, and I will bring the child.'

"I shook hands upon it with Guigolfo and ran home. At dawn I set out; a neighbor wrote a line for me to my parents, telling them I was going, but not saying where. At the Mayor's office I asked in your name for Marc's certificate of baptism. Such documents are free to the public. I got it without any difficulty. That evening I set out for Melun, and in the middle of the night came up with the showman's wagons. The barking of dogs, squealing of monkeys, and crying of an infant greeted me. The manager opened the wagon-door and let me in. The child and myself were given a mattress, and I slept till morning. The two-headed woman undressed the child, felt his limbs to see if they were supple, and throwing him like a ball to the Northern Hercules, said,

"'Good for training!'

"I signed the agreement for both of us with the manager."

"Wretch! wretch," cried André Nicois.

"At length I was avenged," said she; "every day my hatred was being gratified. I saw that child upon whom you had lavished every care and tenderness beaten and starved. He seemed to regard me with the greatest horror. Sometimes he stretched out his little arms, crying, 'Mamma! mamma!' and I struck him, saying,

"'I am your mother.'

"But he turned from me in horror, and covered his face with his hands."

The Naine paused a moment to enjoy the banker's horror and despair, then went on:

"The physical sufferings of the child were nothing to the moral harm done him. When they bruised his body they poisoned his mind, filling it with precocious wickedness. His rosy lips repeated blasphemies, and his childish speech was a tissue of horrors. One day I had some thoughts of sending him back to you. The Northern Hercules asked me to be his wife. It was a temptation. I might have had some taste of happiness. But the Hercules would not have your son. Commonsense, however, forbade me to accept this man, who would no doubt have soon begun to treat me cruelly. The end of our agreement came. I had saved. I had learned many lucrative trades in my travels. I refused to remain in the troupe. I went to Paris, where I was to find the completion of my revenge. I discovered your address. I found that the misery of having lost your child had estranged you from your wife. She no longer loved you; your affection for her was more in appearance than in reality: you had only one idol, gold; one desire, gold; one love, gold—always gold.

"Men spoke of your operations at the Bourse, and envied your happiness. I knew better, and I never envied you. I placed Marc at a modest boarding-school, commanding him to be silent as to the past. Fear or pride made him discreet, and, more wonderful still, he studied. His progress was rapid. I paid his expenses, at first out of my savings, then with my wages."

"You repented then?" said the banker.

"I repent? You shall see. I left the necessary money with the schoolmaster for Marc, and disappeared. I would have wished him to forget me; it would have better suited my plans. At eighteen he had a depraved, perverse, thoroughly evil nature. As a child he had not been innocent; as a man he was utterly bad. At the age when most young men know little of life he was hardened in evil. He was hypocrite enough to disguise his wickedness, and self-controlled enough to await the time for its full enjoyment. He played a double rôle in the world: an honest man by day, he was a thief by night. For the rest, being a pretty, well-dressed boy, paying large sums to his tailor, perfuming his hair, and using rice-powder like a woman, with manners by turns insolent or fawning, he succeeded in obtaining a situation in an honorable house."

"Ah!" said the banker with a sort of relief.

"Do you know the Rue Git-le-Cœur?" said the Naine.

"I believe it is somewhere near the Prefecture," said the banker mechanically.

"Exactly," said the woman. "I do not think you make many purchases there; for you oftener buy diamonds from Falize than old iron from Methusalem. However, if you had done him the honor of going into his shop, you would have found me there, scrubbing the floors or taking the markings from linen when I was not cooking. Methusalem is a jack-of-all-trades. He makes money out of everything—thefts, frauds, *table d'hôte*, and lodging-rooms. I saw your little Marc, then a fine youth of eighteen, come in one day to this table. He was apparently the intimate associate of a thief."

"My God! my God!" cried the banker, burying his face in his hands.

"Up to this time, bad as he was, he had committed no actual crime. He had gone through the police courts, but had not yet come to the convict-prison. He, however, promised so well in the gang he had now joined that Jean Machû gave him the name of Fleur d'Echafaud, which he has ever since kept."

"I am going mad!" said the banker, "I am going mad!"

"Not yet, André Nicois," said the Naine. "You had a friend, a good friend, M. Pomereul."

"Yes, but I lost him by a cruel death," said he.

"His son Xavier was accused of the crime, but was since released. Do you remember that the police, on making a report of the state of the room on the morning after the murder, took from the fingers of Lipp-Lapp, the chimpanzee, a tuft of red hair?"

"Well?" gasped the banker.

"They concluded then, and later on at the trial, that the murderer, Jean Machû, had an accomplice. But Jean Machû would not betray the man who had assisted him. Till yesterday the name of that accomplice was unknown."

"And now—now?"

"M. Xavier, once at liberty, wanted to forget all about it. But there was one that did not forget. Lipp-Lapp, who was wounded by Machû's accomplice, remembered his face."

André Nicois seemed unable longer to follow the Naine: his face grew purple; his eyes protruded. Hasten, Naine, or you will be powerless to touch him further. She threw every word in his face like so many blows.

"Marc was Antoine Pomereul's secretary, and the information given by him first induced Machû, *alias* Rat-de-Cave, to think of robbing the banker's safe. Surprised by the master and attacked by the beast, they killed the one and left the other for dead. No one suspected Marc. I knew, but I bided my time. I feared that I might not be able to prove my charge. The Commune came, and Marc took a bloody part in it. I might have had him shot, but that seemed too easy a death Yesterday Marc was passing along the Chaussée d'Antin, disguised so that no one could recognize him except Lipp-Lapp. With his wonderful instinct, the beast knew him, leaped into the street, pursued and caught him. M. Xavier also recognized him, and he was arrested for complicity in the robbery and murder of Antoine Pomereul."

The banker fell out of his chair, stricken with apoplexy.

And the Naine ran downstairs, crying to the *concierge*,

"A doctor, quick! a doctor! Your master is dying."

So saying, she disappeared down a neighboring alleyway, like a phantom vanishing into the night.

CHAPTER XX.

THE BROKEN IDOL.

THE smoking-room opening from Benedict Fougerais' studio presented a most animated appearance. A dozen or so young men had just risen from an abundant breakfast, the champagne whereof had given them a twofold animation. They were in fact celebrating the sending a model to the government. It was the model of the fountain ordered from the sculptor, representing Hylas and the Nymphs.

If the enthusiasm of Benedict's friends was somewhat exaggerated, it must be admitted that his work was worthy of all praise. From where the young men sat they could see, through the heavily curtained arch of the smoking-room, the group chiselled from a block of white Carrara marble, resting against a background of crimson velvet.

It was a classical work—a perfect representation of that severity of outline made modern by the perfection of form, of which Coysevox dreamed and Clodion revealed the secret. Certainly it required little short of the highest genius to create that polished yet living group, breathing youth, glowing youth. Its author might well exclaim,

" My place is won."

Yes, won among those who crave success from wherever it comes. But changed as Benedict was, he could not look on his work without remorse. Near the group of Hylas was a statue of clay, almost ready to fall into dust. Unfinished and covered with a veil of gray linen, it still attracted the gaze of the artist. It was a plan of a St. Cecilia begun from memory.

"See, old fellow," said one of his companions, "you did well after all to take our advice. If it had not been for that famous supper at which we converted you to mythology, you would have gone back to the Middle Ages, as sure as you live. You would have gone on dreaming, when there is scarcely one of the younger sculptors who can rival you. Dubois is spoiled by affectation, Carpaux is too impetuous. In a couple of years you will be at the head of the new school."

"What success you will have at the Exposition!" said another. "You remember how they gave the medal to Hiolle for his classical figure of Orion? Why, you are sure of it."

"I have just begun my series of articles on the *Salon* of 1873," said an art-critic, "and I will boldly proclaim 'Hylas and the Nymphs' the work of the year. In all my visits to the studios of Paris I have seen nothing to approach this work."

"It means fame, Benedict," said the poet Gildas.

"And happiness," added a novelist.

"To your health, Benedict! to Hylas! to the medal!"

"Thanks, thanks, my friends!" said Benedict, pleased at their enthusiasm, "you give me confidence. One always distrusts himself on the eve of battle. While we are at work the fever of production sustains us; when we have finished we begin to judge what is done."

"It will be the greatest success in ten years," cried a painter.

"It will be called the triumph of Benedict."

"It should be crowned," said Gildas.

"Yes, it should be crowned," cried the others, and two of the young enthusiasts leaped out of the window and brought in branches, which they deposited in the arms of the nymphs.

A general hurrah and another bumper of champagne saluted this offering. But whilst Benedict strove to enter into the mood of his companions, there was a shadow on his brow. He blushed at it; it irritated him, and he strove to shake off by boisterous mirth this reflection of the grief which still gnawed at his heart; but he could not. He believed his success certain. His friends did not flatter him in predicting it. But when he looked at the nymphs, the smile upon their lips seemed to mock the pain at his heart.

"Benedict," said a crayon artist, "will you come to the prison to-morrow?"

"What for?" said he. "I have seen the cell of Marie Antoinette and the chapel."

"Oh, it is only to see a prisoner."

"Who?"

"Why, that double-dyed villain, Marc Mauduit, the accomplice of Jean Machû, who had the honesty to confess his crime before he died."

"And to save that unfortunate Xavier Pomereul," said another.

"An illustrated journal," said the artist, "wants the portrait of this charming youth, who belonged to the Black Cap gang. By my word, I hobnobbed with him one night at the Bouffes, when I was a little excited! But what, in heaven's name, are we coming to, if the most sedate-looking government clerks and the most prepossessing secretaries are ready to steal into our confidence and obtain at once our handkerchief, our friendship, and our watch? They say he has not lost a whit of his coolness in prison. He is a curiosity."

"I say, Paul," said a novelist, "if Benedict doesn't

go, let me go in his place. I want a character for my next novel, and there's one ready made."

"My dear fellow, the simplest way will be to compile Marc Mauduit's notes and documents and make a large volume out of them, entitled 'Memoirs of Fleur d'Echafaud.' You will sell fifty thousand copies, I wager."

"Besides, you will save your imagination so much," said Gildas; "the drama is complete."

"How's that?"

"Well, it seems," said the poet, "that Fleur d'Echafaud belongs to an excellent family. Stolen by a sort of female Caliban, in revenge for his sister's death, the wretch at first placed little Marc in a circus or the booth of a mountebank, or something of that sort. Over and above this education on the tight-rope she had him taught Latin and Greek to disguise him the more. In this new skin he came out as you know, and will end as you can foresee. It seems that this monster of a woman revealed the whole thing to his parents."

"That explains Fleur d'Echafaud's attempt to escape," said the painter. "His family furnished the means, and his early training at the circus did the rest; if his foot had not slipped in climbing a wall, he would have been off to America."

"So you see it is as I said, a perfect drama," said Gildas.

"I must have a talk with my publisher about it," said the author; "in a fortnight it would bring in twenty thousand francs."

"Will you come, Benedict?" asked the crayon artist.

"No, no," said he, shuddering.

Gildas took an opportunity to whisper to the artist:

"Never speak of the Pomereul family before Benedict."

The shade of sadness on Benedict's face was deeper than before.

The young man, however, feeling that he was but a sorry host, made an effort, and rising, filled the glasses of pink crystal with champagne, saying cheerily,

"Keep me company, boys. Let us drink once more to the future, to joy, fame, happiness, to all that can bring us forgetfulness, to all that will give us new life."

Benedict drained the glass, at the very moment that a young man, coming to the door, stopped in surprise upon the threshold. But the sculptor recognized him, and rushed forward eagerly seizing, him by both hands.

"Xavier, old fellow!" he said cordially.

Most of the company knew Pomereul, and greeted him warmly. They had often met him in the resorts most frequented by men of fashion, the theatre, club, racecourse. A series of questions followed to which he found some difficulty in replying all at once: "What has become of you?" "We never see you anywhere." "Are you going to run again?" "Have you been travelling?"

"Good heavens!" cried Xavier, "one at a time. My story will be a surprise to you."

"All the better," said the journalist; "I am never surprised, only animated. You will give me a new vein."

"In the first place, my friends," said Xavier, "I paid my debts."

"Paid your debts?" said a painter. "Can you show your receipts?

"I understand," said the crayon artist; "he payed his creditors to establish a base of confidence for future operations."

"No, you are out there," said Xavier, shaking his head.

"Then explain yourself."

"I paid my debts," said Xavier, "that I might owe nothing to the honest people who had trusted me. And what is still more astonishing is that after paying for everything, furniture, horses, carriages, jewelry, I still had thirty thousand francs."

"But your father left a great deal of money."

"I include my share of what he left," said Xavier. "I can tell you, money goes quick in that little flower-strewn path called Parisian life. We buy at exorbitant prices, we throw money about like princes, we go into all kinds of costly eccentricities, and then some morning comes the crash, and the end of it is we ruin ourselves or our tradespeople. I rather preferred ruining myself."

"But what did you do with the thirty thousand francs?" said one.

"What would you have done with it?" asked Xavier of the author.

"I should have taken the train to Monaco, and spent it there in trying to make more."

"And you?" to the crayon artist.

"I should have gone back for six months to the old life."

"But after that?"

"After that I would have become a Chasseur d'Afrique."

"Well, I am not of the same mind as either of you," said Xavier. "I made up my mind to live on my income."

"Fifteen hundred francs a year? Why, never!"

"But I could earn something besides."

"How? You can do nothing, Xavier."

"I could do nothing; I learned."

"What?"

"Book-keeping, and became cashier of our factory."

"That's a good joke," cried a chorus of voices.

"Do *you* think I am joking?" said Xavier to Benedict.

"No," said Benedict, in a voice of deep emotion.

"Now see," said Xavier, his good-humored voice tinged with bitterness, "we generally say to ourselves and others, when we are throwing money right and left, that 'we are leading a jolly life.' But it is false. We do not get the worth of our money. We eat highly spiced food and drink wines that ruin our digestion. The doctors live at our expense. Our horses do not always come in first on the turf. The cards deceive us. We pass our nights talking nonsense or dealing out bits of pasteboard. The jewellers laugh at us. At thirty we have no fortune, no horses, no illusions. One chance remains to us. Worn out and *blasé*, we marry some young girl who does not understand us, and would despise us if she could know our past life. Too often even this is only a means of retrieving our fortunes, that we may pursue the same career. In a few months we begin to neglect our wife, and there is one more unhappy woman added to the long list. For my part, I followed the example of those savages in some part of Oceanica. They have idols to whom no sacrifice is too costly. They load them with gifts, sending up ardent prayers all the while; but if it happens that the idols do not grant the desires of their worshippers, if they receive their offerings without repaying them in pleasure, martial glory, or happiness, the savages snatch them from the altar, spit upon them, insult them, trample them under foot, and end by setting fire to them or throwing them into the sea. I have done likewise. My idols deceived me. I laughed them to scorn and broke them."

"And are you happy now?" said Benedict.

"Perfectly," said Xavier. "I have sleep, health, good temper. I take an interest in a hundred things that I never knew the value of before. I was a worthless spendthrift, now I am good for something."

"But who worked this miracle?"

"My brother first," said Xavier gravely, "then a young girl."

"A young girl?"

"Yes; I did not tell you all. I am going to be married."

"To an heiress?"

"No, to a poor orphan. I have nothing, yet she is satisfied."

"What is her name?"

"A very obscure one—Louise Dubois. You do not know her. Her father, an honest and honorable man, was our cashier for forty years."

Benedict wrung his friend's hand.

The others, seeing that the breakfast was going to end in a serious conversation, took their leave, and Benedict, with beating heart, found himself alone with Xavier. The young men had not seen each other for two years. Benedict had fought all during the war. When peace was concluded, and Jean Machù's confession had exonerated Xavier, Sabine besought him not to go near Benedict. His name always woke new sorrow in her breast. She knew that he had forgotten her, or was trying to forget; that the talent she was once so proud of had been applied to lower uses. Through the papers she learned of Benedict's new success, and henceforth a gulf opened between them. Loving him too much not to suffer, and too courageous not to struggle against her sorrow, she strove to conceal it from every one. But Xavier was not deceived by his sister's apparent serenity, and in spite of her request and his promise resolved to find out for himself if Benedict did not share in her regret. He knew it was so at the first word Benedict spoke, and at the first glance he gave him. The very way in which he took his hands, the voice in which he uttered his name, sufficed to show that Sabine's memory survived all else. Scarcely were they alone, when Benedict said in a voice of much emotion,

"Why did you never come all this long time ?"

"I knew you were busy and happy," said Xavier.

"Happy!" repeated Benedict, shaking his head.

"To-morrow is the opening of the *Salon*, and you are to exhibit your great work to the judges; but its success is already bruited abroad. Shall I be the only one who has not seen this marvel of modern art ?"

Benedict pointed to the group.

"Go and look at it," he said.

Whilst Xavier was examining the fountain, Benedict threw himself upon a sofa and buried his head in his hands. Xavier stood a long time before the group. When he came back to his friend's side, he said simply,

"It is really very fine, very fine."

But he spoke without enthusiasm, and in a tone which betrayed some hidden emotion.

"Tell me the truth," said Benedict all at once in a troubled voice. "I want to hear from your lips the truth, terrible though it be, perhaps fatal. I want to hear it, even though it puts the last touch to the ruin of my soul. Sabine does not love me ?"

"She has given you up, at all events," said Xavier.

"She never loved me!" cried Benedict vehemently. "She sacrificed me to a mere nothing—a dream—some pride of her own."

"I don't understand you," said Xavier.

"Was it not pride that made her put an end to all that her father had arranged between us? What did I ask of her in that hour of sorrow and affliction except constancy and good faith ?"

"Do you reproach her with the very excess of her generosity ?" said Xavier.

"Yes," said Benedict. "She had no right to drive me from her in her grief."

"She did not want to bring dishonor upon you," said Xavier.

"She has brought worse—ruin," said Benedict gloomily.

"Ruin, when to-morrow you will be famous?"

"Famous! Ah, you, too, with that word on your lips! What is this fame to me? To whom can I offer it? Will any face grow joyful because of my triumph? No; I have toiled, and they tell me I have succeeded; but I worked with pain and a sort of rage. I wanted fame to avenge me, and I sought it no matter where. Do you think I absolve myself, Xavier? No. To-morrow this statue will pass out of my keeping; in six months' time it will stand in open daylight, attracting crowds of sightseers; this evil work will make me rich, but it cannot make me happy. Oh for the pure fame that I once sought for Sabine's sake! Oh for the crowns I once offered, not to pagan deities, but to the Madonna! All is over. I chose this, and I cannot now draw back."

Benedict rose and unveiled the rough cast of his St. Cecilia.

"Look at that clay figure," he said; "it would have been worthy of Sabine and of myself. I saw Sabine as beautiful as that the evening she sang the *O Jesu* of Haydn, which she will never, never sing again for me."

Emotion choked his voice. He made a desperate struggle for composure, failed, sobbed aloud, and threw himself into Xavier's arms, saying,

"Oh my brother, my brother!"

Tears came into Xavier's eyes.

"I can understand," said he. "I have been too weak myself to blame you. On the one hand the saint, on the other the idol, and you prostrated yourself before the latter."

"Xavier," cried Benedict, with the vehemence of deep grief, "can nothing soften Sabine—prayer, promise. repentance?"

"She could not come in here," said Xavier, pointing to the various groups and statues which adorned the room.

"No, no, I know," said Benedict hastily. "But if I purified the sanctuary where she once promised to dwell, if I drove the idol from its temple and broke it with the same hammer that brought it out of nothing, would Sabine come?"

"What are you going to do?" said Xavier, terrified to see that his friend had seized a heavy mallet.

"I am waiting for your answer," said Benedict. "Shall my false glory and to-morrow's success be annihilated? Better so, if I must purchase them at the price of remorse and suffering."

"But this is a work of genius," said Xavier. "You will regret what you did in a moment of excitement, and you will never forgive me or Sabine."

"Would she come back?" cried Benedict again.

"Yes," answered Xavier.

A terrible noise was heard in the studio. Benedict's hammer had destroyed the group from which an hour before he expected so much fame and happiness. "Hylas and the Nymphs" flew into bits, and Xavier stood by in consternation, wondering whether Benedict had gone mad or whether he was merely obeying the imperious voice of conscience. In a few moments naught remained of the fountain but the shapeless remnants strewing the studio floor. And beside them fell Benedict senseless. Xavier hastily called Beppo, laid Benedict on the sofa in the smoking-room, lowered the curtains separating it from the studio, threw the green branches offered to the nymphs at the feet of St. Cecilia, and rushed out of the house. He jumped into a cab, gave an address, and said to the driver,

"Take me there as quick as you can. I will pay you well."

The carriage fairly flew. Xavier rushed up to his sister's room, threw a Spanish lace veil over her head, and, taking her arm in his, said, "Come."

"Where are you taking me?" said she.

"Come," he said in a voice at once tender and imperious.

Sabine obeyed mechanically.

When the coach stopped at the Boulevard de Clichy, and Sabine, entering the court, saw from the appearance of the house that it was specially used by artists, she was disturbed. She timidly pressed Xavier's hand.

"Where are you taking me?" she asked.

He did not answer, but drew her more quickly along.

The door of the studio was ajar. Xavier opened it gently, and Sabine saw at once that it was Benedict's. She would have run away, but Xavier said,

"Stay; if you go now it will not be pride, but treason; no longer virtue, but inconstancy."

Picking up a fragment of the fountain, a charming head of a child, modelled with exquisite art, and which alone would have added to Fougerais' fame, he said,

"This was part of the great work which was not fit for your eyes."

"Oh," said Sabine, her face brightening.

"Now," said the young man, opening the organ in the studio, "sit down and sing."

"I sing?" she said.

"Yes, the *O Jesu* of Haydn."

"Brother," she said, throwing her arms around his neck, "I understand."

She took her place upon the stool, and, in a voice to

THE BROKEN IDOL.

which suppressed emotion lent a new power, she began that song the memory of which had so haunted Benedict.

Whilst Sabine's voice rang out through the room, Benedict, under the intelligent and affectionate care of Beppo, was slowly recovering consciousness. The strain of music seemed to exert a strange influence upon him, as if he wondered from what heavenly sphere came those sounds. Great tears rolled down his cheeks, but they were peaceful and painless tears; he clasped his hands, murmuring, "St. Cecilia."

Feeble and tottering, he arose and advanced to the curtained arch, from which Beppo drew aside the *portière*. Pale as Lazarus arisen from the dead, he leaned forward, looked, stood motionless, and at last cried out;

"Sabine!"

"See," cried Xavier, "your idol broken, the saint has returned."

Sabine did not finish the hymn. The sculptor, still weak, seemed utterly overcome by conflicting emotions. But joy at length triumphed, and when he held Sabine's hand he seemed to revive.

"Will you give it to me?" he said.

She blushed and turned away her head.

"You must ask Sulpice," said she.

"Though I have nothing now," said Benedict, 'and moreover those fragments of marble have ruined me."

Sabine looked at him and smiled.

"Xavier," said she, turning to her brother, "when are you to marry Louise?"

"Why do you ask?" said Xavier.

"Because—I thought—it seemed to me," said she, "that Sulpice might marry us both the same day."

Three months later, in the chapel of the factory at Charenton, a young priest, whose forehead was marked by a scar, celebrated a nuptial mass, and blessed the union of two young couples. The workmen, in Sunday clothes and with joyful faces, crowded the place, and when the newly married came out of the chapel, two young girls offered them beautiful bouquets of white flowers. There was a general shaking of hands and many a moistened eye. Sulpice's discourse on the occasion drew tears from most of his auditors, though few of them understood why he chose a Scripture text concerning idols, to whom men often sacrifice their souls. So well did the noble-hearted priest portray the sweet joys of sacrifice, the power of repentance offered at the foot of the cross, and the mysteries of persecution, martyrdom endured for justice's sake, that all hearts were thrilled with emotion.

Just as the wedding party came out of the chapel, the nasal voice of Pomme d'Api reached their ears. He carried under his arm a bundle of illustrated papers, and cried out,

"Buy the Dying Speech of Fleur d'Echafaud, and the account of his last moments. Only ten centimes, two sous."

THE END.

www.ingramcontent.com/pod-product-compliance
Lightning Source LLC
Chambersburg PA
CBHW030733230426
43667CB00007B/694